Women
and the
State in Africa

Women
and the
State in Africa

edited by
Jane L. Parpart
&
Kathleen A. Staudt

Lynne Rienner Publishers · Boulder & London

Published in the United States of America in 1990 by
Lynne Rienner Publishers, Inc.
1800 30th Street, Boulder, Colorado 80301

and in the United Kingdom by
Lynne Rienner Publishers, Inc.
3 Henrietta Street, Covent Garden, London WC2E 8LU

Library of Congress Cataloging-in-Publication Data
Women and the state in Africa.
  Bibliography: p.
  Includes index.
  1. Women in politics—Africa, Sub-Saharan
2. Sex role—Africa, Sub-Saharan. I. Parpart, Jane L.
II. Staudt, Kathleen A.
HQ1236.5.A357W65 1988 305.4'2'096   88-23974
ISBN 1-55587-223-9 (pbk.)

British Cataloguing in Publication Data
A Cataloguing in Publication record for this book
is available from the British Library.

Printed and bound in the United States of America

Contents _____

About the Contributors   vii

Acknowledgments   ix

1   Women and the State in Africa   *Jane L. Parpart
    and Kathleen A. Staudt*   1

PART 1   THEORETICAL DEBATES

2   Gender Relations, Class Formation, and the
    Colonial State in Africa   *Margot Lovett*   23

3   Gender, Class, and State in Africa
    Robert Fatton, Jr.   47

PART 2   CASE STUDIES

4   Kaba and Khaki: Women and the Militarized
    State in Nigeria   *Nina Mba*   69

5   State, Peasantry, and Agrarian Crisis in Zaire:
    Does Gender Make a Difference?
    Catharine Newbury and Brooke Grundfest Schoepf   91

6   "This Is an Unforgettable Business": Colonial
    State Intervention in Urban Tanzania
    Marjorie Mbilinyi   111

7   Women and the State: Zambia's Development Policies
    and Their Impact on Women   *Monica L. Munachonga*   130

8   The Black Market and Women Traders in
    Lusaka, Zambia   *Karen Tranberg Hansen*   143

9   Zimbabwe: State, Class, and Gendered Models
    of Land Resettlement   *Susan Jacobs*   161

10 Gender Perspectives on African States
    Naomi Chazan   185

Bibliography   203

Index   225

About the Book   229

About the Contributors

JANE L. PARPART is associate professor of history at Dalhousie University, Nova Scotia. She is author of *Labor and Capital on the African Copperbelt* and coeditor (with Sharon Stichter) of *Patriarchy and Class: African Women in the Home and the Workforce* and *Women, Employment and the Family in the International Division of Labour*.

KATHLEEN A. STAUDT is associate professor of political science and assistant dean of the College of Liberal Arts at the University of Texas at El Paso. Her books include *Women, Foreign Assistance and Advocacy Administration* and *Women in Developing Countries: A Policy Focus* (with Jane Jaquette) and a forthcoming collection, *The Bureaucratic Mire: Women's Programs in Comparative Perspective*.

NAOMI CHAZAN is senior lecturer in the Department of Political Science at the Hebrew University of Jerusalem. She is author of *An Anatomy of Ghanaian Politics: Managing Political Recession, 1969–1982* and (with Deborah Pellow) *Ghana: Coping with Uncertainty* and is a coauthor of the text *Politics and Society in Contemporary Africa*.

ROBERT FATTON, JR., is associate professor in the Woodrow Wilson Department of Government and Foreign Affairs at the University of Virginia. He is author of *Black Consciousness in South Africa: The Dialectics of Ideological Resistance to White Supremacy* and *The Making of a Liberal Democracy: Senegal's Passive Revolution, 1975–1985*.

KAREN TRANBERG HANSEN teaches in the Anthropology Department at Northwestern University. She is author of *Distant Companions: Men, Women and Domestic Service in Zambia, 1900–1985*.

SUSAN JACOBS is senior lecturer in sociology at St. Mary's College, Surrey University. She conducted field research in Zimbabwe in 1983–1984, and worked there with the Ministry of Community Development and Women's Affairs. She has published numerous articles on Zimbabwe, including one in H. Ashfar, *Women, State and Ideology.*

MARGOT LOVETT is a doctoral candidate at Columbia University, where she is working on a dissertation that addresses the impact of the rise and fall of male labor migration in western Tanzania on households and communities.

NINA MBA's pioneering book, *Nigerian Women Mobilized: Women's Political Activities in Southern Nigeria, 1900–1965,* is an important landmark in the study of women in Nigerian history. She is currently working on a biography of the Nigerian politician and feminist Funmilayo Ransome-Kuti.

MARJORIE MBILINYI is professor in the Institute of Development Studies at the University of Dar es Salaam, Tanzania, and a founding member of the Women's Research and Documentation Project at the university. She has written extensively on women in Tanzania and is currently coauthoring *I Wish I Were a Man,* with Rebeka Kalindile, an elderly Rungwe peasant.

MONICA L. MUNACHONGA teaches in the School of Humanities and Social Sciences at the University of Zambia and is currently the assistant dean of undergraduates. She has researched and published widely in the fields of women and development, with a special interest in state policy, marriage, and gender relations within the household.

CATHARINE NEWBURY is associate professor of political science and African studies at the University of North Carolina at Chapel Hill. She has spent many years conducting research in rural areas of Rwanda and Zaire. Her publications include *The Cohesion of Oppression: Clientship and Ethnicity in Rwanda (1860–1960).*

BROOKE GRUNDFEST SCHOEPF has worked in Zaire since 1974, when she went to the Université Nationale du Zaire-Lubumbashi to teach rural sociology, economic anthropology, and development studies as a member of the Rockefeller Foundation's field staff. She currently directs CONNAISSIDA, a collaborative medical anthropological action-research project on AIDS in Kinshasa.

Acknowledgments _____

This book has a long history and many debts. The editors began writing on women and the state in Africa in different contexts. Kathy Staudt became interested in the state as she studied women and development policies in Kenya and the United States; she contributed a major piece on the subject to Irving Markovitz's *Studies in Class and Power in Africa* and continues to write on women and the state. Jane Parpart participated in the 1986 Hebrew University conference on state and society in Africa, which culminated in *The Precarious Balance: State and Society in Africa*, edited by Don Rothchild and Naomi Chazan. These separate efforts came together in 1986, at an African Studies Association Annual Meeting panel. Many of the book's contributors participated in that panel (notably Cathy Newbury, Karen Hansen, Monica Munachonga, Nina Mba, and the editors) and benefited from the discussions that followed, and we owe a large debt to all who attended that session. We also gratefully acknowledge the warm and productive interchange among members of the ASA's women's caucus, for those discussions inspired the panel and have sustained us through the vagaries of editing this collection.

This book has also benefited from Lynne Rienner's support and the thoughtful comments of her outside reader; the assistant project editor, Gia Hamilton; and the copy editor, Rose-Marie Strassberg. The editors are grateful for their assistance. The book never would have reached their desks without the tireless help of Evelyn Flynn, secretary at Dalhousie University's Centre for African Studies; Jill Bonar of the University of Texas at El Paso; and Marilyn Bazzett of Scripps College.

Both editors acknowledge the support and help of their spouses, Tim Shaw and Robert Dane'el, who watched children and cooked suppers and even made occasional critical contributions while we engaged in long-distance coediting.

CHAPTER 1

Women and the State in Africa

JANE L. PARPART
KATHLEEN A. STAUDT

To paraphrase a great thinker, "Woman makes her own history, but she does not make it under conditions of her own choosing."[1] Both of us—Parpart, an historian, and Staudt, a political scientist—have written about women making their history in different parts of Africa.[2] Our intellectual interests have now converged on a key point: The male-dominated state warps women's ability to make history on their own terms.

Gender, as we see it, is central to any and all efforts to conceptualize the "modern" state, whether it be its historical origins, current composition, or management of the extraction and distribution of resources.[3] Whether in its indigenous, colonial, or modern forms, the state has been overwhelmingly controlled by men; this control has translated into laws, policies, and spending patterns which not coincidentally benefit men. Women's seemingly personal, everyday experiences are structured by policies, most of which are apparently "gender-neutral." But these policies are in fact experienced very differently by men and women. We have been struck by the absence of attention to women and the state in several different bodies of knowledge.

In this introductory chapter, we focus first on theoretical perspectives into which analyses of gender and the state might fit. Our analysis fits under the broad rubric of political economy, with equivalent attention to politics and economics. We then develop a gendered approach to examine the historical origins, composition, and management of the state, in Africa, in sections designed to raise provocative questions that state-specific contributions in this collection begin to answer. Finally, we summarize the contributors' chapters in this volume.

CRITICAL PERSPECTIVES

Development first preoccupied Africanist literature, but crisis is now the dominant theme. Both of these broad concerns are the stuff of the intellectual agenda of political economy. In one of many volumes on crisis, John

1

Ravenhill begins with a stark summary of conditions in sub-Saharan Africa, "suffering an economic crisis of a magnitude unprecedented in its recent history":[4] economies stagnate. Only in Africa has per capita food production declined in the last two decades. Gains have been made in health care, housing, and education, but crisis threatens them all. Welfare gaps between Africa and the rest of the world are striking, with Africa occupying the bottom rung of countries on standard indicators of well-being, such as infant and maternal mortality, and illiteracy. What explanations and prescriptions do critical perspectives provide for us?

Dependency

Dependency theory focuses on the external constraints to development and crisis. For centuries, Africa has been integrated into a monolithic, world economic system of capitalist accumulation on highly disfavorable terms.[5] From the world trade in slavery through the colonial and contemporary eras, Africa's labor and resources have financed growth outside the continent. The current international economic recession reverberates shocks on dependent peripheral economies. Whether a source for their woes, or a solution, the long arms of the International Monetary Fund are present in many states as indicated in this volume's chapters by Karen T. Hansen (Zambia), Catharine Newbury and Brooke G. Schoepf (Zaire), and Susan Jacobs (Zimbabwe).

For dependency theorists, the Third World state is little more than a comprador elite through which international capital works. Abstract world-systems approaches treat this relationship mechanistically,[6] leaving no independent role for African elites. Some versions of dependency theory argue that upon disengagement from international capitalism, Third World states can begin to work for their people or in solidarity with other similarly situated states through such strategies of self-reliance as those posed in the Lagos Plan of Action.[7]

Questions have been raised about this model. Some Africanist critics of the state reject the bogeyman role for international capital and point a finger at Third World elites themselves. They question the effectiveness of state elites in fostering capitalist accumulation internationally or their commitment to self-reliant development strategies.[8] Some Marxist critics of dependency theory view capitalist accumulation as historically progressive, and call for more attention to internal class conflict and to the role of the national bourgeoisie.[9] Often criticized as overdeterminist, the dependency theory gives analytic short shrift to the human dynamics at the base of international structure, ignoring the possibility that some Third World elites may be able to manipulate the state to benefit themselves and their nations vis-à-vis international capital.

Feminist theorists have expanded and enriched dependency approaches with attention to reproduction and people-dimensions that gives life to pure analysis.[10] Yet, feminist dependency theorists grant little credit to states for forging or mediating international economic relationships. Women appear to be last in a long trail of victims of international capital. Paradoxically, though, theorists view the state as the locus for practice, whether in capitalist societies[11] or those in transition to socialism.[12]

Mode of Production

Mode of production analysis compensates for the overly aggregate nature of dependency approaches. It examines the coexistence of and articulation between different modes of production at their base. The existence of seemingly "traditional" economic systems alongside capitalist development makes Africa a prime region in which to examine the clash between or accommodation of different production modes.[13] However, plagued by obscure terminology, this approach tends toward uncritical economic determinism. Furthermore, it talks around gender rather than focus on it, addressing concepts such as lineage and household. And even this microlevel approach misses the human dynamics at its base.

Moreover, both dependency and mode of production analysts can be faulted for the superficial attention they give to states.[14] Political institutions, political struggles, and the ideologies therein mediate economic factors and help explain variation in people's economic experiences. While economics—whether international or local—undoubtedly influence the opportunities and constraints facing Third World states, economics alone cannot explain Third World realities or the role of the state in creating those realities.

STATIST PERSPECTIVES

Crisis in Africa has also been tied to the arbitrary, corrupt, and heavy-handed state. In this approach, scholars from various ideological perspectives focus on the fragility of democracy, the near absence of political accountability, the state as captured by a ruling class, or the state as stifling economic enterprise. The way in which states are conceptualized bears heavily on the prescriptions implied, whether they be to weaken or strengthen the state.

In both mainstream political science and classical Marxism, state action has been explained in terms of state–society interaction. In the liberal–pluralist conception, states are viewed as neutral umpires, reacting to diverse interest groups and the electorate. In the classical Marxist variant, the dominant class controls the state and uses it for its own purposes. For this volume, Robert Fatton, Jr., analyzes the state as the ultimate organizer and long-term defender of ruling-class interests. Under capitalism, this "captured" state presumably fosters capitalist accumulation.

Women fit uneasily in either view. Women are more than an interest group in a decidedly unneutral setting, and they fit uncomfortably (if at all) in economically based class structures, devoid of attention to the reproductive dimensions of life. In both of these conceptions, theorists pay little heed to the dominance of men in state structures, both in historic and contemporary times. Yet such dominance matters enormously for women, as states institutionalize male control over female sexuality and labor in varying degrees.[15] Our contributors add subtle nuances to this debate, from Jacobs on the "ruling statum's precarious class position" in Zimbabwe, to Fatton's analysis of ruling classes that use gender as they seek hegemony, to Margot Lovett's discussion of class formation itself as a gendered process.

In Africanist Marxist-feminist analysis, states recede into the background. Claire Robertson and Iris Berger conclude: "Women thus have considerable work awaiting them if they are to break the alliance of the local male-dominated upper class with the international capitalist bourgeoisie."[16] While recognizing its male characteristics, the analysis is wedded to an instrumental Marxist-dependency mode. Ideology and political institutions have limited prominence in these conceptions of the state. They ignore the fact that men *outside the dominant class* participate in and benefit from the male-dominated state.

Gender most certainly complicates liberal and class analyses of the state. Analysts can break through these complications by viewing the state as partially autonomous from the dominant class. "Bringing the state back in" has been a rallying cry for political economists of different ideological hues in what Theda Skocpol calls a "paradigmatic reorientation."[17] The political elite shares goals with the dominant class to varying degrees but is separate from that class, acting as mediator for inter-, intra-, and transnational class conflicts.

Much credit for the reorientation is due to the late Nicos Poulantzas, whose writing on the relative autonomy of the state sparked a flurry of theoretical development. Structural Marxists view the state as dedicated to the preservation of the coherence of capitalist society, which occasionally necessitates opposing the dominant class in order to cope with inherent contradictions and to maintain societal cohesion. Poulantzas wrote that the state apparatuses' principal role is "to maintain the unity and cohesion of the social formation by concentrating and sanctioning class domination, and in this way reproducing social relations, i.e., class relations."[18] He argues that ideological and political factors must be incorporated into a class analysis of the state, but did not always succeed in doing so.

Theda Skocpol's historical analysis of the French, Russian, and Chinese revolutions approached the state from a Weberian, institutional direction. She defines the state as "a set of organizations capable of formulating distinctive goals." Wary of reducing explanation to material reality alone, she and other statist theorists highlight political dynamics and ideology—the latter especially relevant in revolutionary transition.[19]

In none of these approaches is gender conflict or male domination of the state central or even peripheral to analysis. On the level of grand theory, Western feminist theorist Zillah Eisenstein has incorporated Poulantzas' theories into a conception of the capitalist patriarchal state which acts in social struggles to create order and cohesion.[20] While analyses like these are insightful, we believe analysis must move beyond highly abstract conceptions about relative state autonomy to historically sensitive, middle-range theorizing in specific states. This is particularly true when studying Third World nations, with their very different cultural traditions.

Everywhere, the political elite is largely male. Just as states mediate class and international conflict, so also do we expect that the state mediates gender conflict. For all the variations in states—weak or strong, more or less autonomous—one constant is that women are *never* central to state power. Accounts render women invisible in state formation, and women occupy official state positions in no more than symbolic numbers. Gender ideology appears to be ever-present, no matter what the state ideology. Women have markedly different access to and relationship with states than men. Our aim is not to solve finally the analytic puzzle of whether the dominant class does or does not control the state as it is to highlight gender in state formation, political participation, and resource allocation. We see class differences among women as crucial for analysis, but do not believe class and statist approaches to be mutually exclusive. We view the idea of abstract relative autonomy of the state, with its mediating role among competing class fractions, as a useful starting point that must move forward to come alive with the human dimensions that historical analysis provides. "States are only human organizations,"[21] absorbing the values, biases, and prejudices of those that "man" them.

Recently, Africanists have been taken with the idea of the partially autonomous state. In Africa, the state dominates much economic effort, and access to the decisions and spoils of state-dispensed credit, export activity, public works, and licensing is essential to power.[22] Contemporary states are built on a tradition and foundation of heavy-handed statism or what Crawford Young terms "the robust trunk of colonial autocracy."[23] States' relations with dominant classes are questioned rather than assumed, as class formation has occurred in different degrees around the continent. Moreover, members of the dominant class—whose overlap with state officials is an empirical question—sometimes hinder the state's capacity for capitalist accumulation, leading critical scholars to call them "pirates," "parasites," and "eunuch capitalists."[24] This is very clear in Marjorie Mbilinyi's contribution for this volume, as beer companies used the colonial state to compete unfairly with women brewers of Dar es Salaam. But whether the dominant class helps the state or not, clearly, political access to the state has profound effects on people's opportunities, resources, and property.[25]

Yet even as women have virtually no power in the state structure, nor do they benefit from the state, neither is gender central to Africanists' analyses.

John Lonsdale, in a staggering synthesis of material on the state in Africa, merely remarks that "women's studies has barely impinged upon studies of the state," as if statist theorists had no analytic responsibility.[26] We think it high time that some convergence be reached in analyses of the state and women.

For us, gender is at the heart of state origins, access to the state, and state resource allocation. States are shaped by gender struggle; they carry distinctive gender ideologies through time which guide resource-allocation decisions in ways that mold material realities.[27] Through their ideological, legal, and material efforts, states foster the mobilization of certain groups and issues. This mobilization usually benefits men rather than women. While over the long haul, state action may submerge and obscure gender conflict, over the short term, the obviousness with which male privileges are fostered may actually aggravate that conflict.

These gender dimensions may cut across class, complicating analysis and making for intricate variations in specific historical settings. However, a gender-sensitive statist focus does not preclude attention to class, but it does elaborate upon and develop a more nuanced class analysis. After all, many state actions concerning gender just do not make economic sense in the short run, apart from ideological interpretation. In promoting male interests, some state action *thwarts* capitalist accumulation among women. Again, Mbilinyi's analysis in this book offers a thoroughly documented example. To be sure, as many feminist theorists have argued, women's specialization in use-valued—as opposed to exchange-valued—work *enables* male accumulation and thereby subsidizes capital accumulation. At some point, though, capital loses as it stifles exchange-oriented accumulation among women. Over the long haul, though, states may have an interest in maintaining gender hierarchy with the effect that subordinate classes reproduce themselves at increasingly lower cost. Here, men's power and gender ideology come into play in full force.

Some danger exists in reifying states and their ability to mold society; Thomas Callaghy, after all, warns that African states are "Leviathans, but lame ones."[28] States are neither monolithic nor unchanging. Constitutional equal rights coexist with institutionalized male privilege; policies to promote female emancipation or women in development stand alongside those fostering female dependency.

In this volume, Jacobs uncovers contradictory policies and the divergent rhetoric and reality of resettlement schemes in Zimbabwe. Women use these contradictions to pursue their self-defined interests. Hansen shows this most clearly for women traders in Lusaka. Often, women aim to extricate themselves from the prevailing political agenda, making an implicit statement about the limited legitimacy which they grant the state. Whether inside or outside state structures, the portrayal of women's political struggles is an important dimension of this collection. Among our contributors, Nina

Mba documents women's political actions in Nigerian history, while Mbiliniyi unearths Tanzanian women's political protests, heretofore buried in colonial documents.

ORIGINS OF THE MODERN STATE IN AFRICA

Much ink has been spilled theorizing about the origins of the modern state as it evolved in Europe and spread elsewhere. Focused on ancient, pristine societies, such theorizing has tried to piece together what remains a genuine puzzle, namely what forces gave rise to the states. While some feminist theorists focus on ancient Sumer, Inca, and Aztec societies, Rayna Rapp calls for analytic attention to state formation in "the bloody laboratory of colonial penetration."[29] From the early colonial period, we can garner insights about how the prevailing capitalist world system affected dependent economies through state institutions.

We believe that Africa is a prime location in which to examine state formation, for its European-derived form has been in place only a century. This time frame permits an examination of living and available memory and documents over a period of continuing, creative flux. More important, Africa is a key location in which to explore the provocative question: Did gender conflict help to shape the character of the state?

Many historical and ethnographic accounts of African societies have emphasized the existence of separate and distinctive gender interests regarding property, resources, and responsibilities.[30] In an era of commercial production and exchange, these separate interests are manifested in husbands and wives who control their own incomes. In other words, household income pooling *cannot* be assumed.[31] Separate interests have also been enshrined in sex-specific institutions which defend or advance the interests of men and women. West Africa in particular is rich with such institutions, though their existence has been documented across the continent.[32] Female institutions, however, have withered with the neglect of a male-oriented state, colonial and thereafter, but are occasionally evoked in crisis (such as the Women's War in Aba) or replaced with new institutions.[33]

Analysts have identified the latter half of the nineteenth century as a time of upheaval, threatening gender controls. Since women started to have access to the courts, they began to use them to their advantage, and the colonial system was initially receptive. Not soon after the beginning of the twentieth century, men began to realize that women were threatening indigenous male control.

Martin Chanock, analyzing case law in Northern Rhodesia/Zambia and Nyasaland/Malawi, makes perhaps the strongest argument that male elders allied themselves with colonial rulers to reestablish control over women through a contrived "Customary Law." In Native Courts, men exerted their most effective power by creating law and applying it to conflict. Utilizing case law, too, Marcia Wright found "no issue more sensitive than the control of women" around the turn of the century as a changing economy opened new opportunities and created a demand for women's productive and reproductive labor.[34] Selected women used legal pluralism to their gain. In the same region, as a response to the sudden ascendance of male power in the late nineteenth century, says Terence Ranger, women created the Mothers' Union to restore their powers.[35]

The richest empirical studies are found in central and southern Africa, where perhaps not coincidentally, diverse marital exchange and property transmission systems confronted one another, and a patrilineal bride-wealth system gradually became ascendant. Lovett's analysis in this volume carefully develops how state formation is a gendered process. Men provided increasingly larger amounts of wealth in exchange for wives, thereby securing greater marital control over wives' labor. Colonial officials had an interest in stabilizing domestic relations and strengthening accumulation processes; they solidified male authority to realize these aims. The stage was thereby set to subsidize men through the maldistribution of state resources to foster male accumulation, an issue to be developed later. Men occupied positions of political authority in overwhelming numbers, thereby facilitating maldistribution patterns. While men used this patriarchal cooperation to wrest power from women, the gender struggle was an ongoing, fluid process, and had to be won each day anew.[36]

WOMEN'S ACCESS TO THE STATE

Women occupy minute numbers of decision-making positions in all African states. While organizational affiliation is high among women, their gains from pressuring states have been minimal. Women are truly outsiders in their relation to the state. Yet the weak or contradictory nature of some states suggests the need for analytic caution in regard to what these minute numbers mean for women.

Women represent half or more of the electorally franchised population in African states and thus potentially half the recruitment pool for political office. Yet during the mid-1980s, women represented only 6 percent of national legislative members in Africa.[37] A United Nations questionnaire nearly a decade earlier found identical figures at the national level, but slightly higher representation (10 percent) at the local level.[38] Women make up only 2 percent of national cabinet or equivalent positions. Typically, they preside over ministries of community development, education, health, social welfare, or women's affairs. Half of the states in Africa have no women in the cabinet at all.[39] Women's limited access to higher education and wage employment offers some explanation for their near absence at the top, though limitations in men's education have not prevented them from assuming even positions as heads of state.[40] Does *regime type* make a difference in women's paltry representation?

Callaghy argues that the "patrimonial administrative state" in Africa is the foundation above which floats a variety of regime types.[41] Its centralized authority is personalized, and a Weberian mix legitimizes it, from patrimonial to charismatic and legal-rational doctrines. Loyalists support personal rulers, using the state as an avenue to upward mobility to become part of a political ruling class. Does this conception represent a Zairianization of Africa? Once committed to moving beyond economic reductionism, political and ideological variables emerge on the analytic agenda. How do women fit into this analytic scheme? Women's studies needs to explore the ideological and institutional conditions under which women's voice in the state and benefits therefrom can occur.

To be sure, African states are difficult to categorize, as there have been dramatic shifts from one regime type to another since independence. It is difficult to predict anything at all about the effects of fleeting regime types on social structure and the sexual division of labor. Most dramatic of these shifts has been the often repeated transition from civilian to military rule, and vice versa. Military institutions, male institutions par excellence, would appear to offer the tiniest pool from which to recruit or appoint women. Still, military rule is diverse, and rulers depend on civilian appointees to varying degrees. In one of the rare studies of women under military rule, in this volume Mba contrasts military and civilian regimes; the former has been more responsive to women's issues on certain issues in Nigeria.

With miniscule numbers of women in official politics, comparison of regime types provides little in the way of analytic conclusions. Such diverse states as Rwanda, Cameroon, Malawi, and Senegal surpass the 10 percent mark for women in legislatures,[42] though not for women in cabinets. Moreover, with token numbers like these, little can be said about whether more women in politics would redirect resources to women generally or would change the character of politics. A tiny, highly visible minority is vulnerable in the male-dominant political game, and absorbing the male political style is a common female survival strategy. To the extent politically active women are linked to or part of the dominant class, women's politics also might be class politics in disguise.[43] Mba's chapter concludes on this dilemma.

The existence of what the United Nations terms women's "national machinery," such as women's wings of national parties, women's bureaus, or women's ministries, has questionable bearing on whether a state is more or less open to greater female representation and a broader political agenda for women. As of 1980, forty-one states had such machineries, many of them starved for staff and resources. Ooki Oooko-Ombaka, in analyzing questionnaire responses from staff in women's machinery, concludes that development strategies still provide only marginal consideration for women.[44] Mba notes that the National Committee on Women and Development was simply the renamed women's unit from the child and family welfare section of Social Development. Zimbabwe's unit is bureaucratically weak, as Jacobs indicates in her chapter.

What does the presence of a women's wing in a national party mean for women's representation in and benefit from politics? In Zambia, the dominant party has a Women's League under its wing (Monica Munachonga describes this in her chapter). Its primary role is to provide support for male politicians, though the few women who have reached high-level politics cluster in traditional women's concerns such as welfare and health. League members police markets to eliminate "profiteering" among traders, many of whom are women. Gisela Geisler's account suggests that the League is not only thoroughly co-opted by the state, but that it often misrepresents women and aggravates divisions among them.[45] Filomina Steady's detailed study of the women's wing of the All Peoples Congress (APC) in Sierra Leone describes how women recruit new members, generate fees for the party, and mobilize supporters for APC leaders. Though theoretically linked to party policy, women have difficulty persuading the party to nominate them as candidates for election.[46] In Mali, the women's wing of the dominant party supports only those women's issues that are consistent with party policy.[47] Whether in single- or multi-party systems, women appear to have limited leverage in mainstream parties.

In socialist states, women fare slightly better in terms of representation in national congresses. Stephanie Urdang's much-quoted remark that women in Guinea-Bissau fought "two colonialisms," Portuguese domination and African patriarchy, is a telling comment on the confrontation of gender ideologies.[48] Mozambique elected 12 percent of provincial-level delegates to its Third Congress party; only 7.5 percent of Central Committee members were women.[49] In a National Congress meeting of the Organization of Angolan Women, participants concluded that "the principle of equality for men and women in society is *not* sufficient to ensure that women are in fact an active element in their country's development or that they participate equally in decision making."[50] In Benin, commodification gave rise to a large number of independent women traders. Prior to the 1970s, the state interfered little in village life, but "witch-hunting" against mostly poor and marginal females became what Georg Elwert calls "the nobles duty for the Marxist-Leninist Revolution." Gender conflict once again came to the surface, and the "revolutionary" state participated in this scapegoating effort.[51]

Whatever a regime's ideology, women's solidarity organizations occasionally attempt to advocate their interests in mainstream politics. Rarely can success be pointed to, as indicated from various studies, be they of market women in Nigeria and Ivory Coast, beer brewers in East Africa, or cooperative members in Tanzania. State discourse helps to shape women's political agenda, often limiting it to manageable legal reforms and defusing gender conflict. (In her chapter, Mbilinyi illuminates divergent discourse concerning what reality is and should be.) More often than not, women opt to withdraw from politics. Their consciously apolitical stance may represent risk calculations that anticipate limited success.[52] In some cases, the more closely linked women's organizations are to the state, the more male-controlled they are. The Women's Commercial Association in Kinsangani requires that husbands consent to women's membership, and speakers admonish women to take better care of their children.[53]

This does not mean women do not vigorously pursue their economic interests. The Kinsangani merchants that Janet MacGaffey analyzes profitably kept their distance from the male-dominated state in a "second economy," thereby preserving traditional freedoms. Christine Obbo discovered that many Kampala women avoided the state in order to carry out various illegal activities.[54] Women sought to evade the state, which, not coincidentally, permitted them to evade new mechanisms of male control.

Still, occasional successes emerge, such as portrayed in Newbury's rich account of the women cassava growers' revolt in Eastern Zaire.[55] We cannot help but wonder if the cast to generalizations about women's politics would change were women in politics and the state more firmly on the intellectual agenda of scholars interested in African women's political power. Perhaps the growing number of women's groups, such as the Zambian Association for Women or The Business and Professional Women's Associations, are an indication of future trends. Certainly women's organizations in Africa are increasingly vocal about the need for more women to enter politics.

MANAGEMENT OF STATE RESOURCES

With states composed almost entirely of men, have men used the decision-making process to consolidate resources and property largely in their hands? Not always would this operate on the basis of crass material interest. Gender ideologies, particularly those that posit men as providers in households in which women serve, provide the rationale for subsidizing men because women have no "need" to support themselves or others. Meanwhile, seemingly "gender-neutral" policies in employment, education, and agriculture invariably have gender-specific effects as shown in the chapters by Jacobs on Zimbabwe and Newbury and Schoepf on Zaire.

We must return briefly to the colonial state where the earliest policy subsidization occurred to men within the rubric of state institutions. Colonial officials subsidized African men, not in solidarity with men per se, but to foster increased male productivity and thereby spur capitalist accumulation. The ideology of officials concerning economic growth required more productivity from men. Yet officials also hoped to generate more revenue from wage labor and cash-crop agriculture to support the state. They established policies to pressure men to enter the wage labor force through taxation, to train men for a commercial economy and the civil service, to consolidate land in men's names, and to subsidize men's farming through credit and extension advice. Lord Lugard and Lord Hailey could not seem to fathom agricultural modernization undertaken with women farmers. Missionaries also shared ideologies with officials, but emphasized marital transformation toward monogamy and lifelong stability, the latter feeding into officials' concern with social stability. Mission programs also subsidized men in agriculture, sometimes with the rationale that this would compensate them for abandoning such privileged traditions as polygyny and open the way to new ambitions.[56] (Lovett's chapter synthesizes the relevant extensive research in Southern and Eastern Africa.)

The state captured men far earlier than women, but in exchange, men acquired resources and used ascendance in state institutions to consolidate control over women. Nowhere is this more clear than in male control over land. Jean Hay documents how the 1930s Luo society, in which land was owned by neither men nor women, was transformed into one in which ownership became a male right. Such processes, well into the middling colonial period, can be linked to gender conflict at the point where the state penetrates rural society. Before this period of male backlash, says Hay, conditions of land surplus and labor shortages enhanced women's negotiating position and evasion of lineage controls over the disposition of surplus production.[57]

Land reform continues to place title deeds in men's names, probably the most significant of all male gains. Moreover, agricultural extension advice, training, and credit are overwhelmingly distributed to men, even in areas where women are the primary farmers.[58] Wage-labor jobs are available in a wider array at higher compensation rates to men as compared to women. Only in education are persistent gender disparities being addressed, though the content of education for women does not often translate into well-compensated employability.[59] As essays in a major volume on women and class in Africa point out, a "widespread feminization of poverty" is occurring.[60]

By no means would we argue that women lack resources altogether, but women's control of resources is more often outside the state rather than within it. They specialize in food production and preparation, notorious for slipping through the grasp of state marketing boards.[61] Hansen's chapter on the "Black Market" is a clear illustration. Women cooperate with one another informally, unregistered and unregulated. Many exist in the gray areas of illegal beer brewing, smuggling, and prostitution. Women, too, can manipulate the state through men, as MacGaffey's work on Zaire demonstrates.[62] Moreoever, women can use Marxist rhetoric to defend their economic interests, and some use the growing public concern for women in development voiced by Western development agencies. Still, women act within an engulfing macroreality, as virtually all chapters herein will show.

Ideology can and does temper the preferential distribution of resources and property to men. Early reports of Ujamaa villages in Tanzania found land rights and wages allocated to male household heads, though these practices began to be rectified in some villages. Official ideology legitimizes the idea that a worker should receive returns for her labor. It gives rise to consciousness expressed in such comments as, "These days there is no more giving of money to the husband, everyone is self-reliant," and "I did not want exploitation and I was given my own plot."[63]

Still, enforcement of ideological directives is uneven. Mozambican collectivist villages are deemed "politically correct" when women are compensated for their labor. We wonder how many are "politically incorrect" on that issue.[64] Of revolutionary Ethiopia, Zen Tadesse says land reform transformed women from tenants of tenants to tenants.[65] In Zimbabwe, the state, despite the misgivings of the Women's Bureau, permits customary land rights to be exercised on land resettlement schemes, thereby perpetuating discrimination against women.[66] As Jacobs shows in her chapter, ideology in the absence of supportive resources may render that ideology meaningless, as in Zimbabwean cooperative resettlement schemes. Socialist rhetoric barely impinges upon the institutionalization of male interests in states dominated by men. Ideologies are plural, as Jacobs reminds us. And peasants, of whom a majority are female, experience daily the pervasive bias against peasant agriculture in virtually all African states, socialist and otherwise.[67]

OVERVIEW OF THE CHAPTERS

We have divided contributions for this volume into two sections; the first addresses theoretical issues that transcend state boundaries, while the second focuses on single states in particular periods.

The two theoretical chapters offer contrasting approaches to understanding gender, states, and classes. Margot Lovett, in "Gender Relations, Class Formation, and the Colonial State in Africa," argues that class and state formation are *gendered* process—which men and women experience differently—rather than preexisting grids into which women fit. Her focus is on Eastern, Central and Southern Africa, from the early colonial period through the 1930s. In careful historical reconstruction, she analyzes the logics and contradictions of colonial capitalist accumulation and social control, differentiating first the gendering of production and reproduction. Lovett outlines not simply the policies and practices aimed at controlling women, but women's challenges to such intentions.

In "Gender, Class, and State in Africa," Robert Fatton, Jr., takes class formation as given and argues that the ruling class controls the state and excludes virtually all women, He presents Marxist and Western feminist analyses of gender relations, class divisions among women, and the state, as well as gendered understandings of Antonio Gramsci. Not yet hegemonic, ruling classes, Fatton suggests, are using gender to consolidate their control.

Following these provocative theoretical accounts with numerous tie-ins to subsequent chapters, contributors provide a continent-wide analytic array of varying states.

Despite the commonality of military rule in Africa, we know little about women's circumstances under these conditions. In "Kaba and Khaki: Women and the Militarized State in Nigeria," Nina Mba compares women's voice in politics across Nigeria's many military governments. Her analysis reveals differences among military regimes that are as great as those between military and civilian regimes. From the first through the last coup, however, women's organizations have grown stronger, and their demands, more substantive. Yet divisions among women are problematic.

In "State, Peasantry, and Agrarian Crisis in Zaire: Does Gender Make a Difference?" Catharine Newbury and Brooke Grundfest Schoepf call our attention to macroeconomic policy reforms and their effects, as well as externally derived remedies to Zaire's agricultural crisis. Gender does make a difference in understanding these relations, and the authors' discussion of the "second economy" reveals women's creative but sometimes desperate attempts to circumvent the clutches of the state.

Marjorie Mbilinyi draws heavily on a critical rereading of colonial documents in "'This is an Unforgettable Business:' Colonial State Intervention in Urban Tanzania." She extracts the starkly racist colonial discourse which describes efforts to control Dar es Salaam residents. Despite all odds against them, the struggles of the people to earn a livelihood emerge, as in the particularly interesting case of resistance to colonial efforts to control what the documents referred to as "old lady brewers."

Monica Munachonga examines both the effects of Zambia's policies on women and women's participation in politics in "Women and the State: Zambia's Development Policies and their Impact on Women." She discusses women's involvement in party politics along with some drawbacks of the Women's League; such politics have made little dent in the policy neglect and legal inequalities which Zambian women experience.

In contrast to Munachonga's broad treatment of women's politics and policies, Karen Tranberg Hansen views neither women nor states as monolithic. As "The Black Market and Women Traders in Lusaka, Zambia" demonstrates, state policies produce unintended consequences such as "black markets"; contradictions abound within administrative instruments and between administrative and coercive apparatuses of the state. Following a sample of one hundred low-income households, which began in 1971 and extended over a fifteen-year period, Hansen finds that household development cycles explain as much or more than state actions. Her analysis reminds us of the folly of treating states in overly deterministic ways.

On the surface, Zimbabwe would seem to be a haven for progressive policies toward women, with its egalitarian ideology, women's ministry, and marital/divorce law reforms which protect women's rights over property and children. Susan Jacobs, in "Zimbabwe: State, Class, and Gendered Models of Land Resettlement," outlines the contradictory effects of laws on women in this "petty bourgeois state." Some unexpected findings emerge from her comparison of two types of resettlement schemes. From interviews, Jacobs learned of women's satisfaction with the well-endowed individualized household settlements, despite women's legal "dependency" on men and high rates of polygyny. Welcoming men's greater work input in agriculture, ploughing, and even household chores, women view themselves as more influential than when living in an extended family situation. In the contrasting resource-poor production cooperatives, with equal membership in the cooperative and work points calculated by labor input, kin authorities dominate structures and women's circumstances change little.

Finally, in "Gender Perspectives on African States," Naomi Chazan discusses how the incorporation of gender allows us to understand African states in general and the relationships between state and society.

In closing, we reiterate the importance of the state in Africa as a central phenomenon which helps to structure people's lives and their beliefs about themselves and one another. There can be no full understanding of either the state or of women without understanding them both. Realistically, we must recognize that men often have used the state to assert and perpetuate patriarchy and to control women's production, reproduction, and access to resources. We must also recognize that they will continue to do so.

Yet it would be a mistake to overdetermine the state's relationship to women. Looking at the origins, composition, and management of resources in the state, women appear almost powerless. But we know from careful, though limited studies up until now, that women are actors who recognize, defend, and advance their own interests in ways that do not fit neatly into mainstream disciplinary concepts. We know, too, that women are becoming more and more organized to act politically at local, state, and suprastate levels. Women act in micropolitics and transborder smuggling as well as in such regional institutions as the Southern African Development Coordination Conference (SADCC), the U.N. Economic Commission for Africa (ECA), and the Association of African Women for Research and Development (AAWORD).

Existing literature on the state without attention to gender is seriously flawed. This collection is the beginning of what we hope will be fruitful endeavors to understand historically specific cases that permit fuller comprehension of the whole of reality in its complex relations between gender, class, and political economy.

NOTES

1. The quote, of course, comes from Marx and is cited in Saul, "The Role of Ideology in Transition to Socialism," 215.

2. Stichter and Parpart, eds., *Patriarchy and Class*; Staudt, "Sex, Ethnic and Class Consciousness in Western Kenya."

3. Although our explicit focus is women, we use gender terminology, both to emphasize social construction and to highlight male-female conflict, the heart of our analysis.

4. Ravenhill, "Africa's Continuing Crises," 1–43.

5. Leys, *Underdevelopment in Kenya*; Amin, *Accumulation on a World Scale*; Wallerstein, *The Modern World System*; and Rodney, *How Europe Underdeveloped Africa*. For critiques, see Smith, "The Underdevelopment of Development Literature."

6. For exceptions, see state-sensitive dependency theorists Evans, *Dependent Developmennt;* and Alavi, "The State in Post-Colonial Societies."

7. For example, selections in Fagen et al., Ravenhill; and Amin, *Imperialism and Unequal Development*.

8. Cooper, "Africa and the World Economy"; Callaghy, *The State-Society Struggle*; Hyden, *No Shortcuts to Progress*, xi; Ravenhill, "Collective Self-Reliance or Collective Self-Delusion"; and Biersteker, "Self-Reliance in Theory and Practice in Tanzanian Trade Relations."

9. Marxist critics include Markovitz, ed., *Studies in Power and Class in Africa*, especially his Introduction, 11ff.; Parpart and Shaw, "Contradiction and Coalition: Class Fractions in Zambia, 1964–1984"; Warren, *Imperialism: Pioneer of Capitalism*; Lubeck, ed., *The African Bourgeoisie*.

10. Beneria, ed. *Women and Development*; Young, Wolkowitz, and McCullagh, eds., *Of Marriage and the Market*. A potential theoretical breakthrough in world-systems/dependency approaches is Smith, Wallerstein, and Evers, eds., *Households and the World-Economy*. While an entire section of the later book is devoted to the state, the section's only rationale appears to be the oblique need to categorize selections with a *national* as opposed to within-nation, case-study focus! The book can be faulted on two key grounds: states are not conceptualized in analysis, and household income pooling is assumed in all but two selections by Diana Wong and Georg Elwert. Beneria and Sen criticize woman-sensitive analysis that is devoid of attention to class in "Accumulation, Reproduction, and Women's Role in Economic Development."

11. See Chapter 3, for example, in Sen and Grown for DAWN (Development Alternatives for Women for a New Era), *Development, Crises, and Alternative Visions*.

12. See chapters on Ethiopia and China in Beneria, 1982, and Fagen, Deere, and Corragio, generally.

13. For English translations of many French theorists who pioneered in this field, see Seddon, ed., *Relations of Production*.

14. A key exception is Bruce Berman, who uses Mode of Production analysis in "Structure and Process in the Bureaucratic States of Colonial Africa."

15. Lerner, *The Creation of Patriarchy*.

16. Robertson and Berger, "Introduction: Analyzing Class and Gender—African Perspectives." In Robertson and Berger, 23.

17. Skocpol, "Bringing the State Back In." Her far-reaching review essay is spun from a 1982 Social Science Research Conference, and the titles of the conference paper and this chapter echo George Homan's 1964 American Sociological Association Address entitled "Bringing Men Back In." We note the source of the echo, for that tone characterizes a volume that excludes women and gender from analysis.

18. Poulantzas, *Classes in Contemporary Capitalism*, 24–25. See also *Political Power and Social Classes* and *State, Power, Socialism*.

19. Skocpol, *States and Social Revolutions*; Krasner, *Defending the National Interest*; Saul, "The Role of Ideology," on ideology.

20. Eisenstein, *The Radical Future of Liberal Feminism* and *Feminism and Sexual Equality: Crisis in Liberal America*.

21. Lonsdale, "States and Social Processes in Africa."

22. See Lonsdale; Callaghy; Kasfir, "Relating Class to State in Africa," 9; and Young, "The African Colonial State": on the growth in the scope and expense of state activities.

23. Young, "The African Colonial State," 57.

24. Schatz, "Pirate Capitalism and the Inert Economy of Nigeria"; Callaghy, "The State as Lame Leviathan"; and Young, "Patterns of Social Conflict: State, Class and Ethnicity."

25. Sklar, "The Nature of Class Domination in Africa," perhaps goes too far in positing political over economic classes.

26. Lonsdale, 5. Parpart, for example, has the only selection on women in Chazan and Rothschild.

27. See, for example, Lewis, "The Debate on Sex and Class." Lewis utilizes historical evidence from Britain and responds to the "either ideology or material base" explanation of others. We hope to see analysis move beyond the either-or approach to encompass how the state mediates both. See Staudt, "The State and Gender in Colonial Africa."

28. Callaghy, "The State as Lame Leviathan."

29. From Staudt, "The State and Gender"; Rapp, "Gender and Class"; Lerner.

30. Hafkin and Bay, "Introduction," 6; Robertson and Berger, 5, 10. For analysis of individual African societies, see Guyer, *Family and Farm in Southern Cameroon*; Oboler, *Women, Power and Economic Change*; Elwert, "Conflicts Inside and Outside the Household."

31. Contrary to most selections in Smith et al. See note 10.

32. See Staudt's review, "Women's Politics, the State, and Capitalist Transformation"; Okonjo, "The Dual Sex Political System in Operation"; Mba, *Nigerian Women Mobilized*; Stamp, "Perceptions of Change and Economic Strategy Among Kikuyu Women of Mitero, Kenya"; Oboler.

33. Van Allen, "Sitting on a Man"; Mba, Ch. 3; and Women in Nigeria Editorial Committee, (WIN), *Women in Nigeria Today.*

34. Chanock, "Making Customary Law"; and Wright, "Justice, Women, and the Social Order in Abercorn, Northeastern Rhodesia, 1897–1903." Also see Chanock's book, *Law, Custom and Social Order.*

35. Ranger, "The Invention of Tradition in Colonial Africa."

36. Maldistribution is discussed in a later section on "Management of State Resources." Parpart, "Sexuality and Power on the Zambian Copperbelt, 1926–1964."

37. Sivard, *Women . . . A World Survey*, 37.

38. O'Barr, "African Women in Politics," 152.

39. Sivard provides a 7 percent figure, but she has no data for twenty-eight African countries. In checking the 1986 *Europa Handbook* and counting names of cabinet members or cabinet equivalents, we found 2 percent.

40. Jane Parpart develops this idea in "Women and the State in Africa." On education, see also Robertson, "Women's Education and Class Formation in Africa, 1950–1980." Notable examples of education not limiting men's rise to political power include Liberia's Samuel Doe and Uganda's Idi Amin.

41. Callaghy (1984).

42. Sivard.

43. Staudt, "Women's Politics."

44. Oooko-Ombaka, "An Assessment of National Machinery for Women"; INSTRAW (U.N. International Research and Training Institute for the Advancement of Women), *National Machineries for the Advancement of Women.*

45. Parpart, "Women and the State"; Schuster, *New Women of Lusaka*; Geisler, "Sisters Under the Skin."

46. Steady, *Female Power in African Politics.*

47. McNeil, "Women of Mali: A Study in Sexual Stratification."

48. Urdang, *Fighting Two Colonialisms.*

49. Parpart, "Women and the State"; Urdang, "The Last Transition?" 13–14; Kruks and Wisner, "The State, the Party and the Female Peasantry in Mozambique," 121–122.

50. Organization of Angolan Women (OMA), *Angolan Women Building the Future*, 30.

51. Elwert. On scapegoating, also see Schuster; Robertson, "The Death of Makola and Other Tragedies, Male Strategies Against a Female-Dominated System."

52. Staudt, "Stratification"; Parpart, "Women and the State." On how the state helps politicize agendas, see Laitin, *Hegemony and Culture.*

53. MacGaffey, "Women and Class Formation in a Dependent Economy," 176.

54. Ibid. State laws require that husbands authorize wives' bank accounts. See also Obbo, *African Women.*

55. Newbury, "Ebutumwa Bw'Emiogo: The Tyranny of Cassava: A Women's Tax Revolt in Eastern Zaire."

56. Staudt, "The State and Gender."

57. Hay, "Women as Owners, Occupants, and Managers of Property in Colonial Western Kenya."

58. See selections in Bay, ed., *Women and Work in Africa*.

59. See note 40.

60. Robertson and Berger, 10.

61. Staudt's "Uncaptured or Unmotivated?" critiques Robert Bates' *Markets and States in Africa* for its inattention to the *gendered* quality of crisis.

62. MacGaffey, "Women and Class Formation," 173–175.

63. Swantz, *Women in Development*, 116.

64. Isaacman and Stephen, *Mozambique*, ch. 5.

65. Tadesse, "The Impact of Land Reform on Women, 18–21.

66. Jacobs, "Women and Land Resettlement in Zimbabwe."

67. Galli, "The Food Crisis and the Socialist State in Lusophone Africa"; Bates, *Markets and States*. See Staudt's critique, "Uncaptured."

PART 1

Theoretical Debates

CHAPTER 2

Gender Relations, Class Formation, and the Colonial State in Africa

MARGOT LOVETT

Over the past several years, gender has emerged as a powerful analytical concept for scholarly investigation. Placing issues of gender at the forefront of analyses of historical processes has enabled scholars to pose new questions about these processes and, as a result, to view them in fresh and innovative ways. This is especially so where issues of state and class formation are concerned.

Until recently, the prevailing approach to analyses of class and state formation implicitly presented these processes as affecting women and men of the same class position or social stratum in similar ways.[1] The possibility that these processes might not be gender-neutral—that there might be differences in the ways in which women and men experienced them—was neither considered nor questioned. As a result, men's experiences and understandings of the state and of class were presented as the only "real" or authentic ones, thus denying the validity of women's experiences which might not fit into this male-defined mold.[2] This chapter rejects such an approach, and argues that if state and class formation are to be fully understood, they must be seen as gendered, i.e., as having differential impacts on women and men.

East, Central, and Southern African women's experiences of the colonial state as it consolidated its rule; as it intervened to largely determine the conditions under which a migrant labor force would be reproduced and controlled; as it promoted cash-crop production and undertook a series of interventions into African systems of land usage and tenure all differed from those of men. This difference ultimately was rooted in the gendered nature of class formation in that under a colonial capitalist system largely predicated on male migrant labor with subsistence wages, production increasingly came to be gendered male, while reproduction conversely became gendered female.[3] The importance of this distinction cannot be overemphasized. The strategic nature of women's structural position as reproductive laborers both subsidized capitalist production and ensured the continuity of those precapitalist social relations on which the edifice of colonial rule was constructed. This situation made it imperative that both the state and capital develop effective means of controlling women's movements and activities. It also determined that, across classes, women's experiences of marriage and of the application of customary law and their access to land, a cash income, and waged work would all contrast with those of men.

This chapter thus examines and analyzes the differences between women's and men's experiences of the state and of class. In so doing, it explores the ways in which state and class formation in East, Central, and Southern Africa during the colonial period was a gendered process. The imposition of colonial rule disrupted crucial precolonial mechanisms of control over persons and inaugurated a period of flux that lasted until after the Great Depression. During these early decades, when the local apparatus of colonial rule was not yet fully effective and the future of settler, plantation, or Copperbelt mining capitalism was still uncertain,[4] women were able to challenge the developing logic of the underlying processes of colonialism and capitalism. Women seized new avenues of power and agency, such as the creation of colonial courts, and also actively constructed other opportunities, such as prostitution and fluid urban marital arrangements, in order to accumulate surplus, gain autonomy, and exercise control over their own labor power, fertility, and sexuality.

During the 1930s, however, the ramifications of the state's and capital's failure to establish effective control over women's reproductive labor became fully apparent. With the depression threatening the future of colonial capitalist production at precisely the point at which Northern Rhodesia and Nyasaland moved to implement the system of Indirect Rule, the severity of women's challenge to the construction and evolution of colonial systems of production and political organization no longer could be ignored. Rural to urban migration of women not only directly challenged the authority of state-appointed chiefs over their people, but, perhaps more disturbing to the state and capital, it presaged the creation of a fully urbanized, proletarianized generation of families, with attendant problems of social control and the demand for social services. Thus, most noticeably during the 1930s, the state, capital, and African men acted at times seemingly in concert to develop and impose new forms of control over women. Among the most important of these were the establishment of Urban African Courts on the Copperbelt and the promulgation of building regulations in Nairobi. The system of Indirect Rule and customary law, conceived during the 1920s, now became fully effective.

Simultaneously, women's previous avenues of accumulation—prostitution, the renting of rooms, and beer brewing—were progressively but decisively closed off. But it must be understood that this was neither a linear nor an uncontested process, for women struggled on both an individual and a collective level to protest attempts by the state and chiefs to confine them within rigidly defined marriages and restrict their freedom of movement out of the rural areas. Women also actively protested the marginalization of their economic activities and attempts by the state and capital to restrict and/or regulate the economic opportunities open to them. Thus, a consideration of changing gender relations and gender struggles comprises an important part of this study.

ECONOMIC NATURE OF PRECAPITALIST SOCIETIES

Prior to the imposition of capitalist production, the distinction between productive and reproductive labor did not exist. In societies based on mixed economies, the sexual division of labor assigned women the major responsibility for agricultural production, while pastoralism and control over the disposal of cattle was the province of men.[5] Both women and men engaged in productive activities that were necessary for the survival of the household, kin group, or community. But while there may have been complimentarity of economic activities during the precolonial period, there was also inequality between the sexes in regard to access to and control of basic resources such as land, especially in patrilineal societies. In such societies, men's direct access to land was guaranteed solely on the basis of membership in a patrilineage, the precolonial landholding unit. Women's access to land was indirect and thus ultimately insecure. Women possessed no independent, autonomous rights to land; rather, their access was mediated through men—either their fathers, adult sons, or, most notably, their husbands.[6] Upon marriage, a husband allocated a portion of his land to his wife on which she was obliged to grow crops for the family's subsistence. The husband retained control over unallocated fields, reserving rights of disposal over the produce therefrom,[7] while his wife generally possessed the right to dispose only of surpluses from her food gardens.[8] These precolonial patterns of authority over basic resources were manipulated and/or invoked by men during the colonial period to justify the gendering of rural class formation. In particular, catalyzed by expanding cash-crop production, and with the active cooperation of the colonial state, men's supervisory rights over land increasingly were transformed into ownership rights. As landowners, men also received modern agricultural inputs. Under the same conditions, however, women's usufructuary and trusteeship (for their sons) rights in land became increasingly threatened and vulnerable.[9] The land reform programs of the 1950s witnessed the culmination of this process.

CONCEPTUALIZING THE GENDERED NATURE OF STATE AND CLASS FORMATION

Borrowing from and expanding upon the work of John Lonsdale and Bruce Berman,[10] it is argued here that colonial states in the area under consideration were forced simultaneously to pursue two contradictory objectives: to ensure capital accumulation while also maintaining social control. Capital accumulation fundamentally challenged precolonial social relations, for it entailed reshaping and reorienting a variety of divergent precapitalist systems of production and social organization in order to generate both cash crops for export and labor for mines, plantations, and settler estates.[11] As such, it required a major transformation of the organization of African productive activities. Capital accumulation further threatened to engender permanent proletarianization and urbanization, both of which were firmly opposed by the state and capital at least until the post-World War II era. Partly because of this opposition, the state actively intervened, most notably through either direct or indirect action intended to generate a labor force, to promote capital accumulation and to shape the nature it would assume in each colony.[12]

The conditions which the state deemed necessary to ensure social control, however, were antithetical to those required for successful capital accumulation. Social control necessitated maintaining and strengthening those social relations of power and privilege on which precolonial, precapitalist societies were constructed, for the state viewed the continued integrity of these existing hierarchies of authority as vital to ensuring the maintenance of social order and stability on which the security of colonial rule depended.[13] But it was precisely the integrity of these social relations—that of the kin group over its members (particularly the authority of elders over women and juniors) and husbands over their wives—which was severely disrupted and weakened by state action undertaken during the early years of the colonial period in pursuit of consolidating its rule and promoting the beginnings of capital accumulation.

Prominent among these actions was the establishment, virtually from the inception of colonial administration in Northern Rhodesia and Nyasaland, of courts to which Africans were encouraged to bring disputes. Rather than upholding the rights of the corporate kin group, which had been the precolonial unit of legal standing, the new colonial courts instead recognized and sought to enforce the rights of the individual. Women were given access to the courts as a means of redressing a variety of grievances, and they were quick to utilize this opportunity to improve their marital situations or, if that proved impossible, to seek divorces. In Fort Jameson district, Northern Rhodesia, the large number of women seeking divorces in the colonial courts caused uneasy state officials in 1904 to prophecy the disintegration of social order and authority. The divorce rate posed a threat to the maintenance of colonial rule, and colonial officials appealed to the local elders to exercise more effective control over their women.[14]

But it was not only the creation of colonial courts that threatened the maintenance of precolonial social relations. Through the imposition of taxes, the use of forced labor to create the bases of colonial administration and infrastructure, the development of a coercive labor recruitment apparatus to ensure capital accumulation, and the imposition of petty commodity production,[15] the colonial state played an integral role in dismantling precolonial hierarchies of power and privilege. In Kenya, the degree of coercion resorted to by settlers in attempting to extract unwilling labor from the African reserves held the potential of "generating African resistance and threatening the basic framework of colonial administration."[16] Therefore, the state intervened in the early 1920s to regulate the conditions under which labor would be recruited, recognizing that labor migration which was not at least tacitly authorized by the chiefs would serve to weaken the latter's authority. The state was particularly apprehensive of the movement of entire families out of the reserves to settle as squatters on European farms, for it understood that these individuals would live substantially autonomous lives, inhabiting areas not only beyond the control of the chiefs but also precisely where state authority was weakest. The state responded to this situation by enacting legislation which augmented chiefs' powers over the movements of their people.[17]

It is thus within the context of state attempts to manage the contradictions implicit in simultaneously promoting capital accumulation and social control that both women and men experienced the state and its formation. But their experiences differed. Because wage rates were often set at a level below the cost of reproducing the daily labor power of a single male worker,[18] social reproduction had to take place predominantly outside the ambit of capitalist relations of production.[19] Whether undertaken in rural areas, mine compounds, or urban townships, under a system of capitalism predicated on cheap (male) migrant labor, women's labor subsidized capitalist production by contributing to the daily reproduction of labor, caring for workers when ill and after retirement, and raising the next generation of migrant laborers.[20]

With a precapitalist sexual division of labor, in which women's contributions to agricultural production were indispensable, and with the fact that with colonial conquest young men—who had been *least* involved in agriculture production—were often rendered substantially "underemployed" (with the loss of such previous activities as defense, hunting, and cattle raiding), both precapitalist and capitalist modes of production articulated to aid in determining that men would enter migrant labor, while women remained engaged in agricultural production in rural areas.[21] For under the colonial rule only male, as opposed to female, labor was expendable if even the semblance of the economic bases of precolonial African societies was to be maintained. The origins of the process whereby production increasingly came to be gendered male, while reproduction conversely became gendered female, thus are to be located in the interaction between the productive logics of the imposed capitalist and existing precapitalist modes of production. Within the new colonial capitalist system, women's continued performance of reproductive labor activities was absolutely vital for capital because it constituted the necessary precondition without which capitalist production simply could not occur. Similarly, women's labor was also vital to the state because it underpinned the social relations on which the system of Indirect Rule was constructed and further relieved the state of any responsibilities for the social welfare of children and the aged. Indeed, the absolute centrality of women's labor to successful capital accumulation and the maintenance of social control made it imperative that the state establish effective control over women's movements and activities.

STATE, CAPITAL, MALE ELDERS, AND SOCIAL CONTROL

The establishment of mechanisms for effective control of its subjects constituted an integral part of the construction and consolidation of colonial state power. Both women and men were targets of social-control measures, but these differed according to their evolving structural positions within the new colonial capitalist economy. Control over young men as actual or potential migrant laborers passed increasingly beyond the kin group to the state itself. It was manifested in the enactment of Master and Servants Ordinances which specified terms of employment and stipulated the punishment for breach of contract, followed by pass laws which controlled the influx of men to urban areas, and vagrancy laws which were invoked to expel unemployed men from towns.[22]

In marked contrast, both the idiom and the locus of social control over women was not the state, but rather the family or kin group.[23] While men were directly controlled within the wider "public" sphere as actual or potential wage laborers or peasant producers, the state sought to regulate women indirectly through the language and authority of kinship. As such, and most notably during the Great Depression when tenets of customary family law were crystallized and consolidated,[24] the state moved to support and buttress the claims of the kin group over its women. But it was precisely during the incipient rural class formation of the 1930s[25] that the bases of kinship authority were most seriously undercut,[26] and that powerless elders and kin groups most insistently clamored for state assistance in keeping "uncontrollable" women in their rural homes.[27] It was clear that more active intervention by the state was needed if women were to be controlled effectively.

Restricting freedom of movement was one of the means by which the state and chiefs sought to control women. Elders realized that women's migration represented "a fundamental challenge to the structural basis of their power"[28] and feared the loss of wealth they received in transfer payments from migrants as bridewealth or in fulfillment of other obligations should women leave the rural areas.[29] In turn, absent married migrants feared the loss of their land rights if their wives did not remain in occupancy to protect them.[30] Chiefs and headmen giving evidence to Northern Rhodesia district officers seeking to establish the jurisdiction of the new Native Courts therefore invoked "tradition" to justify their claims that under customary law they possessed "total powers of control over people's movement."[31] On the basis of this evidence, chiefs were permitted to issue legislation restricting women's freedom of passage out of the rural areas.

From the late 1930s, women seeking to travel outside rural Northern Rhodesia were required to possess a legal marriage certificate or written permission issued by their chief.[32] During this same period, the state moved to assist chiefs' efforts to immobilize women, supporting and at times instigating the establishment of roadblocks where vehicles were searched for women leaving without permission, and pressuring ultimately uncooperative transport companies to refuse to carry unaccompanied women to town.[33]

The same tactics were employed in Kenya, where Nandi males' concern about uncontrollable women intensified during the 1940s. In 1948 the Nandi Local Native Council passed the Lost Women Ordinance which stipulated that written permission of the chief was required before any Nandi female over the age of twelve would be allowed to leave the district, and forbade all African drivers from transporting women or girls outside the district unless they possess a valid travel permit issued by the chief.[34]

However, the combined efforts of the state, African chiefs, and male elders to restrict women to rural areas met with limited success. Women responded by bribing drivers to claim them as their wives or hide them during vehicle searches in order to secure transport to urban areas. They also prevented the preparation of census lists of their villages, perceiving that these would be used as a means of control.[35]

A far more effective mechanism of regulating women used by the state, capital, and African men was marriage. One of the major sources of power held by precolonial elders over juniors had been the control over marriage the elders held. In patrilineal societies, the command elders had over cattle and other goods needed to constitute bridewealth was an especially powerful lever over juniors.[36] But as migrant laborers, young men returned to the rural areas with enough cash to pay their own bridewealth and thus establish themselves at least to some degree beyond the elders authority.[37]

In matrilineal societies as well, the pressures of the migrant labor system changed the way marriages were contracted. The migrant-laborer bridegroom was often physically absent, and brideservice became increasingly difficult to render. It was progressively replaced by what evolved into bridewealth payments.[38] As a result, the bride's kin increasingly lost control over the labor of their new son-in-law.[39] During the 1920s and 1930s, at precisely the time when marriage was gradually losing its character as an institution through which elders exerted power over juniors, it emerged as a focal point of contention between the state, chiefs, and male elders seeking to solidify the existing social order regarding women and unmarried junior migrants whose actions directly challenged it.

The extent of this challenge was apparent during the 1920s, when the male elders of Tanganyika, Nyasaland, and Northern Rhodesia lamented the rising incidence of "marital breakdown and sexual indiscipline."[40] Blame for the now seemingly common occurrence of adultery was attributed to women's new freedom under colonial rule and to the commensurate decline in the authority which chiefs, elders, and husbands previously had wielded over them.[41] That the state soon came to share these perceptions is revealed by actions which it undertook during the 1920s and 1930s to curb women's troublesome independence.[42] Of these, perhaps none was more effective than the creation of a new "customary" marriage law.

Aiming to reverse an unwelcome trend toward increasing marital instability, the state gathered evidence from male elders, seeking to establish the bases for customary marriage contracts. As Martin Chanock has so convincingly argued, "'custom' regarding a basic institution, already irrevocably altered in its working, was to be 'established' by a series of hypothetical enquiries from those who had been adversely affected by the change."[43] The state seized upon the payment of bridewealth as proof of the existence of a legally recognized "traditional" marriage. This pronouncement indeed had the intended effect of increasing marital stability, for it served to bind women more strongly to their marriages.[44]

Simultaneously, male-dominated Native Courts were created and given jurisdiction over marital cases.[45] They quickly declared that henceforth they would only enforce a husband's marital rights and award him compensation for his wife's adultery in cases where bridewealth had been paid.[46] This was followed by the establishment, between 1936 and 1938, of Urban Native Courts on the Copperbelt which aimed to stabilize urban marriages by bringing them within the ambit of "tradition."[47] Control over urban marriages was further cemented during the 1940s when the state acquiesced to rural elders' insistence that all such marriages be contracted and registered in the rural areas. The 1947 Northern Rhodesia Draft Marriage Ordinance made registration compulsory, and by the 1950s, only registered marriages were considered legal.[48] As late as 1955, a raid on Ndola's African locations carried out at the request of rural chiefs resulted in nearly forty women being arrested, taken before the Urban Court and fined because they did not possess marriage certificates. They were charged as unmarried women who had left their rural homes without the required chiefly permission.[49]

But the state's initial steps, taken during the 1920s and 1930s, to more firmly situate women within marriage coincided with what was perhaps women's most sustained challenge to that institution's efficacy as a mechanism of control. Centered in the newly developed mine compounds and urban townships of the Copperbelt, this challenge consisted, quite simply, of informal mine marriages, which took place without the participation of respective kin groups or the transfer of bridewealth. Because they were not sanctioned by the kin of the parties involved, these extremely fluid marriage arrangements posed an especially powerful threat to the authority of the elders and to the maintenance of rural social relations.[50] They also increased women's autonomy. Because the urban courts would not hear marriage cases contracted outside "custom" and no bridewealth had to be returned at divorce, women were able to easily leave unsatisfactory informal marriages. They were just as easily able to contract new marital arrangements, for women's reproductive labor services were in high demand at this time, and temporary marriages flourished in the Copperbelt mine compounds during the 1930s.[51]

Women's presence on the Copperbelt was allowed, if not actively promoted, by capital, which quickly recognized that married laborers were healthier and tended to remain at work longer, and were therefore ultimately more efficient and productive than unmarried workers. As such, it encouraged workers to bring their wives with them to the mines, took an extremely lax attitude toward marriages, (acknowledging as legitimate unions arrangements in which a woman had lived with and cooked for a worker for just one week[52]), and was extremely unsympathetic to attempts by chiefs to forcibly repatriate to the rural areas any woman they considered an unlawful wife.[53] Yet it must not be assumed that capital was unconcerned with controlling women. As had the state and African men, capital sought to establish effective mechanisms of control over women in order to ensure continued benefits from their labor power.[54] And like the state and African men, capital also chose to do this by pushing women into marriages, however temporary or informal.

As noted by George Chauncey, this was achieved by restricting certain economic activities within the compounds solely to those women whom capital recognized as legitimately married, with the intent of financially penalizing women who did not form "steady relationships" with miners. Single women were denied access to company land on which to plant a garden, and after the mid-1930s, were barred from the compound markets where they had sold their produce.[55] After 1944, capital sought increased control over the movement of single women, making the possession of a pass mandatory for any unmarried women desiring to enter the compounds.[56] In addition, only married women were entitled to reside in houses that provided the space for illicit beer brewing and sales. But while such efforts may have forced women into marriages, during the 1930s, these were mostly temporary ones. Thus women had the best of both worlds—access to company-sanctioned economic opportunities while simultaneously retaining a degree of autonomy and economic independence.

URBAN RESIDENCE,
REPRODUCTION, AND ACCUMULATION

Mine compounds and urban townships served as loci of economic opportunity and independence for women into the 1930s, in part because these areas were precisely those in which precolonial patterns of authority were inoperative.[57] Individuals who resided in such areas at this time were substantially beyond the existing forms of control wielded by chiefs, elders, and king, while new mechanisms of regulation had yet to be developed and imposed. By the first decade of the twentieth century, Ndebele women were firmly settled in Bulawayo, and Kikuyu and Kipsigis women began shortly thereafter to migrate from their rural homes to Nairobi.[58]

Engaging in prostitution (and often in its complimentary activity of beer brewing) was the primary means by which many of these women established themselves as integral parts of the emerging urban African petty bourgeoisie during the first twenty-five to thirty-five years of the twentieth century.[59] Prostitutes frequently accumulated the wealth necessary to construct and operate lodging houses which served urban migrant laborers. As early as 1914 in Bulawayo Location, where Africans paid the municipality a monthly rent for stands on which they erected their own dwellings, women owned 106 of the 115 stands rented out by absentee landlords.[60] During the 1920s, "a few women and Asian families" virtually monopolized the provision of the location's housing.[61] Prostitution during this period thus enabled unmarried women to achieve financial independence and security, acquire property and transmit it to heirs of their own choosing, and in some cases diversify into other activities such as retail trade.[62]

But for present purposes, what was distinctive about prostitutes was their success in carving a niche as petty-bourgeois accumulators by providing reproductive labor services to migrant workers. In addition to the sale of sex, prostitutes were remunerated for cooking a worker's food, washing his clothing, and providing him with bathwater and a bed in which to sleep[63] (i.e., for sending him back to work rejuvenated).

The urban presence of prostitutes, however, revealed a major contradiction in the state's policy on rights of urban residence for Africans. Access to urban housing was viewed as temporary, being restricted in theory solely to those Africans employed in town.[64] Because urban wage-labor opportunities for women remained negligible until well into the post-World War II period,[65] the state's policy effectively gave only men legal rights of urban residence. While the urban presence of men employed for wages was thus easily justified, the presence of self-employed women unaccountable to husband, employer, or the state—as women were not required to carry passes[66]—was harder to rationalize. The colonial state did, however, recognize that prostitutes provided daily reproductive labor services which neither it nor capital were willing to assume, and as such initially tacitly condoned the urban presence of these women.

As revealed through the experiences of Nairobi prostitutes, the state, however, only tolerated certain kinds of prostitutes. During the 1930s, Nairobi prostitutes comprised two distinct groups: *malaya* women who were Islamized, urbanized, and committed to accumulating urban property which they would pass on to their designated heirs; and *wazi-wazi* women, predominantly Haya from Tanzania, who functioned in a very real sense as long-term migrant laborers, sending the proceeds from their work home to their families to augment the lineage property of their fathers, and returning to their rural homes upon retiring. While *malaya* women formed an important part of the developing African urban petty bourgeoisie, comprising a substantial proportion of the just over 50 percent of Muslim residential property owners in the "unofficial" African location of Pangani in 1933, *wazi-wazi* women were transients who lacked similar intentions of consolidating themselves as a class.

During the 1930s, Luise White argues, "the state moved to legislate the African petty bourgeoisie out of existence"[67] by attacking African urban property ownership. This attack came in two stages. In 1936 the state finally carried out its long-delayed intentions of demolishing Pangani, offering property owners either lifetime leases to houses which could neither be sold nor passed on to heirs, or £50 compensation at a time when the estimated cost of building a four-room mud and pole house was £78. Of 239 Pangani landlords, all but a few of them single women, 175 accepted the lifetime leases. The second and final stage came in 1938 when the state banned the construction of mud and pole lodging houses. This effectively rendered urban property ownership illegal for Africans, as the £250 cost of building a four-room stone house undoubtedly was beyond the means of the petty bourgeoisie.[68]

While the basis on which *malaya* women were able to constitute themselves as a class (their ownership of property) was destroyed by the state, no such moves were made against *wazi–wazi* prostitutes. Quite simply, by the end of the 1930s, the state had made it clear that it would tolerate only that form of prostitution which did not lead to urban capital accumulation and thus class formation. So long as urban prostitutes functioned simply to reproduce male labor power on a daily basis, the state permitted their activities. But it refused to countenance their accumulation of immovable property which would be transmitted to future generations, for it was this that would decisively reproduce them as a class.

The fortunes of Bulawayo prostitutes and other nascent petty bourgeois women followed remarkably similar lines. As in Nairobi, the Southern Rhodesian state did not move against them directly, but rather undercut their attempts to consolidate their class position by attacking their status as property owners.[69] But Bulawayo's petty bourgeois women confronted a second threat to the maintenance of their economic position, that being African men. Women's status as uncontrolled prostitutes and providers and occupiers of urban housing generated pronounced gender antagonisms as well as class ones. Both petty bourgeois and emerging working-class men repeatedly appealed to the state to regulate these women, who were viewed as usurping privileges (such as the right of urban residence) which properly should be reserved for men.[70]

Women's protests against the efforts of the state and African men to expropriate their property were sustained and vocal.[71] But ultimately they lost. Both the Kenyan and Southern Rhodesian colonial states viewed urban areas as temporary places of work and therefore residence for Africans, and, as such, set definite limits on urban women's abilities to accumulate. The state deemed rural, not urban, areas as the proper locus of accumulation by Africans.

GENDERING OF CLASS FORMATION I: MARGINALIZATION OF WOMEN'S URBAN ECONOMIC ACTIVITIES

Accumulation was not in fact the outcome of the economic activities of the majority of urban women. Whether residing as squatters in illegal settlements or attached to male workers through a variety of marital arrangements, the economic position of the majority of urban women was steadily eroded over the course of the twentieth century. During the post-World War II period, urban women lived overwhelmingly within conditions of widespread poverty. Wages of individual male workers rarely provided for their own support, and married women quickly discovered that their contributions to household income were essential to ensure the family's subsistence.[72] Yet the income-generating activities available to them were few, often low paying, and generally extensions of reproductive labor activities performed with the household.

Women not only contributed to the support of their families, but they also continued to service the emerging urban working class and thus subsidize capitalist production by maintaining gardens whether in mine compounds or on the fringes of urban areas, using the produce therefrom both for household consumption and for market sale. Other contributions included selling cooked food and firewood, illegally brewing beer or distilling liquor, and engaging in prostitution.[73] But by the end of the colonial period, rather than having consolidated themselves as entrepreneurs who traded to accumulate, the majority of urban women functioned as petty traders who entered the market on an irregular basis purely in order to survive.[74]. This situation was the outcome both of the gendering of reproduction as female and of attempts by the state, capital, and African men to control women by restricting or regulating the economic opportunities available to them.[75]

With the likely exception of prostitution, beer brewing was perhaps the single most lucrative economic activity open to women.[76] It was also the first to be appropriated by the state, which quickly realized that acquiring a monopoly over the preparation and provision of beer would increase municipal revenue, serve as a direct means of regulating workers by ensuring that drinking occurred within a supervised environment, and finance, both to its benefit and to that of capital, a variety of urban social-control programs disguised as recreational or welfare schemes.[77] To pursue these objectives, official beer halls were established in Bulawayo in 1911, Nairobi in 1921, and on the Copperbelt mines in 1929 when the Roan Antelope beer hall opened and the state concomitantly proclaimed illegal the brewing, sale, or possession of beer within three miles of the mine compound.

In the mining and administrative centers of the Copperbelt, in contrast to Nairobi or Bulawayo, the state's ban on individual beer-brewing predominantly affected women who were at least nominally married, being either temporarily or more permanently attached to men as wives, for it was solely in the married quarters that women found access to houses within which beer could be brewed and sold in relative security.[78] It is probable that during the 1920s and 1930s the majority of such "married" beer brewers were in fact informal wives who used this activity to increase their own economic autonomy. It also seems likely that during the 1940s, when, as a result of the combined efforts of the state, capital, and African men, women became more firmly situated within increasingly stabilized urban marriages,[79] this pattern began to change. By the late 1950s such women no longer brewed beer to augment their independence and economic self-sufficiency, but rather to supplement their husbands' wages.[80]

State establishment of official beer halls thus fundamentally restricted women's ability to accumulate. Although illicit beer brewing flourished, the profits from this activity were now uncertain and insecure, as women were compelled to pay out part of their earnings as bribes to location or compound police if they hoped to persuade these officials to ignore their activities. Women were also subject to periodic raids, arrest, and fines, and in such areas as Ndola's African locations, they and their families faced eviction from their houses if women were caught brewing or selling beer.[81]

The state benefited at women's expense from its attempts to monopolize the preparation and sale of beer in at least two ways. Not only were women brewers forced to transfer a part of their income directly to the state in the form of fines and bribes, but through their patronage of the beer halls, male workers now redistributed to the state at least a portion of the surplus formerly expended on the purchase of beer from women brewers, thus further undercutting women's economic position. Taken together, women's restricted access to an independent income from beer brewing, their inability after the 1930s to accumulate urban property from prostitution, their relegation to petty trade, and the lack of waged labor opportunities open to them have been interpreted as proof that urban women's dependence on men increased during the colonial period.[82] But while it is correct to say that women's economic position steadily declined during this time, it is not always correct to conclude that this decline directly translated into a rise in dependence upon men.

Rather, any perceived increase in women's dependence must be analyzed in terms of the class position of the women concerned. While an interpretation of increased dependence may hold for emerging middle-class women who become increasingly domesticated,[83] it would not be correct to so categorize the experiences of nascent working–class women.[84] Due to the ambiguous structural position occupied by the post-World War II urban African working class, for whom (unlike its counterpart in developed capitalist economies) the wage was incapable of fully providing for the reproduction of labor, workers and their families remained dependent upon women's agricultural production and/or on income they earned outside capitalist relations of production in order to subsist on a daily basis and to reproduce themselves generationally as a class. As such, it would be more accurate to describe the relations of these women with their male partners as interdependent, a relationship in which the economic position of each was exceedingly fragile, and each accordingly needed the other in order to survive. But the reality of such interdependence was masked by the existence of a gender ideology which viewed the man as the head of his household. The interdependence was further concealed by the husbands' seeming power within the family as exemplified by their withholding from their wives knowledge of the precise amount they earned in wages, often retaining total control over such income and grudgingly distributing it piecemeal for the purchase of food or household items if and when they saw fit.[85]

But male power within the household was in many cases only apparent. Miners living in married quarters were subject to eviction if their wives deserted them; they were dependent upon their wives to collect their rations, cook their food, prepare their bathwater, wash their clothing, and clean their houses. In other words, men relied upon women's reproductive labor services to maintain a certain level of health and wellbeing which would not otherwise be possible for them to achieve. That women often withdrew these services is revealed in part by incidences of wife beating,[86] which, rather than being seen as evidence of women's powerlessness, may instead be viewed as men's responses to women's exercising what power they possessed within the marital situation.

Gender struggles within individual households over access to and distribution of the (male) wage, control of women's income from beer brewing or petty trade, and regulation of women's freedom of movement and sexuality[87] may thus be seen as indicating the degree to which both husbands and wives maneuvered for positions of control and autonomy within a larger economic situation which rendered them largely powerless and uneasily interdependent. But because they occurred with the "private" domestic domain, the root causes of such struggles were masked. Rather than reflecting a pathology peculiar to particular marital situations, gender struggles within the household must be understood as resulting from those wider structural stresses rooted in the developing colonial capitalist economy described above which bounded the lives of emerging working class families in the post-World War II period. These struggles and tensions were systemic. They were not isolated aberrations.

STATE INTERVENTION INTO
AFRICAN LAND USAGE AND TENURE

The gendering of rural class formation had its origin during the first decade of the twentieth century, with the earliest efforts by the colonial state to promote peasant cash-crop production. By now it is widely recognized that throughout the colonial period, the state oriented such efforts almost entirely toward men, excluding women from access to agricultural extension services and credit.[88] State actions enabled men to enter the money economy as ostensible producers of agricultural commodities, and aided in denying women similar status, despite the fact that their labor more often than not had heavily contributed toward producing what was considered their husbands' crop.[89] But the internal logic which drove the process by which rural class formation was gendered has yet adequately to be analyzed. It is not sufficient to offer an explanation primarily on the level of ideology, i.e., to assert that the state targeted men as cash-crop producers because it adhered to Western concepts of gender in which men were dominant, thus implying that the state acted as it did because it was "patriarchal" or sexist in nature.[90] Rather, it is necessary to seek an answer in the actual practices and gender biases of the state as they unfolded and interacted with precolonial African patterns of social organization and control over resources.

Reminiscent of its attempts to ensure social control, the state directed its initial interventions into African patterns of land usage at men who stood at the apex of existing hierarchies of power and authority. Meetings with chiefs and influential male elders were arranged by colonial officials to urge the adoption of export cash crops and to distribute the necessary seeds, at times free of charge. As the state in turn gave these men the responsibility of apportioning information and seeds and organizing production as they saw fit,[91] the pattern whereby cash-crop cultivation was to be supervised by and the proceeds thereof controlled by men, while women increasingly would be relegated to food-crop production and largely denied the opportunity to command a cash income, was established from the outset.

The state was assisted in its attempts to gender production as male by missions and settlers. All three played a role in introducing such technological innovations as the ox-drawn plough and the tractor, and in helping to ensure that men, not women, would be taught to employ them. Early in its rule, the state established government farms and agricultural training centers at which young men, prominent among them the sons of chiefs, received instruction in the use of the new technology.[92] Ploughing demonstrations were organized, and colonial officials encouraged chiefs to purchase these implements. Missions and settlers provided young men with practical experience in handling such tools, and they returned home to introduce them into their communities.[93] State efforts additionally served to ensure that rural areas would indeed become the locus of accumulation for Africans, and aided in determining that those Africans who so benefited would be men.

If emerging male control over more advanced agricultural technology, as well as over the proceeds of cash-crop production, are to be fully understood, precolonial patterns of social organization and production and the command of resources must be examined. It was these practices that were invoked by men in the name of "custom" to justify women's exclusion from new economic opportunities and control over resources under altered colonial capitalist circumstances. One of the explanations given as to why women did not possess, or at times even utilize, ploughs is that the oxen needed to pull them were owned by men; presumably, by extension, ploughs were to be as well.[94]

Male appropriation of the income gained through the sale of cash crops was similarly justified on the basis that the fields on which such crops were planted were unallocated land traditionally considered "men's fields," the proceeds of which were men's to dispose of as they liked.[95] When it came to the adjudication of land claims in western Kenya prior to consolidation and registration during the state-initiated land reform programs of the 1950s, women's exclusion from the advisory groups formed to assist in determining rights to land was explained by invoking "tradition": men and not women decide land disputes. Women likewise were not registered as landowners because "'it is customary: men own land and women do not own land.'"[96]

However, it is also undeniable that throughout the colonial period, state programs to establish and extend cash-crop production were designed and implemented with built-in gender, and later class, biases. The colonial state believed that women were conservative and neither willing nor able to adopt new methods of cultivation.[97] It was further convinced that agricultural development would come about only if security of tenure were vested in the hands of individual men who consequently were able to transmit their land to their son(s).[98] In order to encourage those farmers whose existing practices most closely approximated its own biases, the state undertook, most notably in the post-World War II period, a series of interventions intended to support nascent capitalist farmers. Variously called Master, Improved, or Progressive Farmer schemes, these programs extended loans to targeted farmers for the purchase of agricultural implements or inputs; offered them the services and technical advice of extension workers, who also distributed to them literature containing relevant information; and emphasized crop rotation, the use of manure, and soil conservation measures.[99] Agricultural extension workers who toured villages did not approach women, who in any case generally lacked the literacy needed to benefit from printed technical information.[100] The effect of such state intervention was to deepen and accelerate already existing economic differentiation and rural class formation. It further served to exacerbate gender struggles and antagonisms.

Already apparent during the 1930s, the expansion of cash cropping and developing land shortages combined to bring about a rise in the value of land as property.[101] By the post-World War II period, this translated into the increasing fragility of women's access rights to land, as evidenced in part by emerging conflicts and gender struggles within the household over the allocation of land between "men's" and "women's" crops (i.e., cash versus food crops, and the control of women's labor). While continuing to be responsible for food-crop cultivation, women were now expected to labor on their husbands' cash-crop fields as well.[102] Women's labor burden accordingly was intensified, and they progressively lost control over the products of their labor as well. As husbands often retained sole rights to dispose of the income gained from cash-crop sales,[103] wives came to function in a role somewhat analogous to that of unpaid laborers on their husbands' farms.

State-initiated land-reform programs of the 1950s, which instituted a system of individual land tenure, solidified the gendering of rural class formation, in part by issuing individual land title deeds solely to men in the overwhelming majority of cases. Lacking title deeds as collateral, women were unable to secure loans to develop "their" land or diversify into marketing or retail trade; further, women lacked the sources of income which would enable them to purchase land when such a market developed.[104] As reproducers, women's publicly recognized identity was defined within the sphere of subsistence farming on land to which continued access was uncertain, while men's status as producers was established through their appropriation of women's labor for the cultivation of cash crops over which women ultimately had no control. By the end of the colonial period then, the distinction between reproduction and production finally had become institutionalized.

CONCLUSION

This chapter has argued that the unfolding of state and class formation shaped both men's and women's experiences during the colonial period. But although identical processes patterned their daily lives, men and women were affected by them in sometimes quite dissimilar ways. In order to contextualize, analyze, and affirm the validity of women's experiences of those processes, this disparity must be acknowledged. The analytical concept of gender is invaluable in helping us to do so.

Proceeding from the outset with a commitment to the importance of gender allows us to see that state formation not only had differential impacts on men and women, but that state actions and policies in turn helped to determine the nature of twentieth-century class formation and gender relations. Seeking to consolidate its rule and develop effective control over its colonial subjects, the state directed its earliest efforts at promoting cash-crop cultivation at existing (male) sources of power and authority, was instrumental in establishing the migrant labor system and the parameters for the conditions under which the social reproduction of the labor force was to occur, and later intervened to limited women's freedom of movement to urban areas by helping to create and apply "customary" marriage law.

Ultimately, however, it was men's and women's evolving structural positions within the developing colonial capitalist economy which proved most important in determining the manner in which the state related to them and thus molded their experiences of the state as well as of class. As reproducers, women both subsidized capitalist production and underpinned those social relations on which the state had based its rule. Men as producers were targeted for migrant labor and were the beneficiaries of state efforts to alter precolonial systems of land usage and tenure, while women were denied both this status and corresponding opportunities to command a cash income.

Thus, men and women were affected by the processes of state and class formation in disparate ways. Women's experiences of the proletarianization process quite obviously differed from those of men. While the majority of women did not enter migrant labor or initially work for wages, the early dynamics of proletarianization enabled them—as prostitutes and beer brewers in urban areas and mine compounds where they directly serviced the migrant labor force, and even if only temporarily—to accumulate. Similarly, women's experiences of "peasantization" were categorized by their relegation to subsistence farming, the appropriation by men of their labor and their loss of control over the products thereof, and by their increasingly uncertain access to land. In order to more fully understand the ways in which women's and men's experiences of the state and of class differed across regions and historical periods, more detailed local studies which pay careful attention to issues of periodization are needed.

NOTES

1. Studies that include analyses of gender, class, and state formation are Bujra, "Urging Women to Redouble Their Efforts," 117–140; Robertson,

Sharing the Same Bowl, Introduction; Scott, "Gender: A Useful Category of Historical Analysis"; Acker, "Class, Gender, and the Relations of Distribution." On state formation, see Staudt, "Women's Politics," 193–208; Parpart, "Women and the State."

2. For an analysis of male bias in the experience of class in early industrial England, see Scott, "Women in *The Making of the English Working Class*."

3. The distinction here between productive and reproductive labor is merely conceptual. According to orthodox Marxist theory, women's domestic labor, which reproduces labor power on both a daily and a generational basis (and in underdeveloped capitalist economies includes agricultural production both for subsistence and for sale) is not considered productive labor. According to this perspective, only labor activities that create surplus value are designated productive. For a discussion of the domestic labor debate, see Fee, "Domestic Labour," 1–8; Seccombe, "The Housewife and her Labour under Capitalism" 5–24. While dissatisfied with the gendered definitions of orthodox Marxist theory, the terms productive and reproductive labor have been retained here because they denote a useful theoretical distinction between types of labor.

4. Anderson and Throup, "Africans and Agricultural Production in Colonial Kenya," 329–330; Vail, "The Political Economy of East-Central Africa," 239–246; van Zwanenberg, *Colonial Capitalism and Labour in Kenya*, Chapter 1 and 227–285.

5. Henn, "Women in the Rural Economy," 1–18.

6. Hay, "Women as Owners, Occupants, and Managers," 110–123; Okeyo, "Daughters of the Lakes and Rivers," 186–213.

7. Harris and Harris, "Property and the Cycle of Domestic Groups," 127, 140; Gulliver, "The Arusha Family," 201; LeVine, "The Gusii Family," 68–69.

8. Dixon-Fyle, "Reflections on Economic and Social Change," 425; Hay, "Luo Women and Economic Change," 95; Oboler, *Women, Power, and Economic Change: the Nandi of Kenya*, 172; Winans, "The Shambala Family," 46.

9. Bryceson and Mbilinyi, "The Changing Role of Tanzanian Women in Production," 62; Wright, "Technology, Marriage and Women's Work," 104–105.

10. Lonsdale and Berman, "Coping with the Contradictions: the Development of the Colonial State in Kenya, 1895–1914," 487–505, and "Crises of Accumulation, Coercion and the Colonial State," 55–81.

11. Lonsdale and Berman, "Coping," 488.

12. Lonsdale and Berman, "Crises," 58, 61; Cliffe, "Labour Migration and Peasant Differentiation: Zambian Experiences," 336. For a theoretical contribution, see McIntosh, "The State and the Oppression of Women," 260.

13. Lonsdale and Berman, "Crises," 79; Wright, "Justice, women, and the Social Order," 38.

14. Chanock, *Law, Custom and Social Order: The Colonial Experience in Malawi and Zambia*, 35–36, 104, 172–173.

15. Bernstein, "African Peasantries," 423.

16. Lonsdale and Berman, "Crises," 81.

17. *Ibid.*, 79.

18. This was evidenced in part by high levels of malnutrition and the presence of diseases related to dietary insufficiency among workers. See Phimister, "African Labour Conditions and Health in the Southern Rhodesian Mining Industry, 1898–1953," 102–150; Tambila, "A Plantation Labour Magnet: the Tanga Case," 36.

19. Chauncey, "The Locus of Reproduction: Women's Labour in the Zambian Copperbelt," 135–164; Deere, "Rural Women's Subsistence Production," 9–17; Jackson, "Uncontrollable Women in a Colonial African Town: Bulawayo Location, 1893–1958"; Wolpe, "Capitalism and Cheap Labour-Power in South Africa," 425–456.

20. Beneria, "Reproduction, Production and the Sexual Division of Labour," 219; Cliffe, "Labour Migration," 342; Deere, "Rural Women's Subsistence Production"; Stichter, "Women and the Labor Force in Kenya, 1895–1964," 45.

21. Bryceson and Mbilinyi, "The Changing Role," 94, 107; Stichter, *Migrant Laborers*, 10; Tosh, "Lango Agriculture during the Early Colonial Period," 422; Vail, "The Political Economy," 228.

22. In Kenya, the Master and Servants Ordinance, first enacted in 1906, and the Registration of Natives Ordinance, enacted in 1915, legislated the pass system. See Lonsdale and Berman, "Crises," 70–71 for enumeration.

23. Wright, "Justice, Women," 46.

24. Chanock, *Law, Custom*, 11.

25. Cliffe, "Labour Migration," 340–341; Dixon-Fyle, "Reflections," 431, 435; Mandala, "Capitalism, Kinship and Gender," 155; Raikes, "Rural Differentiation and Class Formation in Tanzania," 294.

26. Both property and the proceeds from labor migrancy became increasingly individualized, and elders progressively lost control over juniors. See Chanock, *Law, Custom*, 190–191; Lovett, "From Wives to Slaves," 6; Mandala, "Peasant Cotton Agriculture," 39–40.

27. Chauncey, 156; Jackson, 18, 34–35; Lovett, 8; and van Onselen, *Chibaro*, 181.

28. Chauncey, 152.

29. Ault, "Making 'Modern' Marriage 'Traditional,'" 185.

30. Cliffe, "Labour Migration," 341; Hay, "Women as Owners," 119–120; Lovett, 7; Stichter, *Migrant Laborers*, 68.

31. Chanock, *Law, Custom*, 113.

32. Parpart, "Class and Gender on the Copperbelt," 143–144.

33. Chauncey, 159; Ault, 183.

34. Oboler, *Women, Power*, 174.

35. Chauncey, 160; Ault, 183.

36. See Beinart, "Joyini Inkomo: Cattle Advances and the Origins of Migrancy from Pondoland," 199–219; Harries, "Kinship, Ideology and the Nature of Pre-Colonial Labour Migration," 142–166; and Meillassoux, *Anthropologie economique des gouro de Cote d'Ivoire*, chapters 7 and 8.

37. Lovett, 6; and Mandala, "Peasant Cotton Agriculture," 39–40. Migrants' potential independence depended in large part on the ready availability of unclaimed land. Where elders controlled land allocation,

migrants' potential autonomy was limited.

38. Chanock, *Law, Custom*, 180.

39. Ault, 185–186; Wright, "Technology, Marriage," 60.

40. Chanock, "Making Customary Law," 59. See also Chanock, *Law, Custom*, 193–194.

41. Bryceson and Mbilinyi, "The Changing Role," 103.

42. Chanock, *Law, Custom*, 145–150.

43. *Ibid.*, 183.

44. *Ibid.*, 172–182, citing Elizabeth Colson on the Plateau Tonga of Northern Rhodesia and Monica Wilson on the Nyakyusa of Tanganyika; Isaacman and Stephen, *Mozambique: Women, the Law and Agrarian Reform*, 7. As her kin were required to return the bridewealth upon divorce, an unhappy wife was often pressured by her family to remain in an unhappy marriage.

45. Chanock, *Law, Custom*, 115, 189.

46. Ault, 189; Perlman, "The Changing Status and Role of Women in Toro," 572.

47. Ault, 187–188; Parpart, "Class and Gender," 143–144.

48. Chanock, *Law, Custom*, 212–214; Parpart, "Sexuality and Power on the Zambian Copperbelt, 1926–1964."

49. Epstein, *Urbanization and Kinship*, 281–282.

50. Ault, 192–195; Chauncey, 153; Epstein, 284; Parpart, "Sexuality and Power," 8.

51. *Ibid.*, 8; Parpart, "Class and Gender," 152.

52. Chauncey, 140–141; Parpart, "Class and Gender," 149.

53. Hansen, "Lusaka's Squatters," 124; Chauncey, 158–159.

54. Chauncey, Parpart ("Class and Gender"), and others cite such a conflict as existing between the state and capital over women's presence in urban areas. But in a sense, this conflict was more perceived than real. Neither the state nor capital wanted these women to form the nucleus of a permanently urbanized population; both wished them to return to their rural homes when their services were no longer required, and both sought to control them. But while the state might be sympathetic to, and supportive of, efforts by chiefs and male elders to repatriate their women from urban areas, capital was quite antagonistic to these attempts. This cannot be interpreted as capital fighting for women's rights, but rather as evidence of the degree to which capital directly benefited from women's urban presence. Capital's conflict with the state revolved around the issue of which groups—it or the state and male elders—would benefit form controlling women's labor.

55. Chauncey, 149–151.

56. Parpart, "Class and Gender," 151.

57. Bujra, "Women 'Entrepreneurs,'" 220; Chauncey, 136, 153; Jackson, 10; Thornton, "The Struggle for Profit and Participation," 70, 80.

58. On Bulawayo, see Jackson, 10. On Nairobi, see Bujra, "Women 'Entrepreneurs,'" 217.

59. Jackson; White, "A Colonial State and an African Petty Bourgeoisie," 167–194.

60. Jackson, 38.

61. Thornton, 71.

62. Bujra, "Women 'Entrepreneurs,'" 224, 231, 233. Woman-woman marriage was one of the means by which prostitutes designated heirs.

63. Chauncey; White, "Women's Domestic Labor" and "A Colonial State."

64. Cliffe, "Labour Migration," 331; Epstein, 25–26; Hansen, "Negotiating Sex and Gender in Urban Zambia," 223; Jackson, 15; Thornton, 70; and van Zwananberg, "Urban Poverty in Nairobi," 195. Housing was often tied to jobs. See Epstein, 31; Bettison, "The Poverty Datum Line in Central Africa," 22.

65. Bujra, "Women 'Entrepreneurs,'" 222; Epstein 35, 58; Hansen, "Negotiating Sex," 228–229; Stichter, "Women and the Labor Force," 46, 57, 59.

66. Lonsdale and Berman, "Crises," 70–71; Thornton, 76. In Kenya, passes were to be carried by all males over the age of sixteen. I believe women were exempt from the pass laws because the system was designed primarily to control a migratory labor force. As such, the state viewed men—not women—as the actual or potential workers such passes were intended to control.

67. White, "A Colonial State," 171, 181.

68. *Ibid.*, 182, 185.

69. The state engineered an end to African property ownership in Bulawayo by initiating a municipal rebuilding scheme in Bulawayo Location in 1919; promulgating building regulations in 1927 that were designed to make new construction of privately owned dwellings increasingly difficult; and finally, acquiring in 1929 a monopoly on the provision of African housing, banning Africans from further building in the location, and classifying all location inhabitants as tenants who henceforth were unable to rent out huts because they no longer owned them. See Jackson, 40; Thornton, 72–73, 77.

70. As cited in Thornton, 71, a 1916 petition by the petty-bourgeois Loyal Mandebele Patriotic Society to the Bulawayo Town Clerk argued: "In the Bulawayo Location nearly all the stands and huts are occupied by single women who should not be there at all, for the reason that these locations are established for male servants who are working in town." As cited in Jackson, 33, an Industrial and Commercial Workers Union member giving evidence before a 1930 government commission believed that strict measures needed to be taken to combat prostitution in Bulawayo Location. "Today prostitutes are permitted to hire cottages from the Municipality simply because they are able to pay rent and they have cottages in preference to working men; this should not be allowed." See also Jackson, 23, 28.

71. The Bantu Women's League was formed in 1924 to mobilize protest among women householders against the municipal rebuilding scheme. See Thornton, 75. Women also protested their new status after 1929 as location tenants to the state in petitions and evidence before government commissions. See Jackson, 40.

72. Parpart, "Sexuality and Power," 8. In research conducted during 1957 and 1958, David Battison found that 22 percent of single men (either unmarried or having a wife who resided elsewhere) who worked in Lusaka had incomes below the Poverty Datum Line, as compared with 65 percent of childless couples, 78 percent of couples with one or two children, and 87

percent of couples with three children. Similarly, in Blantyre-Limbe, 83 percent of families were unable to maintain a minimum standard of consumption solely on the income represented by the male worker's wages. See Bettison, "The Poverty Datum Line," 23, 32. In Ndola in the late 1950s, Epstein discovered that location dwellers generally existed on the margins of poverty, with monthly expenditures exceeding the income represented by the husband's wage. See Epstein, 53.

73. For women's gardens, see Chauncey, 139; Epstein, 59; Hansen, "Negotiating Sex," 229; Hay, "Luo Women," 103; Parpart, "Class and Gender," 150. For sale of cooked food and firewood, see Bettison and Rigby, *Patterns of Income and Expenditure, Blantyre-Libme, Nyasaland*; Nyirenda, "African Market Vendors in Lusaka," 42–43; Parpart, "Class and Gender," 150; and Southall and Gutkind, *Townsmen in the Making: Kampala and its Suburbs*, 55, 137–139. For beer brewing and liquor distilling, see Epstein, 31; Bettison and Rigby, 27, 63, and 120; Parpart, *Working Class Wives and Collective Labor Action,* 5; Rothman, "The Liquor Authority and Welfare Administration in Lusaka," 29; Southall and Gutkind, 22, and 58. For prostitution, see Hansen, "Negotiating Sex," 228; Parpart, "Class and Gender," 150–151; Southall and Gutkind, 61–62, 85.

74. In Lusaka in the late 1950s, A. A. Nyirenda calculated that 82 percent of the women vendors at the Main Town market were married. Unlike male traders, they came to the market only on an occasional basis "to sell some of their domestic supplies when they are in need of money." Nyirenda, 42–43. See also Hansen, "Negotiating Sex," 229.

75. Even when employment opportunities were available to women, husbands opposed them, believing women's first responsibility was to care for them. See Epstein, 58; Hansen, "Negotiating Sex," 228.

76. Women could at times earn a pound or two in a single brew, a profit that equaled or exceeded male workers' monthly wages. See Parpart, "Class and Gender," 149.

77. Chauncey, 146; Parpart, "Working Class Wives," 7; Rothman, 27; Thornton, 76; and van Zwanenberg, "History and Theory," 191. Such social control programs included the establishment of halls, cinemas, and playing fields.

78. Chauncey, 146; Parpart, "Working Class Wives," 5. For Ndola, see Epstein, 311.

79. In 1931, about 30 percent of the Copperbelt mine workers lived with their wives. By 1961 this figure had increased to about 80 percent. See Parpart, "Sexuality and Power," 3.

80. Parpart, "Working Class Wives," 5.

81. Bujra, "Women 'Entrepreneurs,'" 223; Southall and Gutkind, 59–60; Epstein, 25, 61; Hansen, "Lusaka's Squatters," 124; Jackson, 12; Rothman, 33.

82. See, for example, Epstein, 120; Hansen, "Negotiating Sex," 219–237; Parpart, "Class and Gender."

83. Bettison and Rigby found that as a husband's wage rose, his wife's contributions to her family's income correspondingly declined. Emerging middle-class wives lacked independent sources of income and were financially

dependent upon their husbands. *Patterns of Income*, 74, 88, 92, 99.

84. Though perhaps a bit uneasy, the definition of "working class" has been extended here to include petty traders and other women who, while not working for wages, nevertheless stand in an exploited and unequal relationship to capital. For a discussion of this issue, see Robertson, *Sharing the Same Bowl*, Introduction.

85. Parpart, "Sexuality and Power," 6; Epstein, 75, 77; Parpart, "Working Class Wives," 9. Malnutrition was not uncommon among the wives and children of male workers. See Parpart, "Class and Gender," 152–153.

86. Epstein, 69–70; Parpart, "Sexuality and Power," 10.

87. For women's struggles to gain access to their husbands' wages and have a measure of say in their distribution, see Epstein, 57; Lovett, 3; Parpart, "Class and Gender," 152–153; Parpart, "Working Class Wives," 9. For control of women's income, and for control of women's freedom of movement and sexuality, see Epstein, 62, 74; Hansen, "Negotiating Sex," 226.

88. Boserup, *Woman's Role in Economic Development*, 54–55. Muntemba, "Women and Agricultural Change in the Railway Region of Zambia," 83–103; Oboler, *Women, Power*, 160.

89. Bryceson and Mbilinyi, 100; Harris and Harris, "Property and the Cycle," 149; Oboler, 161–162; Winans, 45–46.

90. Muntemba, 85.

91. Maxon, *John Ainsworth and the Making of Kenya*, 187–189; Tosh, 424; Wrigley, *Crops and Wealth in Uganda*, 14–16, 40, 48.

92. Fearn, *An African Economy*, 84.

93. Maxon, 217; Dixon-Fyle, "Reflections," 428–429; Muntemba, 88.

94. Dixon-Fyle, "Reflections," 429; Hermitte, "An Economic History of Barotseland, 1800–1940," 312–313; Peters, *Land Usage in Barotseland*, ix; Raikes, "Rural Differentiation," 309.

95. Gulliver, "The Arusha Family," 201; Harris and Harris, 140; LeVine, "The Gusii Family," 69. This distinction apparently held even when cash and food crops were planted in the same field. See Oboler, 161–162.

96. Okeyo, "Daughters," 207, 210.

97. Boserup, *Woman's Role*, 54; Chanock, "Agricultural Change and Continuity in Malawi," 404.

98. *Ibid.*, 404.

99. Coulson, "Agricultural Policies in Mainland Tanzania," 78; Dixon-Fyle, "Agricultural Improvement and Political Protest on the Tonga Plateau," 585; Muntemba, 91–92; Oboler, 171; Raikes, "Rural Differentiation," 297, 306.

100. Muntemba, 93–94; and Stichter, "Women and the Labor Force," 49.

101. Bryceson and Mbilinyi, 104–105; Chanock, *Law, Custom*, 230–231.

102. Bryceson and Mbilinyi, 100; Harris and Harris, 149; Oboler, 161–162; Winans, 45–46.

103. Harris and Harris, 140; LeVine, "The Gusii Family," 69; Oboler, 162.

104. Boserup, *Woman's Role*, 58–61; Chanock, "Agricultural Change," 403–404; Okeyo; Dixon-Fyle, "Reflections" 430; Muntemba, 96.

CHAPTER 3

Gender, Class, and State in Africa

ROBERT FATTON, JR.

The vital role which the state plays in post-colonial and late-industrializing nations has generated a vast literature on the nature, scope, and function of state activities. The state is increasingly portrayed as a bureaucratic apparatus of domination endowed with an autonomy of its own as well as with its own material interests and political agenda. In this literature, the state is no longer an agent of social classes and no longer reflects their relative power; the state is now above society and struggling against society itself.[1] A stronger conceptualization even contends that the state is capable of opposing the fundamental interests of the ruling class.[2] This chapter contends that such a conceptualization is seriously flawed.

While it is true that in exceptional situations the state may achieve a relative autonomy from the ruling class, the state in a class society is the ultimate organizer and defender of the long-term interests of the ruling class.[3] The existence of a ruling class requires the existence of a state whose role is to preserve and reproduce the social, political, and economic structures of the ruling class's dominance. This is not to say that the state always fulfills this role; it may be constrained by the ruling class itself and/or transnational agents, and/or it may be challenged by the subordinate classes. The capacity of the state to protect successfully the position of the ruling class, the capacity of the state to be effective, is directly dependent on the degree of hegemony which the ruling class itself has achieved.[4] Thus, to make sense of the state is to decipher the relations of class power, the processes of class formation, and the hegemonic propensity of the ruling class. Before "bringing the state back in" it is crucial to "bring classes back in."

This chapter aims to do precisely that in the political context of Africa. Special attention is paid to the hegemonic projects of the ruling class. It will be argued that ruling classes exist throughout Africa, but that they have yet to become hegemonic. Their domination and their rule express more the threat and use of direct violence than their moral, material, and intellectual leadership. Ruling classes are in the process of constructing their hegemony; in this quest they are using gender as a means to consolidate the closure of classes. While still fluid and in flux, entry into the ruling class is increasingly difficult and virtually blocked to independent and autonomous women.

In Africa, the construction of ruling class hegemony has the effect of conflating male power with class closure. Women are not totally excluded from the ranks of the ruling class, but their quest for status and wealth depends inordinately on aligning themselves with powerful men. In the absence of such alignments, women tend to withdraw from the public arena to build their own parallel and independent spheres of survival. The emancipation of women is thus linked to the struggle against ruling class hegemony; it requires both a feminist and a class consciousness.

WOMEN AND CLASS

The state in Africa is the prime instrument with which a class can hope to become a ruling class. To be outside the state is to be condemned to a subordinate and inferior status. In Africa, class power is state power; the two are fused and inseparable. State power, however, is conspicuously male power, and this in turn implies that African women have been marginalized.[5] This is not to say that women have accepted their marginality; on the contrary, they have developed conventional and unconventional methods of struggle against patriarchal domination. As Christine Obbo has observed:

[W]omen . . . too wanted power, wealth and status . . . and this created tension and conflict between the sexes. Women found that, because men depended on them for achieving these goals themselves, they regarded any direct attempt by women to seek the same goals as women becoming uncontrollable! The need to control women has always been an important part of male success in most African societies. The women, however, whether married or single, had definite strategies for achieving economic autonomy and hence improved social conditions—strategies such as migration, hard work and manipulation. Migration involved mobility and hence escape from obstacles to individual progress in favour of creating or taking up more options. Hard work brought direct rewards for their labour and enabled them to feed, support and rear their children. Through manipulation the woman engaged in "strategic planning" and thus mobilized needed resources and engaged in certain actions that led to institutional change.[6]

Despite such strategies, women's access to political and economic resources has been severely constrained by pervasive and overwhelming patterns of male domination. Male domination should not, however, obscure the profound inequalities and class contradictions dividing women. If women are repressed and exploited, they certainly do not experience repression and exploitation equally. The lives of women are decisively determined by their social class.[7] The life chances of the peasant women are clearly enormously different form those of the privileged women of the emerging urban bourgeoisie. Indeed, the latter has the power and the wealth to force men of lower classes into submission and obeisance. In this perspective, while all women suffer from patriarchy, rich and poor women bear its burdens unequally and differentially.

The position of women in the social order is thus significantly dependent on class affiliation; in general, however, women obtain this affiliation not on their own but on account of their father's and/or husband's social status.[8] To a large extent women's connections into the male world determine her class membership. There are exceptions, however; Janet MacGaffey has found in her study of entrepreneurs in Kisangani that "instead of becoming increasingly impoverished, [women] are in fact doing very well for themselves. . . . [They] have succeeded in asserting their autonomy and have become members of [the commercial middle class] individually and not just as dependents of men."[9]

These few successful women should not mask the overall African reality that men and women of the same class are fundamentally unequal. In general, a woman's access to state resources and hence to class power hinges upon her male linkages. Women therefore lack the political and material autonomy that transforms individuals into full citizens. Women's subordination in the public and political realms of society is reinforced by the equally repressive environment of the private and intimate domain. This domain that Catharine MacKinnon has identified as the "common ground of [women's] inequality" and as the "sphere of battery, marital rape, and women's exploited labor,"[10] embodies the most immediate site of male supremacy. To this extent all women share the common experience of degradation, humiliation, and isolation that inheres in the private and intimate domain. The private, as it were, becomes a political battlefield; women's oppression is also the politics of women's personal lives and of highly individual relations of subordination. "Sexual politics" as MacKinnon suggests, is at the core of the women's struggle for equality, but her stress on its centrality detracts her from analyzing the material matrix that envelops it.

Analyses of this kind, as Michele Barrett observes, have "tended to ignore the ways in which private oppression is related to broader questions of relations of production and the class structure."[11] These analyses claim to be advances over Marxism, and to embody its "final conclusion and ultimate critique,"[12] but in reality they are more a retreat from class than a conceptual and theoretical revolution. Radical feminism brings valuable insights to Marxism, but it does not supersede it. Women's oppression can be better apprehended with the tools of Marxian materialism. As Lise Vogel has argued:

> [S]hared experiences of and cultural responses to female oppression
> may produce a certain degree of solidarity among women across class

lines. While this solidarity has a basis in reality, and can be of serious political import, the situations of women in the dominant and exploited classes are fundamentally distinct from a theoretical perspective. Only women in the subordinate class participate in the maintenance and replacement of the indispensable force that keeps a class society going—exploitable labor power.[13]

Women thus have a contradictory insertion into the social structure: while they all suffer from the effects of patriarchy, they do not experience equally the ravages of class domination, nor do they share the same aspirations and interests. The woman's struggle for emancipation is articulated within the totality of social struggles and thus within the parameters of the class struggle. This does not imply, however, that sexual relations should be equated with class relations. As Roberta Hamilton has remarked, "Marxists must consider the consequences for women in *any social system* of bearing the greater burden of perpetuating the species. . . . Men have conquered the world because they had nature on their side. The social repercussions of this, how men and women spend their lives, how they experience their sexuality, are translated into privileges not only for rich men but for all men."[14]

Men's biological advantage, however, need not crystallize into patriarchal relations of power. Such relations must be approached in their historical specificity; they are the product of particular historical conjunctures, modes of production, and class relationships. While the procreative function of women is obviously transhistorical, it does not necessarily and inevitably generate patriarchal forms of domination.[15] Thus, it is impossible to go beyond women's biological inequality and to contemplate their liberation without traveling decisively beyond the confines of class societies. This is not to say that patriarchal discriminations will suddenly vanish with the advent of a socialist society; these discriminations are so deeply embedded in the social and cultural fabric of all African societies that even in the most committed Afro-Marxist and socialist states the process of women's emancipation is hesitant, contradictory, and limited.[16] As MacKinnon has forcefully argued:

> If seizures of state and productive power overturn work relations, they do not overturn sex relations at the same time or in the same way, as a class analysis of sex would . . . predict. Neither technology nor socialism, both of which purport to alter women's role at the point of production, have ever yet equalized women's status relative to men. In the feminist view, nothing has.[17]

Gender is therefore relatively autonomous from class, but this by no means implies—as MacKinnon does[18]—that it can be studied and apprehended across the boundaries of and independently from class. The establishment of the simple dichotomy of male/female to explain woman's oppression does not suffice; in fact, it obscures the internal contradictions of the women's struggle for liberation. While women suffer similar patriarchal impediments, they do not have the same aspirations, desires, and needs. Urban women and peasant women, bourgeois women and proletarian women, old women and young women have more contradictory interests and lifestyles than could ever be surmounted by their common experience of sexual submission. As Janet Bujra has noted:

> To discuss the implications for women of capitalist class formation is consciously to reject the simplistic notion . . . of "African women" as a homogeneous category. The condition of women in Africa has of course always been culturally diverse. . . . [W]omen cannot be thought of as a single category, even though there are important and occasionally unifying struggles in which they may engage. At the same time women cannot be simply analyzed "as men": gender is almost invariably a relevant social category. The point is that gender differences find differential expression at different class levels— gender is qualified by the places women occupy in newly emergent classes.[19]

In this perspective, the conquest of important political positions by upper-class women would not significantly alter the reality of sexual oppression. The feminization of African ruling classes might contribute to the partial erosion of patriarchal ideology, but it would certainly not end class domination, nor engender more democratic practices. The mere incorporation of women into the strategic locations of the state will not stop such domination and practices. In fact, legal changes and the ushering in of socialism would not suffice. A separate and fundamental transformation of the ideological, political, and economic foundations sustaining the confinement of women into domestic labor is required. As Lise Vogel has put it:

> As an obstacle to effective equality for women, domestic labor has a stubborn material presence that no legislation, by itself, can overcome. A major index of socialist society is, then, progressive reduction of the disproportionate burden on women of domestic labor. Two paths toward this goal are available. First, domestic labor itself can be reduced through the socialization of its tasks. Second, the domestic labor that remains to be done outside public production can be shared among women, men, and, in appropriate proportion, children. Because domestic labor cannot be substantially reduced, much less eliminated, overnight, socialist society must take both paths in order to assure women of real social equality.[20]

The struggle for women's equality therefore entails a multidimensional attack against the resistant traditions and entrenched interests of male supremacy. This is all the more urgent in Africa where women's subordination is more pervasive, acute, and accepted. In what follows, I am fully aware of the theoretical and empirical dangers stemming from an analysis that generalizes African problems, and may not do justice to regional, national, and political specificities. Macroanalyses, however, are necessary. It is hoped this essay will serve as a guide for further investigation into the nature of political and sexual domination in Africa, and perhaps as a means of struggling against that domination.

HEGEMONY AND EXIT

African ruling classes will remain nonhegemonic for the foreseeable future however masculine or feminine they may be. So far, they have been incapable of legitimizing their exploitation; they have failed to establish the "moral authority of suffering and injustice," as Gramsci says. They lack hegemony. The concept of hegemony, as Gramsci defines it, characterizes:

> The "spontaneous" consent given by the great masses of the population to the general direction imposed on social life by the dominant fundamental group; this consent is "historically" caused by the prestige (and consequent confidence) which the dominant group enjoys because of its position and function in the world of production.[21]

The question of hegemony, however, is not merely material stuff; it is also a politics of moral and intellectual leadership. To assert its hegemony, the ruling class must be able to defend its own corporate interests by universalizing them, by ensuring that these interests can "become the interests of the . . . subordinate groups."[22] To this extent, hegemony implies consent rather than domination, integration rather than exclusion, and co-optation rather than suppression.

The ruling class must therefore establish its leadership at the ideological and cultural levels to neutralize popular challenges and indeed gain the consent of the broad masses. It must develop its own "organic intellectuals" to direct and organize its world view and aspirations.[23] Organic intellectuals are managers of legitimation; they contribute to making the class to which they belong into the leading and hegemonic class of society. They disseminate the dominant ideology to integrate the subordinate classes into the ruling class's way of life. The transformation of corporate class interests into the general interest requires the intense labor of cultural imagination, diffusion, and penetration of the organic intellectuals. It is such labor which imparts to the masses their proper ideological code of conduct and beliefs.

A ruling class is therefore hegemonic when it has established its intellectual, moral, and material leadership over society, and when it has succeeded in persuading subaltern classes that positions of subordination and superordination are just, proper, and legitimate. This requires certain concessions from the ruling class, concessions which, while not fundamental, contribute to the political co-optation of popular sectors and the progressive expansion of the productive process. In this instance, the ruling class "really causes the entire society to move forward, not merely satisfying its own existential requirements, but continuously augmenting its cadres for the conquest of ever new spheres of economic and productive activity."[24] This is the moment of "historic unity" when the ruling class has established its material, ethical, and political leadership over society, and when the relationships of superordination and subordination are accepted by all as organic and not contradictory, and as legitimate and not exploitative. When such a situation crystallizes, the ruling class has achieved hegemony.

Hegemony, however, does not entail the absence of the ruling class' capacity to exercise domination or coercion. What it does signify is that domination is legitimate and eclipsed by the politics of consent and leadership. What is important therefore in the study of hegemony is not whether ruling classes rule without a coercive capacity of intervention, but whether such coercive capacity has achieved predominance over their ethical and intellectual leadership. Hegemony crystallizes when consensual politics becomes so powerful that subordinate classes accept the rule of the ruling class, the given social reality, and their place within it as tolerable, legitimate, and just. Subordinate classes, however, have not so much a "false consciousness" inhibiting their determination to change and transform the historical order, as an embryonic consciousness which manifests itself only "occasionally and in flashes." The consciousness which dominates their historical conduct is not theirs. It is "borrowed" from the ruling class and "is not independent and autonomous, but submissive and subordinate."[25]

Not surprisingly, women have been victimized by the hegemony of the male vision of the world. It is a vision that has led women to accept many of the patterns and processes of their own subordination. Christine Obbo has found that measures bent on improving the conditions of East African women have been opposed not only by men, but by women—in particular, elite women.[26] Simone de Beauvoir's description of the predicament confronting European women seems equally valid for African women:

> The privileged place held by men in economic life, their social usefulness, the prestige of marriage, the value of masculine backing, all this, makes women wish ardently to please men. Women are still, for the most part, in a state of subjection. It follows that woman sees herself and makes her choices not in accordance with her true nature in itself, but as man defines her. . . . Representation of the world, like the world itself, is the work of men; they describe it from their own point of view, which they confuse with the absolute truth.[27]

The liberation of women hinges therefore on the emergence of a feminist consciousness as a source of moral anger and self-affirmation, and as an alternative to the male-constructed reality. The development of such a consciousness, however, faces many obstacles. As Pepe Roberts has pointed out:

[S]exual identity—concepts of masculinity and femininity—are culturally produced and culturally specific. They are, however, so deeply embedded in our lived experience that . . . they constitute the limits and substance of common sense. They are the most difficult to challenge and change because they appear to be the most natural of all "human" attributes.[28]

In Africa, where patriarchal traditions are so ingrained in the fabric of society, women's struggle for emancipation is replete with contradictions, ambivalence, and silence. This is not to say that women fail to resist and protest, but that their resistance and protest are easily co-opted or suppressed by the structural, political, and ideological powers of male supremacy. Moreover, because the male-dominated African ruling classes lack hegemony, they have been unable to take into account the interests and aspirations of women and subaltern classes. The reformist and "universalist" reach of African ruling classes is severely limited, and thus the state is always prepared to "silence even the murmurings of women" and the voices of peasants and workers. As noted previously, however, African women themselves, and those of the elite in particular, have contributed to the silencing of women's opposition to male domination. In this instance, the hegemony of the male world view has penetrated women's consciousness and debilitated the feminist struggle for emancipation.

While the male world view may have contributed to fill partially the hegemonic fissure, African ruling classes are nonetheless struggling to compose and articulate a more encompassing and complete hegemonic system. This in turn compels them to take direct charge of the state itself, to staff it, and consequently to obliterate the political space required for the effective exercise of statecraft. Paradoxically, because state power and class power are one, the state has lacked the relative autonomy necessary to effect those reforms and concessions necessary for the preservation of the rule of the ruling class. With their eyes fixed on immediate and selfish interests and their hands in direct control of the levers of the state apparatus, African ruling classes have been unable to take the long view and organize, in an appropriately flexible way, the conditions of their own continued dominance. Because those staffing the main agencies of the state form the ruling class, and are part of the ruling class by virtue of this very fact, their relative independence in deciding how to serve the long-term interest of their own class is seriously inhibited.

The nonhegemonic status of African ruling classes deprives the state of the relative autonomy that makes reform possible, despotism unnecessary, and liberal democracy viable. The state is almost exclusively an authoritarian structure of dominance; expressing the narrow corporate interests of the ruling class, it has failed to become integral. The integral state is the state of a hegemonic ruling class and as such it is capable of "expansion." It is capable of integrating and co-opting potential allies and antagonistic elements into its own institutions. The integral state is thus relatively autonomous since it can extract certain sacrifices from the ruling class and make certain concessions to popular classes. The integral state, however, is not above society; it is integral precisely because the ruling class has achieved hegemony. In other words, the integral state can emerge only when the ruling class has consolidated its rule to the point where its material, intellectual, and moral leadership is unquestioned or at least consensually accepted by the subordinate classes. Thus, hegemony makes possible the integral state.[29]

In African conditions where hegemony is nonexistent or embryonic, the state is not likely to take seriously into account the interests of those classes over which the ruling class seeks to impose its domination and authority. Also, to the extent that the state is the systemic concentration of man's power, it codifies, institutionalizes, and legitimizes patriarchy. As MacKinnon has argued:

> [The] State is male in the feminist sense. The law sees and treats women the way men see and treat women. The . . . state coercively and authoritatively constitutes the social order in the interest of men as a gender, through its legitimizing norms, relation to society, and substantive policies. It achieves this through embodying and ensuring male control over women's sexuality at every level, occasionally cushioning, qualifying, or de jure prohibiting its excesses when necessary to its normalization. Substantively, the way the male point of view frames an experience is the way it is framed by state policy.[30]

Not surprisingly, the rule of most African ruling classes is authoritarian, brutal, and violent. Compliance is the result of coercion and not consensus, and popular resistance is seldom frontal and revolutionary. Resistance takes the form of withdrawal from the public realm rather than confrontational assaults against the state. "Exit"[31] is the preferred means of voicing discontent since it does not necessarily provoke the immediate exercise of state repression. It embodies the more common reaction of the most marginalized groups and classes of society. Not surprisingly, women whose independent access to the state is limited and whose struggle for sexual emancipation is neglected tend to exit from the conventional political arena. As Kathleen Staudt has observed:

> With both their marginality in conventional politics and the depoliticization of their issues . . . many women withdraw or are alienated from contemporary politics, preferring instead to manage what is left of their own affairs autonomously. While the ability to remain autonomous suggests the still limited power of the state, women's autonomy also magnifies gender participation gaps in conventional politics and thus women's continued marginality in those politics.[32]

Such withdrawal from politics, as well as the general phenomenon of exit, demonstrates that African ruling classes are nonhegemonic since they are unable to penetrate certain popular political and economic spaces existing independently of state authority. The study of the state presupposes therefore the analysis of classes and, in particular, the degree of hegemony which the ruling class has attained. It is hegemony, or the lack of it, which determines the nature of the state and the scope of its autonomy. Instead of approaching politics from a "state-centered model," this chapter seeks to reaffirm the primacy of class and gender in the shaping of society and in the authoritative allocation of values. To do otherwise is to assume that the state can stand undisturbed above society and impose in an antagonistic manner its own policies and preferences on a recalcitrant male-dominated ruling class. It is to assume that the ruling class can exist without ruling; it is to assume that the ruling class does not exist at all. In reality, the state is neither a balloon floating freely in midair nor an omnipotent autonomous organism. It is grounded in class and gender practices and ligatured to the exercise of class and male domination. This is particularly so in Africa, where both an intense process of class formation and an ambivalent but increasingly assertive feminist struggle are taking place.

While still fragile and weak, African ruling classes are clearly discernible. Their conspicuous lifestyles and life chances distinguish them from the vast majority living in poverty. Irving Leonard Markovitz defines them as an "'organizational bourgeoisie': a combined ruling group consisting of the top political leaders and bureaucrats, the traditional rulers and their descendants, the leading members of the liberal professions, the rising business bourgeoisie, and the top members of the the military and police forces." Markovitz then argues that the members of the organizational bourgeoisie are "located at pivotal points of control in those overarching systems of political, social and economic power . . . the nation-state and capitalism."[33] They have integrated the private and public spheres into their own corporate domain for the advancement of their productive and political power. As a result, women's politics have been traversed by the aspirations and projects of the male-dominated organizational bourgeoisie. Indeed, the struggle for female emancipation has tended to be controlled, shaped, and articulated by the women of the organizational bourgeoisie whose privileged resources and political connections have given them a certain influence over state policies.[34] As Staudt has indicated:

> Women have not been universally disadvantaged, thus suggesting the importance of sex and class interaction in politics. . . . [Very] rarely do women activists in conventional politics articulate genuinely redistributive issues. Rather, their issues benefit themselves in a particular class . . . women's politics is another dimension of class politics, wherein the political process is used to advance the interests of those already privileged.[35]

The power to advance the interests of the privileged class is inextricably tied to their control of the state. Class power in Africa is fundamentally dependent on state power. Capturing the state is the best and perhaps exclusive means for acquiring and generating the material wealth necessary to become a ruling class. The absence of a hegemonic African bourgeoisie grounded in a solid and independent economic base and successfully engaged in the private accumulation of capital has transformed politics into material struggle. State power provides the fundamental opportunity to build class power in a context of great and increasing scarcity. Not surprisingly, once an incipient ruling class takes over the state, it monopolizes it for its exclusive material and political gains and uses it for the violent exclusion of potential rival groups.[36] In this sense, the power-holders inside the state constitute the dominant fraction of the African ruling class, but they are a dominant fraction in formation, and accordingly rule without having achieved hegemony. As Frederick Cooper has remarked: "[African ruling classes may] be better defined by their project than by their current situation. . . . But it is not a project that has been altogether successful."[37]

The fragility of the ruling classes' project is directly related to the peripheral nature of African societies. The dependent and backward character of African capitalism has contributed to the material and hegemonic fragility of most African bourgeoisies and thus to authoritarian political forms of governance.[38] Such authoritarian forms, however, mask the ruling classes' relative incapacity to transform their power into effective political, economic, and cultural policies. The African state has yet to develop the means and resources with which to penetrate all the sectors of society. Authoritarianism coexists therefore with a definite lack of authority.[39] This paradox of African politics can be partly explained by the articulation of different modes of production.

It is in this perspective that Goran Hyden has introduced the concept of an "uncaptured peasantry" capable of resisting and neutralizing state policies.[40] The uncaptured peasantry operates its own "peasant mode of production" as a separate material and institutional structure. Such a structure constitutes the kin-based "economy of affection" which represents an alternative "space" to the dominant state system. This alternative space allows the peasantry to "exit" the demands and policies formulated by central political authorities. Thus, in Hyden's perspective, the state is incapable of sustaining and reproducing existing social relations and, specifically, of controlling the labor force in the interest of any program of economic growth. Suspended in midair, without roots, in a strong indigenous bourgeoisie and without the power to enforce the systemic an authoritative allocation of values, the state is "soft" and impotent. The state is thus incapable of imposing the structures of capitalist or socialist modernity.[41]

What Hyden fails to recognize, however, is that the economy of affection is paradoxically an inevitable phenomenon of the transition to capitalism. Indeed, the proletarianization of male labor that this transition entails has been subsidized by the living that females could eke from the land.[42] While the partial separation of labor from what Marx called "the objective conditions of its realization—from the means of labour and the material for labour"[43] forced adult African men into the cash nexus of migratory wage labor, it confined African women to the household and compelled them to "surperengage" in agricultural work to supplement their husbands' meagre wages. As a result, only males' labor was defined as work since it obtained a wage; unpaid females' labor no longer qualified as work.[44]

In this perspective, far from being an impediment to capitalist development, the economy of affection contributed to such development by facilitating the emergence of cheap wage labor. Simultaneously, by fostering the separation of consumption from production and labor from housework, the transition to capitalism further consolidated the existing ideology of female subordination. Indeed, the transition has introduced into African societies a profound chasm between public and private realms. This chasm largely corresponds to the sexual division of labor: women are confined to the privacy of the household wherein they perform their "natural functions" of mothering and wiving, and men are catapulted into the public world of "real production and real work" wherein they lord it over economy and politics.[45]

Alice Clark's comments on the working life of the European women at the dawn of capitalism define well the predicament of contemporary African women: "Thus it came to pass that every womanly function was considered as the private interest of husbands and fathers, bearing no relation to the life of the State, and therefore demanding from the community as a whole no special care or provision."[46]

While some African women have gained a certain degree of independence from the male-dominated network of finance and politics, this independence is being challenged and is difficult to sustain in changing economic circumstances. As Claire Robertson has argued in her study of women and class in Ghana:

> Increasingly . . . it is only the disadvantaged [women] who make fulltime trading their occupation, although many of the advantaged use it to supplement their incomes. In the face of educational disqualification from many jobs, trading remains a live option but also bears the stigma of low social status. The paradox is that, while many women aspire to the male-dominated elite, most will remain in female networks where they are economically independent from men, and poor as a consequence. Westerners should not mistake such independence for privilege. That women have been able to survive so far has largely depended on the strength of those networks. However, socioeconomic forces are weakening that strength and making it logical for younger women to trade off economic independence for the anticipated greater security of dependence on a man. Unfortunately, neither the weakened female networks nor the marital situation offer most women the long-term security they are seeking for themselves and their children.[47]

Increasingly drawn as custodians of the private realm and excluded from the public domain, African women have lost a significant amount of whatever power they may have enjoyed in some precolonial societies. Indeed, colonialism and the transition to capitalism have both enhanced the ideology of female subordination that had been sustained by patriarchal religious practices and the weight of reactionary traditional customs.[48] This in turn has contributed to the massive underrepresentation of women in the strategic locations of the state and thus to the accentuation of women's powerlessness. In spite of certain changes, the legal structure of most African states continues to discriminate against women in "matters concerning land, marriage, divorce and inheritance."[49] The underrepresentation of women in the state has therefore reinforced the existing sexism of male-dominated organs of power. Not surprisingly, many women have opted to withdraw from state institutions to engage in autonomous activities of simple survival.[50]

The capacity of women and the peasantry in general to withdraw from the domain of the state has prompted Hyden to advance the thesis of the softness of the African state. For Hyden, therefore, African politics are a politics without ruling classes and a politics marked by the absence of institutionalized power. This, however, does not preclude the existence of authoritarianism, dictatorial rule, and tyranny. Paradoxically, as Hyden himself acknowledges, the soft state creates the perfect terrain for these arbitrary and violent forms of governance.

The question this inevitably brings to mind is why and how can the state unleash its arbitrary violence, particularly against the lower and working strata of the population, if it stands in midair, uncontrolled by any ruling class? Hence, the important issue is not whether the state is soft, but whether it is soft for, or harsh against, particular groups and classes. In short, whose benefits are best served by the softness of the state? It is true that in most African countries social discipline is weak and power lacks institutionalization, but this general systemic weakness favors in disproportionate ways the interests of the privileged ruling circles. In fact, the soft state is neither neutral nor in midair. It unleashes its power, often violently, to defend the interests of the dominant faction of the ruling class. It depoliticizes the subaltern groups by eliminating their independent organs of representation and by reducing their participation in decisionmaking. The emergence of the one-party state throughout Africa is the means to these ends. In addition, the one-party state is the vehicle through which material resources are acquired and distributed since the state in Africa is the fundamental agent of capital accumulation and extraction.[51] In these circumstances, it is not surprising that the struggle for controlling the state, in conditions of monolithic political structures and generalized material scarcity, becomes Hobbesian, violent, and deadly.

Such a situation of political insecurity has transformed the one-party state into a system that breeds disorder rather than order. This in turn has generated a process of escalating repression as those ruling the state have sought to maintain and preserve their absolute monopoly of power. Political instability in Africa is therefore rooted more in the extreme politicization of the state as an organ to be monopolized for absolute power and accelerated economic advancement than in the softness of the state as Hyden would have it. To characterize the state as soft is to miss the class relationships and class struggles that provide the social context that molds and shapes the state itself. Thus, if the state in Africa is relatively weak in terms of its capacity to impose its authority on all sectors of society, it is nonetheless powerful enough to unleash its violence against particular groups and classes.

Rooted in male dominance, the state also marginalizes women and uses them as scapegoats for masking persistent systemic failures and illicit political practices.[52] Robertson's remarks concerning Ghana are illustrative of a continental phenomenon:

> [G]ender identity is increasingly being used by the government of Ghana in an ideology which objectifies women traders into a class which can be blamed and persecuted for causing the enormous economic problems. . . . The persecution heightened during the first Rawlings government. In a symbolic act on August 18, 1979, soldiers bulldozed [the women's traders] Makola No. 1 Market and reduced it to a pile of rubble. "That will teach Ghanaian women to stop being wicked," a soldier said.[53]

Male-dominated ruling classes have therefore used gender ideology as a means of legitimizing their governance and enlisting the support of males from subordinate classes. By instilling fear of female economic competition and autonomy, ruling classes have reinforced sexism and eroded the solidarity of the oppressed. The relative hegemony of patriarchal ideology has tended to mollify women's resolve and women's confidence in their quest for emancipation. As Pepe Roberts has pointed out:

> Women who struggle to maintain some economic independence from men may be accused of making their husbands impotent, or of prostitution or of neglecting their children and "causing" juvenile crime. Similarly, women who vigorously dislike polygyny are confronted with claims that it is the natural birthright of the African (man). While there has been scope for individual acts of resistance, however, the exercise of individual strength often increases a woman's personal vulnerability. Those who are not deterred by male fantasies of female aggression encounter the moral crusades, the denigration and the violence against women who force their way out of male control.[54]

The hegemony of gender ideology is not only grounded in the weight of cultural traditions but also in the material conflicts generated by the processes of capitalist (under)development. African men generally regard women's participation in urban labor as an unwelcome source of competition in an already overcrowded job market. Simultaneously, men stereotype female wage-earners as lazy, gossipy, incompetent, and morally depraved workers who have failed to maintain the "good" spartan habits of rural existence. As Obbo has observed:

> Fear and frustration in personal or professional relationships with individual women lead men to lash out at all women, particularly those in wage employment. Any attempt at self-reliance and economic independence is interpreted as a challenge to male juridical supremacy and, therefore, bad for African society. Most men expect the impossible—an educated women who will blindly obey their wishes and who will stay in the rural areas cultivating food. The good woman stays at home in the village because, if she is in town, she is a source of worry for her husband.[55]

Such patriarchal prejudices have contributed to persisting and pervasive discriminatory state policies. Reflecting at best a benign neglect of any feminist agenda, these policies hinder and limit women's access to capital, land, and credit. The impotence of the state to enforce new and more egalitarian rules of conduct is thus biased impotence. It is an impotence that consistently favors and enhances the power, interests, and status of the male-dominated privileged classes.

In this instance, it is significant to note the tolerance of the state toward the illegal acquisition and reproduction of wealth through the rapidly expanding black markets of Africa. The phenomenon of the black-market economy known as the *magendo* in East Africa indicates that the softness of the state is more a symptom of ruling class interests than institutional weakness and fragility.[56] The *magendo* persists because it serves the material and political purposes of the ruling class. It constitutes a source of wealth and a means of ascending to membership in the ruling class. Accordingly, in spite of its autonomy from the formal structures of state power, the *magendo* depends inevitably on the power-holders for its continued survival and expansion. The state will not close down the *magendo* operations because they are too profitable for both state agents and *magendo* entrepreneurs.

The relative autonomy of the *magendo* from direct state control has, however, enticed women into its illegal network. Providing a niche where patriarchy has yet to consolidate, the *magendo* has attracted enterprising women in search of material improvement. This has involved activities ranging from selling goods without a license and gin distilling to prostitution.[57] That such "services" do not frontally challenge patriarchal structures, and in fact satisfy men's visceral pleasures, has made women's participation in the illegal *magendo* economy acceptable to the state.

In contrast to this rather symbiotic relationship between state and *magendo*, the state/peasant relationship has been characterized by domination and subordination in spite of the peasant's capacity to exit. Indeed, the fact that peasants enjoy certain means of exit from governmental policies should not conceal the negative and pervasive impact of the state on their livelihood and mode of production. The peasants' exit is a choice of last resort, reflecting their desire to avoid the adverse effects of official policies.[58] It is not an indication of the peasants' victorious independence from state interference. Peasants, like women, withdraw from the public realm precisely because of the harshness of state decisions. As Staudt has observed, when rural women organize to defend their economic interests, they do so outside the conventional political realm, but this limits their capacity to obtain badly needed state services. "This autonomy may be an asset in organizational effectiveness but [is] a drawback in extracting the increasingly valuable resources distributed in the policy arena."[59] Thus, the exit of both women and peasantry is more a symptom of the hard-centered nature of the state than of its softness.

The concept of the soft state is therefore misleading because it masks the authoritarian character of most African states and the uneven and biased impact of state intervention. In this instance, it is preferable to allude to Gramsci's notion of the integral state, a state in which crystallizes the "organic relations between . . . political society and 'civil society'."[60]

Because the African state has yet to become integral, the ruling classes have failed to obtain the "spontaneous" consent of the masses to the general direction they wish to impose on society. In these circumstances, social discipline and order are imposed by direct domination on those who do not consent either actively or passively to the rule of the governing classes. Thus, while the state cannot effectively expand the domain of its authority to obtain the obedience of all its subjects, it has the capacity to crush fundamental political challenges. It possesses sufficient coercive might to repress serious contending and opposing "voices."[61] In fact, the means of exit represent a safety valve for the continued survival of most African political systems. Exit embodies the safest and most profitable expression of discontent as the popular articulation of voices is much too costly and dangerous in the African context of authoritarian one-party states.

In Africa, most ruling classes have restricted so stringently the level of voice that the masses have found in exit the only means of expressing their opposition without risking the brutal suffering of state repression. Hence, it is the incapacity of the ruling classes to tolerate and institutionalize a relatively high level of voice that has paradoxically contributed to the development and persistence of exit. Such an incapacity indicates the failure of the ruling classes to control, shape, and guide political participation; it is symptomatic of their nonhegemonic status. African ruling classes have been unable to impose their "intellectual and moral leadership"; they have been besieged by a continuous and persistent "crisis of authority." They lack the necessary legitimacy to establish an integral state which can command obedience without the pervasive use of force.

CONCLUSIONS

I have argued that the African state has a limited organic autonomy because the ruling class is a ruling class in so far as it is capable of occupying directly the main offices of the state. The ruling class expresses its class power through its unmediated control of state power. Such a fusion of state and class powers reflects its nonhegemonic character. Accordingly, coercion rather than persuasion, domination rather than leadership, and corruption rather than legitimacy constitute the stuff of African politics.

This grim depiction of African politics is not meant to lead to fatalism and resignation, but to indicate the enormous obstacles to African emancipation. The structures of ruling class and male domination, and the atrocious realities of severe deprivation and crude forms of underdevelopment are well entrenched in most African societies. These unsettling and cruel social phenomena are not, however, all there is to African politics. Indeed, the existence of these phenomena is an invitation to popular struggles, revolts, and revolutions. Oppression and repression have always generated opposition and challenge; there is therefore no reason to believe that African men and women will continue to put up with being the victims of injustice.

This is not to say that a continental revolution of the poor and exploited, let alone a genuinely socialist revolution, is imminent but that popular pressures that are disruptive of the existing order are in the making. In this perspective, the women's struggle for equality, however contradictory and hesitant it may be, is a source of hope and progress. As Bujra has observed:

> The existence of *women's* organizations in Africa is not . . . unthinkingly to be equated with the existence of any specifically *feminist* consciousness, or any desire to transform the class or economic structures of postcolonial society. Women's liberation is disruptive in its challenge to male prerogatives; organizations such as these reinforce the status quo. They serve petty bourgeois class interests more than they serve women. To dismiss them out of hand because of this would be shortsighted, however. For, despite their primary significance as institutions of class control, such organizations, in bringing women into communication with each other, can provide arenas of struggle within which women who are poor and subordinated can speak out and exert pressure on those who enjoy the rewards of postcolonial society.[62]

Thus, the march leading to the emancipation of women is difficult and full of detours, but the emergence of popular challenges to patriarchal forms of domination is a clear indication that African women have begun the journey. The journey, however, will remain incomplete if the politics of class fails to guide the politics of gender.

This chapter posits also the need for a study of the state as an organ of domination ligatured to the hegemonic project of incipient ruling classes.

The state, however autonomous it may be, cannot transcend the parameters of class power. In Africa, it is the vehicle to such power and the means to protect, maintain, and reproduce it. Finally, I contend that while class and state power are manifestly male power and thus contribute to the political underrepresentation and economic marginalization of women, they nonetheless fragment female unity. Indeed, class appurtenance and class interests divide women and overcome the solidarity generated by their common experience of suffering patriarchal abuses. Let me thus join in the old-fashioned pleas for the analytical primacy of class in analyzing society, the state, and gender.

NOTES

1. Callaghy, *The State-Society Struggle.*
2. Block, "The Ruling Class Does Not Rule," 6–28; Evans, Rueschemeyer, and Skocpol, *Bringing the State Back In*; Nordlinger, *On The Autonomy of the Democratic State.* Nordlinger asserts (p. 203): "the democratic state is frequently autonomous in translating its own preferences into authoritative actions, and markedly autonomous in doing so even when they diverge from those held by the politically weightiest groups in civil society."

Skocpol, *States and Social Revolutions* and "Political Responses to Capitalist Crisis," 155–201, in which Skocpol contends (pp. 199–200) that "No existing neo-Marxist approach affords sufficient weight to state and party organizations as *independent* determinants of political conflicts and outcomes . . . so far, no self-declared neo-Marxist theory of the capitalist state has arrived at the point of taking state structures and party organizations seriously enough."

3. Milliband, *Marxism and Politics* and *Class Power and State Power*, 3–78. Poulantzas, *Political Power and Social Classes* and *State, Power, Socialism.* For a survey of state studies see Carnoy, *The State and Political Theory.*
4. On the concept of hegemony see Gramsci, *Prison Notebooks.*
5. Hay and Stichter, *African Women*; Parpart, "Women and the State in Africa"; Staudt, "Women's Politics, the State, and Capitalist Transformation in Africa," 193–208.
6. Obbo, *African Women*, 5.
7. Parpart, "Women and the State," 224–225; Staudt, "Sex, Ethnic, and Class Consciousness in Western Kenya," 151, 162, and "Women's Politics," 203–204.
8. Parpart, "Women and the State," 221–222; Little, *African Women in Towns*, 76–101; Obbo, 39–52.
9. MacGaffey, "Women and Class Formation in a Dependent Economy: Kisangani Entrepreneurs," 161–165.
10. MacKinnon, "Feminism, Marxism, Method, and the State: Towards Feminist Jurisprudence," 657.

11. Barrett, *Women's Oppression Today*, 79.

12. MacKinnon, "Feminism, Marxism, Method, and the State: An Agenda for Theory," 544.

13. Vogel, *Marxism and the Oppression of Women*, 148.

14. Hamilton, *The Liberation of Women*, 104.

15. McDonough and Harrison, "Patriarchy and Relations of Production," 11–41.

16. Staudt, "Women's Politics," 202–204; Urdang, *Fighting Two Colonialisms*.

17. MacKinnon, "An Agenda for Theory," 523.

18. MacKinnon, "Agenda" and "Towards Feminist Jurisprudence."

19. Bujra, "Urging Women to Redouble their Efforts," 118.

20. Vogel, 173.

21. Gramsci, 12.

22. *Ibid.*, 181.

23. *Ibid.*, 5, 12, 181–182.

24. *Ibid.*, 60.

25. *Ibid.*, 327.

26. Obbo, 6, 160–161.

27. de Beauvoir, *The Second Sex*, 154–161.

28. Roberts, "Feminism in Africa: Feminism and Africa," 180.

29. Gramsci, 52.

30. MacKinnon, "Towards Feminist Jurisprudence," 644.

31. The notion of exit is developed in Hirschman, *Essays in Trespassing: Economics to Politics and Beyond*.

32. Staudt, "Women's Politics," 207.

33. Markovitz, *Power and Class in Africa*, 8.

34. Staudt, "Women's Politics," 208.

35. *Ibid.*, 203.

36. Ake, *A Political Economy of Africa*, 181.

37. Cooper, "Africa and the World Economy," 20–21. Some African ruling classes have a higher degree of hegemony than others. Countries like Senegal, Kenya, and the Ivory Coast have ruling classes whose rule is in the process of becoming hegemonic. See Fatton, *The Making of a Liberal Democracy: Senegal's Passive Revolution, 1975–1985*; Fauré and Médard, *Etat et bourgeoisie en Côte d'Ivoire*.

38. Ake; Rodney, *How Europe Underdeveloped Africa*.

39. Callaghy, "The State as Lame Leviathan: The Patrimonial Administrative State in Africa."

40. Hyden, *Beyond Ujamaa* and *No Shortcuts to Progress*.

41. Hyden, *Beyond Ujamaa*.

42. Bujra, "Urging Women to Redouble their Efforts," 124–127; Staudt, "Women's Politics," 193–194; Henn, "Women in the Rural Economy," 1–18.

43. Marx, *The Grundrisse*, 471.

44. Markovitz, "The Consolidation of Power," 190.

45. Staudt, "Women's Politics," 193–201; Hamilton, *The Liberation of Women*, 26–27.

46. Clark, *Working Life of Women in the Seventeenth Century*.

47. Robertson, *Sharing the Same Bowl*, 224.

48. Strobel, "Women in Religion and in Secular Ideology," 87–101.

49. Parpart, "Women and the State," 218–220; Hay and Wright, *African Women and the Law*.

50. Parpart, "Women and the State," 220–221; Hirschmann, "Women and Politics in Commonwealth Africa"; Staudt, "Women's Politics" 205–207.

51. Ake.

52. Parpart, "Women and the State," 219–220; Wipper, "African Women, Fashion, and Scapegoating," 338–339, 346–347.

53. Robertson, *Sharing the Same Bowl*, 243–244.

54. Roberts, "Feminism in Africa," 181.

55. Obbo, 9.

56. Kasfir, "State, Magendo, and Class Formation in Uganda," 95.

57. Obbo, 123, 128, 131–132, 136; Parpart, "Women and the State," 222.

58. Bates, *Markets and States in Tropical Africa*, 87.

59. Staudt, "Administrative Resources, Political Patrons, and Redressing Sex Inequities," 403.

60. Gramsci, 52.

61. On the concept of voice, see Hirschman, *Essays in Trespassing*, 224.

62. Bujra, "Urging Women to Redouble their Efforts," 137.

PART 2

Case Studies

CHAPTER 4

Kaba and Khaki: Women and the Militarized State in Nigeria

NINA MBA

Of the twenty-six years Nigeria has been an independent state, seventeen years have been spent under military governments. By 1990, the earliest possible date for a return to civilian rule, over two-thirds of Nigeria's independent political history will have been "militarized." What are the implications of the militarization of the state for women in Nigeria? Are the policies of male-dominated military governments toward women substantially different from those of male-dominated elected representative governments? Does military government alter the legal and administrative systems in ways that enhance or diminish the status of women? Are there more educational and economic opportunities for women under military rule? Is the participation of women in government and their access to political power augmented or decreased?

Although there is a body of literature on military coups, military governments, and military political cultures in Africa, scant attention is paid to the position of women vis-à-vis the military. Nor is much attention paid to the attitudes and policies of the military toward women. Nonetheless, this literature needs to be examined briefly.

Military rule in Africa is generally seen as an aberration, with no antecedents from the traditional colonial or anticolonial past. Yet, in Nigeria, there were precolonial models of military rule, a good example being the rule by army leaders in Yorubaland in the nineteenth century during the Yoruba wars "though with no repudiation of the supremacy of the civilian ethic and a

---

Kaba is Yoruba for "a woman's dress" and is used here to denote women. It has become customary in Nigeria to refer to the civilian government as "men in *agbada*"—this term is derived from the Yoruba *Ijoba alagbada*, literally, "government of the owners of the *agbada*" (the flowing robes worn by Yoruba men)—and the military government as "men in khaki," or the Yoruba *Ijoba ologun*, literally, "government of the owners of the war" (i.e., warriors). In some situations, *agbada* also bears the connotation of ill-gotten and ill-used political power.

gradual return to civil rule."[1] In these military governments, women were sometimes rewarded with important chieftaincy titles, as in the case of *Iyalode* Efunsetan Aniwura of Ibadan.[2]

The colonial army, surely never "apolitical," was committed to maintaining the colonial order and used force against political opponents of the British administration, including women. Such force was used in 1925 during the dancing women's movement and in 1929 during the Women's War, both in the Eastern Provinces of Nigeria.[3] As in subsequent military governments, the colonial order relied heavily on the civil service to implement policies and to provide some link with the people.

Military and colonial governments strengthened the power of the center, practicing what Afigbo terms "bureaucratic centralism." Regarding the similarities between the condition of Nigeria in 1959 and 1979, Afigbo observes:

> Each period of bureaucratic centralism saw noticeable advances—or what looked like advances—in economic and social development, . . . followed by an arrangement under which a bunch of brawling politicians are made to run the country under a federal constitution.

While transitions from both colonial/bureaucratic dictatorship to independence and from military/bureaucratic dictatorship to civil rule in 1979 were "smooth," later to be followed by complete breakdowns of the new systems, the colonial regime provided Nigeria with training in the game of politics. The fourteen years of military rule allowed no such experience. It was no wonder that politicians in the Second Republic were afflicted with the "Rip van Winkle syndrome."[4]

Similarities also exist between colonial and military states in their policies and attitudes toward women, often invisible to these male rulers. Regardless of the wide-ranging real or theoretical origins of coups, military regimes often proclaim themselves as "modernizers." Such orientations and objectives can be assessed. Was the emancipation/equality of the sexes perceived as an aspect of modernization? If a regime saw itself as the custodian of the constitution, did it implement legal rights of women in the constitution? If a regime came into power as a result of a palace coup, did it pay any attention to women who constitute a negligible part of the armed forces? This chapter will examine each military regime chronologically, focusing on its policies toward women. Women's position in the First Republic, 1960 to 1965, provides a basis for comparison.

Nigeria inherited the British parliamentary system of government, with a bicameral federal legislature and four regional legislatures which were contested for by three major political parties and several minor ones. Although one country, Nigeria had two different electoral systems: women in the southern regions have been enfranchised, in stages, from 1950; women in the Northern Region were not. The political party in power in the Northern Region, the Northern People's Congress (NPC), was a cadre party, open only to Northern men, who were predominantly Muslim and believed either in the seclusion of their women or in the relegation of women to the domestic sphere. The NPC was also in power at the federal center and in coalition with the NCNC (National Council of Nigeria and Cameroons), which was committed to suffrage for women. However, no amount of political pressure could shift the NPC's opposition to enfranchisement of women. Therefore, in the 1959 federal elections, only women in the south could vote and contest elections. Ironically, representation in the federal legislature was based on population, the North having 174 members; the East, 73; the West, 62, and Lagos, 3. Yet the North was given these seats based on the 1953 census total population rather than the eligible voting population. This was accepted by the South for the sake of obtaining independence in 1960 as a unified country.

In the south, very few women contested the elections and none won a seat in the House of Representatives. Therefore there were no women in the federal cabinet. One woman was appointed to the Senate (each regional government nominated twelve members) and a second was appointed in 1964. In the 1961 regional elections, three women were elected to the Eastern House of Assembly. There were no female ministers in the regional governments. The two Southern-based parties had women's wings, but there were no women in the top positions in the party. Several women were elected to local government councils in the South.

The National Council of Women's Societies (NCWS), a nonpolitical body of women's associations, was formed by elite women in 1959 and had branches throughout Nigeria. Its aims were to promote the education, welfare, and status of women. It was recognized by the federal government as the organization representing women and received an annual subvention. While it included both elite and market women, its executive committees were comprised primarily of elite women. The NCWS emphasized its nonpolitical and nonpartisan national posture.

Women were marginally represented in the federal and regional civil services. In 1954 there were only twenty-three women in the senior civil service. It was only with regional self-government in 1956 that married women were employed on a permanent basis. There were no women in the judiciary, though there were female lawyers. In the armed forces, there were a handful of Nigerian women nurses in the medical corps. Such was the position in the First Republic.

THE FIRST COUP: JANUARY 15, 1966

By the close of 1965, the political system had broken down. There was civil war in the Western Region, and the federal government had lost control of the country. The ethnic conflicts that polarized the political system also divided the armed forces, as politicians used indigenization to promote their kinsmen.

The general officer in command, Major-General Ironsi, excluded all civilian political leaders from participation in the government. This action did not deprive women of any power since they had none in the First Republic. At both the federal and regional levels, top civil servants were either appointed or co-opted into the executive councils. Since there were no top female civil servants, women were not represented. Ironsi relied most on several advisers who were outside the government, senior academics and professionals—all men.

Although Ironsi's regime was short-lived (he was assassinated in a countercoup on July 29, 1966), it set the pattern of military government in Nigeria, and that pattern excluded women. It was not a deliberate policy; women were just not there in the eyes of the military rulers—not in the armed forces, not in the civil service, and not in the professions. Political parties were banned.

THE SECOND COUP: JULY 29, 1966

Lt. Colonel Yakubu Gowon led a different style of government than Ironsi, bringing a number of politicians into government though there were no women among them. With greater dependency on the civil service, the era saw emergence of the "super permanent secretaries," who wielded more power than some top military officers and civilian ministers. B.J. Dudley describes the relationship between the military and the bureaucracy as "symbiotic," leading to a greater centralization of political power than ever before. The result was that the bureaucrats developed a vested interest in perpetuating military rule. To do so, the civil service sought "to insulate the military authorities from the people with the consequence that the military becomes all the more isolated and remote from the people they were supposed to govern."[5] With no women at any level of government, the military was indeed very remote from women.

The civilian-appointed commissioners in the cabinets of the four regional governments (changed to twelve states in 1967) were also committed to maintaining the military in power. These were not politicians as found at the federal level, but "new men" chosen either for their technocratic capability or area of origin in order to ensure local acceptance of the regime. It was not until 1970 that the civilian administrator of the East Central State appointed a woman commissioner, novelist Flora Nwapa. Subsequently, a woman commissioner was appointed in North Eastern State, D. Miller; two were appointed in Oyo State, Folake Solanke and Ronke Doherty; while Kofoworola Pratt was appointed in Lagos State.

In 1967 the Eastern Region seceded, declaring itself Biafra; civil war ensued from July 1967 to January 1970. Biafra was divided into provinces and governed by male civilian administrators. Women were, however, more involved in wartime administration in Biafra than in Nigeria. Women were recruited into the civil militia and promoted to officer cadres; the militia exercised political and military power at different times and places. Women were also recruited into the Intelligence and Propaganda Directorates and several held responsible positions. At the war fronts, women were active in the medical corps. The Biafran government sponsored a delegation of three women to the United Kingdom and Europe on a diplomatic mission.

The civil war had a long-term, significant effect on the economic activities of women. It marked the emergence of a large number of women as food-contractors. In Biafra, where food supplies were desperately short and all able-bodied men liable to arbitrary conscription, women were forced to obtain foodstuffs for their families. They dominated the internal trade in unoccupied food-producing areas and even undertook "attack trade" (crossing through enemy lines into Nigerian-occupied territories to purchase goods). The Biafran army gave out many contracts to women to provide foodstuffs for the soldiers. When the war ended, a number of women who had been farmers, teachers, and typists had become traders and contractors, and found these occupations more lucrative and satisfying. After the war, the task of reconstructing war-damaged areas resulted in a flood of contracts provided by the Federal Rehabilitation Commission. Many were given to women who acquired the nickname "emergency contractors."

With the end of the war came the beginning of the oil boom. Nigeria's income from petroleum exports skyrocketed from 26 to 82 percent of total revenue. The consequence of the oil boom was "to convert the military political decision-makers and their bureaucratic aides into a new property-owning, rentier class working in close and direct collaboration with foreign business interests with the sole aim at expropriating the surpluses derived from all for their private and personal benefit."[6] The combination of military rule and oil boom created a new dominant property-owning class and generated commercial capitalism.

Quite a few women became members of this class as a result of their relationships to top military officers, civil servants and office holders. The sobriquet "cash madam" became much in vogue to describe wealthy women contractors and suppliers who were beneficiaries of contracts awarded by the military government. However, the majority by far of the nouveau riche were men.

Gowon's regime, having ensured the unity of the country and a peace "without victors or vanquished," announced that there would be a return to a civil government in 1976. During 1973 discussions concerning the future civil government, Gowon announced that when elections were held, women in the Northern States would vote. This announcement was severely criticized in the North by traditional rulers and the Northern intelligentsia. This opposition is confirmed by a 1972 public-opinion survey that showed "there was still considerable opposition in the North to giving women the franchise even among the educated civil servants and students who constituted most of the Northern sample."[7] Gowon amended his position by saying only educated women would vote, which led to an outcry from women who objected to an educational qualification that was not required for men.

Gowon's dilemma came to an end when in 1974 he postponed the return to civil rule indefinitely. The level of corruption and abuse of office by military and civil office holders exceeded all previous bounds. Political power at the state level became highly personalized, with governors acting as autocratic monarchs in their domains and addressed as "Excellency." The military government wound up being far worse than the civilian government it had overthrown. Because the military government had destroyed the former political system, opposition could only come from within—that is from dissatisfied military officers.

THE THIRD MILITARY COUP: JULY 1975

General Murtala Mohammed seized control through a countercoup, and the army was shown as playing its "custodian" role. The Gowon regime had allegedly allowed the country to drift and some sort of direction had to be taken. The new regime embarked on a purification of the government and civil service, the demilitarization of the political system, and the demobilization of the army. Fears within the ranks over the latter led to an abortive coup in February 1976. Mohammed was assassinated and replaced by Lt. General Olusegun Obasanjo, who continued the policies of the Mohammed regime.

COMPOSITION OF THE MILITARY GOVERNMENT

The power of the civil service was drastically reduced; the "super permsecs" (permanent-secretaries) were restricted to advisory functions. A massive purge of the service led to the removal of about ten thousand civil servants,[8] with the demoralization and humiliation of the civil service being the long-term result. The loss of its political power under Obasanjo continued under the presidential system of government. With some improvement in women's access to education, more women were recruited into the service once it was subordinated. The gross underrepresentation of women in the civil service continued, but there was some improvement in the position of women in the top echelons.[9]

While the civil service was disengaged from an active political role, Obasanjo's regime continued Gowon's policy of appointing civilian commissioners at the federal and state levels. These were generally professional and technical experts, not politicians. At the federal level, there were eleven civilians and fourteen members from the armed forces and police,[10] none of which was female although by 1975 there were many women professionals and academics to consider. At the state level, it appears to have been unofficial policy that there should be one woman commissioner in each state. Most states appointed one female commissioner; in each case, the women were also professionals.[11] The government made a number of major policy decisions based on the reports of exclusively male commissions appointed by the government.

RETURN TO CIVIL RULE: CDC

When the male-dominated military government returned to civil rule in 1979, it ignored women in its fifty-man Constitution Drafting Committee (CDC). The criteria for selection were professional competence and equal representation from the nineteen states. Of the fifty members, nineteen were university teachers, twelve lawyers, twelve businessmen, six holders of political office. Less than 40 percent were Muslims.[12]

The CDC was criticized as being too bourgeois and too intellectual, but the most widespread criticism of the composition was the absence of women on the panel, especially given the number of women lawyers and academics. The *Daily Times* editorial of October 7, 1975, summed up the general view:

> It is rather odd that not one woman was found qualified to represent the female population on the panel. In a country where about 50% of the population is female and part of this is made up of lawyers, educationists, sociologists, administrators and scientists the omission of our womenfolk is an error that is not too late to put right.

Was the absence of women an "omission" or a deliberate policy to exclude women from the body responsible for shaping the country's political future? Although Mohammed had reduced the political power of the permanent secretaries, he and Obasanjo relied heavily on the political division of the Cabinet office for the formulation of the political program. The military government refused to amend the membership, despite the general criticisms, numerous articles in the press by aggrieved women and a press release by the NCWS protesting the exclusion of women. In the view of the military government, the opinion of women was neither relevant nor necessary. However, the government was not completely impervious to public opinion and NCWS lobbying: it did recognize the special interests of women in subsequent phases of the political program.

RETURN TO CIVIL RULE: LOCAL GOVERNMENT

Local government was completely reorganized in 1976 and made the "third tier" of government. Each local government unit included between 150,000 and 800,000 people which were to have specified functions to be administered by an elected council elected on a popular vote. Traditional rulers were involved in the councils in varying ways and degrees in different areas. Both federal and state governments were obliged by statute to provide revenue allocations for the local government councils which also had the power to raise revenue locally.

The federal government issued the Draft Local Government Edict No. 189 of 1976, which included the Local Government Electoral Regulations. The Edict was adopted by each state, which also added its own supplemental listing of local government areas, but there was general uniformity in the provision of the Edict. The qualifications of an elector, according to the Edict, were fourfold: *He* (used throughout the Edict, but refers to men and women) must be over the age of eighteen, have been born in the area, be a resident of the area and be able to prove payment of tax. According to the Electoral Decree, men and women were elegible to vote, subject to the above qualifications, throughout the nineteen states of Nigeria. This meant that the Obasanjo military regime had fulfilled Gowon's verbal pledge that women in the Northern States would vote in the next election, twenty years after their southern sisters. With one stroke of the pen, backed by the inherent coercive powers of a military regime, the politically delicate and explosive issue which neither the colonial nor First Republic governments had been able to solve was settled.

No statement was issued regarding the reasoning behind this aspect of the Edict. It was probably not due to Obasanjo's personal commitment to the equality of women.[13] Gowon, a Christian Northerner, had supported the enfranchisement. All evidence suggests that Mohammed, a Muslim Northerner married to a Yoruba woman, would also have supported the measure. As a government committed to efficient management, rationalization of the economy and administration, and national unity, it must have appeared retrograde and divisive to retain the one country-two electoral laws system and exclude women from suffrage.

There was some resistance to the enfranchisement of women. In the November 11, 1976, issue of the *Daily Sketch*, the Ministry of Information, Sokoto State, declared that women would not vote in that state. The federal government issued a statement clarifying the edict, reiterating that women were eligible to vote. During the elections in the Northern States, there were separate booths for male and female voters, and voting was extended until late at night to enable women in *Kulle* (seclusion) to come out to vote.

Candidates for the local government elections were subject to much more restrictive qualifications than were voters. Teachers and civil servants were disallowed from contesting "with the result that, particularly in the Northern states most members turned out to be illiterate, unable to read or write even in the vernacular."[14] The restrictions affected women more adversely than men since a large proportion of likely candidates were teachers. Nonetheless, a number of women did contest, and quite a few were successful. One of the most spectacular victories was that of Sawaba Gambo, veteran politician of the colonial period and First Republic, who was unopposed in Sabon Gari,

Zaria. She claimed that her nomination papers were completed, filed, and paid for by a group of young men and women in her ward and that another local government area in Zaria had invited her to stand.[15] Altogether, five women were successful in Kano and Kaduna states and one in Niger State. Eight women were successful in Anambra State, as were a handful of women in most other southern states, including future political leaders Biola Babatope in Mushin, Lagos, and Chief Janet Akinrinade in Iseyin, Oyo State. However, these women represented but a tiny minority of the 299 local government councils.

Although the enfranchisement of Northern women was a democratic step, other aspects of the elections were most undemocratic. Only in seven of the nineteen states were the elections direct, and there about 50 percent were returned unopposed. Voter registration fell far below expectations. Voter turnout was very low; in Kaduna State it was estimated at 16 percent. As a result, the councils became heavily unrepresentative.[16]

CONSTITUENT ASSEMBLY

The councils were designed to provide "civic training" and lead to development in the local areas. In the immediate short run, they served as electoral colleges for the election of the Constituent Assembly (CA), the next stage in the political program. The CA was to approve the Draft Constitution produced by the CDC. Representation in the CA was by states according to their estimated populations. Altogether, 203 members were elected by the local councils, acting as electoral colleges. "In effect this meant that it took the votes of an average of some 60 unrepresentative councillors to elect one member of the CA."[17] Eighty-five seats were unopposed (ten out of the eleven in Borno, six out of seven in Nigeri), while the remaining 118 seats were contested by 340 candidates. In Oyo State, every single seat was contested.[18]

The elections were hotly contested, with numerous malpractices because the CA was seen to be—and indeed was—the stepping-stone to political office. The majority of those elected were businessmen and contractors, former politicians, commissioners, retired military and police personnel, professionals, and academics. The only woman elected was Chief Janet Akinrinade, a large-scale tobacco leaf farmer and contractor, in Iseyin/Kajola, Oyo State. "If the CDC/CA could be said to be representative of any group at all, that group would be the elite of Nigeria society—contrasting with the first republic where the consensual basis was that of the political class."[19] As a result of their lack of education and wealth, compared to men, women represented only a fraction of that elite.

Seven members of the CA were chairmen of CDC committees. Twenty members were appointed by the military government: sixteen of them were "experts" in the area of constitution-making and four were female, appointed to appease women and those men who had criticized the exclusion of women in the CDC. Thus, out of a total membership of 250, five were women; this figure turns out to be 2 percent of the membership representing over 50 percent of the population. It is not known what criteria were used in selecting the women members, but they did represent the main ethnic groups: Jummal Jarma (Hausa), Faustina-Kariba Braide (Rivers), Abigail Ukpabi, a graduate teacher (Igbo), and Toyin Olakunri an accountant (Yoruba).

Though few in number, three of the women were very articulate and active members, succeeding in at least one important amendment. The draft constitution had a chapter on Fundamental Rights, Section 35, which concerned the right to freedom from discrimination. The draft declared that no person should be discriminated against on the basis of community, ethnic group, place of origin, or political opinion. Mr. Ukpabi moved an amendment that no person should be discriminated against because of their sex. She was supported by Chief (Mrs.) Akinrinade, and a number of members spoke out in support of the amendment. After a prolonged debate, the amendment was passed.[20] This was a very significant victory for women in Nigeria because the full prohibition reads that

> a citizen of Nigeria of a particular community, ethnic group, place of origin, sex, religion or political opinion shall not by reason only that he is such a person be subjected either expressly by or in the political application of any *law in force in Nigeria*. [emphasis added][21]

This means that any discrimination against women in customary or Islamie law is unconstitutional and justiciable. Thanks to the female members of the CA, the constitution provided complete equality for women. The enforcement of the constitutional prohibition against discrimination is another matter altogether, and it should be made the subject of legal action in the future if such a provision is included in a future amended or new constitution.

The women members of the constituent assembly proposed that a commission on women and children be included in the list of statutory commissions (such as the Federal Judicial Services, Police, Defence Council, and National Population), but this was rejected on the grounds that a commission not contained in the draft constitution would not be accepted. Another motion to have one woman from every state nominated into the Senate was also rejected after it was decided that the Senate must be a fully elected body. The women members participated in debates on other issues, but it appears from the proceedings that members expected them to discuss "women's issues" only.[22]

The Constituent Assembly submitted the amended constitution at the end of 1978, and the final constitution was published in January 1979. It contained seventeen amendments that were added by the military government. It is this and the unrepresentative nature of the constituent assembly that leads Nwabueze to observe "whether Nigeria's new constitution is an original act of the people or an act of the federal military government is very much a matter for argument."[23]

After October 1978, all military commissioners were withdrawn from the federal and state cabinets, and civilian commissioners were appointed as deputy chairmen of State Executive Councils. In Ogun State, Commissioner Womiloju Idowu was the Deputy Chairman, the only woman of nineteen states to hold the post. While the Constituent Assembly was still in session, the Federal Electoral Commission (Fedeco), set up in 1977, completed voter registration in August 1978. It reported eligible voters to number 47,710,680, of which 24,465,683 were women—51.3 percent of the electorate. On September 21, 1978, the ban on political associations and activities was lifted; in two months, fifty-two political associations were formed.

POLITICAL PARTIES

In the initial excitement, several women rushed to announce the formation of all-women political associations. Sawaba Gambo declared her intention to run for president and to form an all-women party which would ally with other parties. Simultaneously, Laila Dogonyaro announced that she would form a national party, whereas Gambo's would be confined to Zaria only.[24] This kind of public rivalry between two women leaders in the North was indicative of the state of intense bitterness as deals were made, promises offered, and alliances betrayed in the formation of political parties. As Olufunmilayo Ransome-Kuti had discovered in 1959, no small women's party is viable.[25] Sawaba Gambo eventually joined one of the main parties, GNPP (Great Nigerian People's Party), while Dogonyaro joined the National Party of Nigeria (NPN). Likewise, Bimpe Ajiboye's "association for female rights" formed in Ilorin merged with the women's wing of the NPN.[26] The Nigerian Women's National League, formed by Regina Agbakoba in Onitsha, led a peripheral political existence, as did Feliz Mortune (also of Onitsha) and her National Democratic Action Party.

Though nonpartisan, the League of Women Voters, formed in late 1978 under the auspices of the NCWS, was one example of women's successful and long-lasting independent political activity. The president was Mrs. Pratt (former Lagos state commissioner and president of the NCWS); the secretary, Priscilla Kuye, a lawyer. The objectives of the League were "the education of women on how to exercise their civil rights . . . so they can identify persons and parties likely to do their best for women . . . (to create) a strong forum to raise the status of women and involve them in policy making . . ."[27] The League organized meetings of women at the usual NCWS venue where talks were given about the importance of voting and the need for women to be active in any political party and influence that party to consider women's interests. The meetings were well publicized, especially in the markets where leaflets were distributed. One such read:

> Women of Nigeria this is your chance to make your contribution to the progress of your beloved country. Do your civic duties. Don't fail Nigeria, don't fail the generation yet unborn. Don't sell your conscience, shake off your apathy. Come out and vote for the party of your choice. To vote is a *must*.

The League and the NCWS stressed the nonpartisan nature of their activities, and the NCWS ruled that no executive member could also hold office in a political party. Branches of the League were formed in Anambra and Imo states, thanks largely to the President of the NCWS, Anambra state, Oyibo Odinamadu. She had also been very active in the Unity Party of Nigeria (UPN) and was appointed a national vice-chairman of UPN. At that point, the NCWS Anambra state voted Mrs. Odinamadu out of the presidency of the branch on the grounds of her involvement in partisan politics. She was succeeded by Dr. Helen Chukwuma, who, ironically, was to become equally active in the Nigeria Peoples Party (NPP) and appointed a commissioner in the NPP-controlled government.[28]

In the midst of this activity, the League of Women Voters was suddenly invited by the chairman of Fedeco to discuss its registration. A delegation, including Dr. J.O. Akande of the University of Lagos, explained to the Federal Electoral Commission (Fedeco) that it was not applying for registration as a political party but as a women's political education movement. In late 1979, the League received a letter from Fedeco stating that it was not eligible for registration and that it had contravened Section 77 of the Electoral Decree.

The League replied that it was not subject to the electoral decree and that it was just like any other association or movement registered under the Land Perpetual Succession Ordinance. "Whilst the League believes that it is its duty to educate Nigerian women to vote, to exercise their civic rights in the interests of the nation, this can in no way be deemed as canvassing for votes for any candidate."[29]

The League seems to have fallen victim to the general hysteria over the registration of parties and Fedeco's overzealousness. It should have been quite obvious that the League could never have applied for registration since, as an all-female body, it contravened the requirements that there should be no discrimination on the basis of area, ethnic group, religion, or sex. However, the publicity generated by Fedeco's action made the NCWS executive uneasy—lest the NCWS be seen as involved in partisan political activities. The League had begun moves to register under Land Perpetual Succession Ordinance using land owned by the NCWS, but the executive decided to suspend action. Despite a minority in favor of continuing the League's work, it gradually ceased to function even before the 1979 elections and was not revived for the 1983 elections.

Since independent partisan political activity by women was soon seen as a nonviable option, women reverted to the practice, well established in the 1950s, of participation in the women's wings of the five political parties registered by Fedeco. Following the pattern of the First Republic, the parties of the Second Republic also had women's wings. Women's wings registered women, ensured their votes for the party, and campaigned for the party's candidates, especially in rural constituencies. The wings were represented in the national executives, but the representatives were not part of the policy-making caucuses of the national executives. The only national office held by women of any party was the rather nebulous office of vice chair, of which there usually were several. Oyibo Odinamadu of the UPN and Hajiya Gambo Sawaba of the GNPP both held such positions. Women were more adequately represented in the state executives of the parties, which is understandable considering the number of states in Nigeria.

The parties nominated far fewer women as candidates for election than men. No woman was ever fielded as a presidential candidate; one woman, Bola Ogumbo, was selected as a running mate (to Aminu Kano, presidential candidate for the People's Redemption Party, PRP). There were several running mates for state gubernatorial elections (Odinamadu for UPN Anambra State; Ndidi Edewor, Nigerian People's Party [NPP], Bendel State; and Janet Akinrinade, NPP, Oyo), but no female gubernatorial candidate. In the Senate elections, only four of the 475 candidates who contested were women, none of whom was successful. In the elections for the Federal House of Representatives, there were about ten female candidates out of a field of two thousand, three of whom were successful (Biola Babatope, UPN; Justine Eze, NPP; and V. Nnaji, NPP). In the elections for the state houses of assembly, there were roughly 42 women candidates out of 5,000; only five were successful.

Why did the parties nominate so few women candidates in 1979 and 1983—as had been the position in the 1959 and 1964 national elections and the 1960, 1961, and 1965 regional elections? According to the parties, the electorates are prejudiced against women in government and will not vote for women; women do not have the stamina and strength to cope with the rigors of campaigning; male party members themselves are prejudiced against female candidates; and there are too few women of "timbre and calibre" (i.e, of education, social status, and wealth) to constitute a pool of talent from which the parties can draw.

In the elections, only 16.8 million votes were cast, representing just below one third of the electorate. This was the lowest turnout in Nigeria's electoral history. According to the Fedeco Report, in the elections for the Federal House of Representatives, Mushin Central Constituency in Lagos State, Biola Babatope won with 42,083 votes, but the turnout was 12.5 percent of the registered voters. In the same election, Justine Eze, of the Uzo Uwani constituency in Anambra State, won with 16,945 votes and a 41 percent turnout. In the State Houses elections, Mrs. N.V. Emodi, in Onitsha constituency, won with 3,914 votes; 46 percent of the registered voters actually voted. One explanation for the low voter turnout was that the newly enfranchised eighteen-year olds and those previous nonvoters below the age of thirty-five seemed indifferent. There is no breakdown by sex of voter turnout, so no accurate assessment can be given as to how women voted, though the impression of most observers recorded in the media was that as many women as men voted.

THE SECOND REPUBLIC

In the new civilian government that took office on October 1, 1979, under President Shehu Shagari, there were three women Federal Ministers (Mrs. Oyegbola, National Planning; Mrs. Ivase, Education; and Mrs. Akinrinade, Internal Affairs) and one woman commissioner in just about each state government. In terms of the numbers of women holding formal political office and participating in the political system, the second republic measured greater success than the first republic and the military regimes. However, in terms of improvement in the condition of life of women and men, the implementation of constitutional rights and liberties for women and men, and the proper management of the human and national resources of the country, the second republic measured greater failure than the first republic and the military regimes. The second republic betrayed the trust of the citizens in an elected representative government. It established "a continuous record of irregularities—of the perversion of the relationships and procedures established by the constitution, of the transgression of constitutional limitations and restraints and of abuse of power."[30]

Is participation in bad government an advantage for women? Several women politicians were found guilty of abuse of office by the subsequent military government, but since there were far fewer women than men in office, their numbers are correspondingly slight.[31] Several women in politics were also active in the opposition to the abuses of government, notably Biola Babatope.

The record of the Shagari government vis-à-vis women's issues was very poor. The constitution was a product of the military regime; its implementation was frustrated by the civil regime. Islamic and customary laws continued to discriminate against women. In the response to constant demands from the NCWS and other women's bodies for the creation of a women's commission or bureau (turned down by the Constituent Assembly), the Shagari government set up the National Committee on Women and Development in 1981. The committee was simply the women's unit of the child and family welfare section of the Directorate of Social Development in the Ministry of Social Development, Youth and Sports. Corresponding state committees were set up in the state ministries. The function of the committees was purely advisory. The NCWS, the members of the committees on women and development, and various women's professional bodies lobbied the Shagari government to upgrade the committee to a technical department with executive functions, as called for by the Lagos Plan of Action 1980 and various UN resolutions. The civil government was as impervious as had been the military governments.

RETURN TO MILITARY GOVERNMENT

Just as in January 1966 and July 1975, so too on December 31, 1983, the military intervened to save the nation from mismanagement, abuses, and disorder and to restore probity, discipline, and the economy. At that point, the intervention was viewed as necessary by all except members of the Shagari government. "Given the mood of total disillusionment among the people induced by intolerable hardship and their desire to be rid of those who had brought it to them, the change could not have been other than welcome."[32]

The military government, headed by Major General Buhari, set up a structure of administration similar to that of previous regimes in which civilians were incorporated into the federal and state executive councils headed by military governors. The top policymaking body was the Supreme Military Council. Needless to state, there was no woman member of the SMC, which was a military/police body, with the exception of the civilian attorney general. By 1984, the highest-ranking women in the armed forces were a colonel in the army, one wing commander in the air force, one commander in the navy (all from the medical corps), and the first and only Assistant Inspector General of the police force (as of 1986). Once again, no woman was appointed to the federal executive council, but Buhari insisted that each state government should have one women commissioner. This was implemented in all states; women became the attorneys general in two states. It would appear that military governments feel that women can operate only on the local and state levels.

However, this time around the pattern was more oppressive than before, The civil service, including the cabinet office, was relegated to the background. The government relied far more on a greatly expanded National Security Organization (NSO), which had no women in the higher ranks. Under the Buhari regime, the state was more militarized than ever before. Military tribunals were set up to try civilian offenders, though judges were included in the tribunals. A number of draconian measures were introduced. The government was insensitive or indifferent to public opinion except when it was offended by that opinion expressed by the press. It then reacted repressively.

The initial euphoria again gave way to disillusionment in the public and to rivalries and tensions in the armed forces. The result was the fifth coup, which took place on August 27, 1985, with Major General Babangida as head of state. The structure of administration continued: the same exclusion of women from the federal government continued, as did the policy of having one woman commissioner in the executive councils of the state governments generally comprised of about ten civilian commissioners.

Later on, however, Babangida adopted a more liberal posture toward women. He announced that one in every four nominated local-government councillors should be women and that one woman should be on every government board or panel; this policy is being implemented gradually. The first woman vice-chancellor, Professor Grace Alele-Williams of the University of Benin, was appointed in early 1986. Subsequently, Babangida defended this appointment on a visit to Benin University. "Let it be known that here in Benin I believe we have started what appears to be a silent revolution to bring women directly into the mainstream of the government and administration of higher institutions." The Babangida regime sees the emancipation of women as part of its "crusade to guarantee equal opportunities to all, irrespective of sex, class, religion, or ethnicity."[33] Unlike previous military rulers since Gowon, Babangida's wife (who happens to be from Bendel State, while Babangida is from Niger State) plays the role of "First Lady" in public and has shown evidence of commitment to women's issues and associations. She has formed an *ad hoc* committee of professional women to advise her on ways to improve living conditions of rural women.

Like the Obasanjo regime, that of Babangida is committed to the return to civil rule in 1992 and to involving the citizens in preparing for a new political order. There is greater freedom of the press, the powers of the NSO have been divided among several bodies, and government slogans promise the restoration of human rights. In order to ensure civic participation at all levels, a political bureau was set up in January 1986 to coordinate a national political debate throughout the country, not just another CDC meeting in closed sessions in Lagos. It has seventeen members, two of whom are women—Hilda Adefarasin is president of the NCWS; the other is an academic.

Women's associations have participated in the political debates and made vehement and innovative demands for much greater political power for women. The NCWS organized a symposium in Lagos in May 1986 on the political future of Nigeria. Speakers from a number of women's associations under the umbrella of the NCWS condemned the "tokenism" of the past governments and demanded at least 30 to 40 percent of the positions in legislatures and cabinets. They criticized the past roles of women as "the three C's: concubines, contractors and aides to corruption." A resolution was passed calling for the revival of the League of Women Voters. The NCWS organized similar symposiums in a number of the states of Nigeria.[34]

Besides its increasing political awareness and articulateness, the NCWS also continues to lobby for the removal of legal and administrative disabilities of women. For instance, it is very concerned that women are not allowed in practice to stand surety for bail, that married women have to obtain the consent of their husbands when applying for passports, that women are discriminated against in taxation assessment, and that women in the civil service receive half the annual leave allowance of their male counterparts. The NCWS lobbies for making credit facilities accessible to rural women and has set up a free legal-aid counseling service, operated by lawyer members. It has prepared a detailed critique on customary laws of divorce and inheritance and on maintenance payments in both customary and ordinance divorce cases.

A lot of this activity by the NCWS is interpreted negatively by women's associations outside its framework. Although the Council of Muslim Women is affiliated with the NCWS, a recently formed (1984) organization, Muslim Sisters of Nigeria, criticizes the NCWS as being "Christian and Zionist" [sic].[35] It defends the Sharia code on marriage and divorce and considers the NCWS elitist and pro-establishment.

The latter criticism is also made by the radical feminist academic organization of Women in Nigeria (WIN), formed in 1982 at Ahmadu Bello University, Zaria. WIN views the NCWS as elitist and philanthropic, arguing that "a pre-requisite for a solution to the problems facing women in Nigeria is that women must organize themselves to fight against the oppressive conditions which deprive them of their basic human rights. The fight against women's oppression must be carried on in alliance with other groups and forces which are struggling against all forms of exploitation in society."[36] A member of WIN, Biklisu Yusuf, a newspaper editor in Kano, demands:

> We should stop dancing backwards by voting anti-feminists to represent us at those important places. Dancing backwards is allowing only the men to legislate on our problems, problems that are close to our hearts. Women wear the shoes so they know where it pinches. Therefore dancing forward is electing women to legislative houses and executive posts.[37]

The diversity and depth of women's political ideas, as expressed in the political debate under the current military regime, testify to the greater maturity and sophistication of their political consciousness compared with the past. Their experiences of a militarized state and of a disastrous return to a constitutional civil state have shown that Nigeria has not yet solved its central problem of how to govern itself under a government popularly elected by and administered for the benefit of all men and women. Women realize now that participation in government is not enough: they must help to fashion the form of government and make it responsible and accountable.

Simultaneously with the articulation of women's political thinking under the auspices of the NCWS is the demonstration of the continued viability and vitality of a more traditional form of political action, namely mass mobilization by communal and market women's associations in defense of their interests. These associations of women as daughters, wives, and traders show the strength of the congruence between women's public and domestic worlds in Nigeria. They continue to provide the basis for the mobilization of the masses of women in the political system of the militarized state as they did in the precolonial, colonial, and postcolonial periods of Nigeria's history.

Just as the women in Lagos and Abeokuta demonstrated against the payment of taxes in the 1930s and 1940s,[38] so in 1984 and 1985 did the women traders in Abeokuta, Sagamu, and Ijebu-Igbo demonstrate against an Ogun State government levy of ₦50 on selfemployed persons such as mechanics, tailors, taxi drivers, and traders. Among those categories, only women traders took action. In Abeokuta, about two hundred women marched to the palace of the traditional ruler (*Alake*) of Abeokuta in a manner strongly reminiscent of 1948. All markets were shut and "for hours they rained abuses and poured scorn on the state's administration."[39] A number of women were arrested and heavily fined. In 1948, the *Alake*, though still powerful, was the agent of the colonial administration that imposed the taxation; in 1984 the *Alake* had negligible authority in the state government. Nonetheless, the women preferred to voice their grievances to the person representing the local authority who is most accessible and familiar to them.

But how effective is such a mode of political protest when the traditional ruler is himself subject to the state government?[40] The Ogun state government did not amend the levy and other taxes imposed to raise revenue for its near bankrupt treasury. The women's demonstrations were unsuccessful in terms of their main objective and in leading to the formation of an organization to represent the women's demands.

Since Independence, mass action by women in the informal sector has continued, but it has been sporadic, uncoordinated, and unsustained. Compared to the colonial period, the scope and vitality of women's collective action is much diminished. It is far more localized and materialistic, and has not produced long-term leadership. The women have generally reacted only to measures by government, both civil and military, that threaten their economic interests.

The gap between urban and rural women, between the "formal" and "informal" sectors, and between the "elite" and the "masses" is very wide. Urban, educated middle-class women have the national leadership potential but not the mass support needed for effective political action. Besides, the majority of such women insist on the depoliticization of "women's issues" and operate within the framework of voluntary associations which cannot enforce sanctions on their members. Urban market women and rural community-based women have the potential for mass mobilization and can enforce effective sanctions, but they lack the national leadership and political objectives.

At both levels, women remain marginal to the state, whether militarized or civil, unless new organizations of women emerge that attempt to fuse the gender ideology of the female intelligentsia with the skills of the middle-class female meritocracy and the militancy of the mass female associations. Such organizations must transcend religious differentiation among women. The organization, Women in Nigeria, and the increased politicization of the NCWS augur well for the development of new political posture by women's organizations.

CONCLUSION

The militarized state greatly augments the power of the central federal government vis-à-vis the state governments and over society. The main objective of increased state power is to weld the component ethnic groups into a viable national union and to contain any ethnic or class movement which threatens the unity of the state. The result is a military nationalism at home (and also abroad) that serves the corporate interests of the military and those groups with which the military must ally in order to govern. The allies of the military are the civil-service mandarins, big-business barons, bourgeois technocrats, and pseudopoliticians.

Within this ruling class, there is such a close convergence of military and civil roles that it is fashionable to talk about the "militarization of the civilians" and "civilization of the military." Thus, when civil government was restored in 1979, it flouted the constitution the military government had helped to produce and adopted the military method of summary executive action, popularly known as government with immediate effect. There is, further, a two-way traffic between the military and civil routes to power: the military in government needs to secure the goodwill of the civilian public lest dissatisfaction be used by a dissident military faction as rationale for a countercoup. Civilian governments are aware that if they fail to execute military-favored policies, they will provide the conditions which could lead to military intervention.

Colonial and militarized states affected women similarly in terms of structures and styles of government. Both operated a bureaucratic centralism in which women were either not represented or only marginally so. In both systems, government was remote from the people; women protested the defense of their own interests to the agencies of government closest to them. The colonial and militarized states adopted policies which promoted the interests of certain class factions of women.

The colonial government partially enfranchised Nigerian women; the first Nigerian civil government preserved the status quo for political reasons;

the second military government, free from those political considerations, completed the enfranchisement of Nigerian women. The current military government appears to want institutionalized civilian input in government; whether to ensure its stability or to accelerate the return to civil rule—or both—remains to be seen. As part of this process, it seeks to co-opt women into the state system at several levels. This military commitment to the incorporation of women into the militarized state at least at the local, state, and institutional levels is strong enough to overcome the ethnic, cultural, and sexist prejudices which would handicap a civilian government in Nigeria. Finally, the predisposition of the military government toward the integration of women is reinforced at the international level by the new gender consciousness generated by the U.N. Decade for Women. Given proper political organization and agitation by Nigerian women, women's prospects of augmenting their political power in the militarized state are favorable. This will provide them with a much stronger starting position for the race to political power whenever there is a return to a demilitarized state.

NOTES

1. Ajayi and Ikara, *Evolution of Political Culture in Nigeria*, 5.
2. Awe, *Iyalode Efunsetan Aniwura*.
3. Mba, *Nigerian Women Mobilized*, Chapter 3.
4. Afigbo, "Nigerian Politics in the 1980's."
5. Dudley, *Introduction to Nigerian Government*, 86.
6. Dudley, 16–116.
7. Peil, *Nigerian Politics*, 133.
8. Yahaya, "The Struggle for Power in Nigeria," 265.
9. In the federal civil service, the first female Permanent Secretary, Francesea Emmanuel, was appointed July 1, 1975; the second, Stella Odesanya, in 1981. In 1987, there were about ten female federal permanent secretaries. The first female head of state of the civil service, Teju Alakija of Oyo State, was appointed in 1981. There are several female permanent secretaries in most state civil services. The first woman ambassador, R.T. Mohammed, was appointed in 1977. Several high court judges are women, as are many magistrates and state counsels.
10. Yahaya, 265.
11. In 1975 in Oyo State, however, the NCWS convened a meeting of "concerned" women in Ibadan and passed a resolution demanding not one token woman commissioner but a 30 percent representation of women in government. One of the leaders at that meeting was Dr. Bolanle Awe of the University of Ibadan. Shortly afterwards, she was offered commissionership by the governor of the Western Region, Colonel Jemibewon. Dr. Awe refused to accept a token appointment and led a delegation of women from NCWS to explain her stand to the military governor. He offered to appoint a second commissioner, Mrs. Adesida, saying that appointing any additional females

would be too progressive compared to sentiments of the rest of the country. This was acceptable, and Mrs. Adesida and Dr. Awe were appointed commissioners. The governor also appointed one women to each local government council. When new states were created in 1976, Mrs. Adesida became a commissioner in Ondo State, and her vacated seat in the Oyo state cabinet remained unfilled. Therefore, Dr. Awe ended up being the lone women commissioner after all! (Interview with Professor Balanle Awe.)

12. Dudley, 159.

13. An incident that reveals Obasanjo's personal attitude occurred in February 1978 when he inaugurated the National Advisory Council on Education. Asked by Oyibo Odinamado why so few women (three out of thirty-three) were appointed to the council, Obasanjo replied, "Yes, so few, yet so many madam. While we want our women to be fully involved in our national life, we also want them to take care of our homes" (*Punch*, February 2, 1978).

14. Dudley, 112.

15. *Sunday Times*, December 12, 1976.

16. Dudley, 160.

17. *Ibid*.

18. Kirk-Green and Rimmer, 19.

19. Dudley, 161.

20. *Proceedings of the Constituent Assembly of the Federal Republic of Nigeria*, Official Report, Vol. III, 2334–2342.

21. *Ibid*.

22. Toyin Olakunri took part in debates on other issues as well; in particular, she moved an amendment on Section 10, Directive Principles and Objectives of Economic Policy, proposing much greater economic autonomy for partially indigenized enterprises. The amendment was strongly criticized by supporters of foreign investment, but as Mrs. Olakunri complained, the issue was distorted because of her sex. "I think the question should be to analyze rather than being sentimental and supporting a woman's amendment." The chairman did not help matters with such comments as, "I would myself be very reluctant to discourage a lady" (Proceedings, Vol. III, 2400–2401).

23. Nwabueze, *The Presidential Constitution of Nigeria*, 2.

24. *Nigerian Standard*, September 26, 1978; *Daily Times*, October 2, 1978.

25. Mary Hudung Princewill, formerly one of Ofunmilayo Ransome-Kuti's assistants in the all-female Nigerian Women's Society in the 1950s, declared that the only woman who could have been president in 1979 was the late Mrs. Ransome-Kuti. Princewill complained that she was edged out of the local government elections by men and that the only solution was to join a party. She in fact became an UPN candidate in Jos (*Daily Times*, October 9, 1978).

26. *Daily Times*, October 5, 1978.

27. *Daily Sketch*, December 14, 1978.

28. Anambra State was NPP oriented: UPN had a negligible following. This explains the apparent contradiction between the objectives of the League and NCWS (i.e., encouraging women to be politically active) and the removal of Mrs. Odinamadu for her successful political activity. What was really the focus of objection was her allegiance to UPN. Admittedly, as a party office

holder, it would have been diplomatic for Mrs. Odinamadu to resign her presidency, but this could have been affected by her "Ladies Agreement" had she been an NPP office holder. Mrs. Odinamadu had been a member of the Biafran Women's diplomatic delegation.

29. Information from Professor Akande, Mrs. Kuye, and *Punch* (January 17, 1979).

30. Nwabueze, *Nigeria's Presidential Constitution*, xi.

31. Whether women in office are as corrupt as men, or less so, is a vexing question. Traditionally, women were the purifiers of their society: the self-image of women as expressed in NCWS resolutions stresses women's greater moral strength and probity. But the record of women in office is not free of confirmed corruption. Peil considers that there is no reason to expect otherwise: "Since one of the most consistent findings of this study is the lack of difference in attitudes between men and women, greater participation of women in politics seems unlikely to lessen corruption" (Peil, 1976, 63).

32. Nwabueze, *Nigeria's Presidential Constitution*, xii.

33. *Guardian*, May 8, 1986.

34. The NCWS Anambra State held its own political debate in July 1986. Its communiqué also criticized tokenism, demanded that 50 percent of policy-making decisions be made by women, and the involvement of women at each stage of elections. It suggested the elimination of party politics at the local level, with representatives selected by town unions, age grades, etc., then second level elections to state legislatures. It also insisted that "upstarts should not be allowed—wife beaters, home breakers should not resort to politics" (sic) (*Daily Star*, July 2, 1986).

In Imo State, the Ogbe Progressive Women's Association in the Ahiazu local government held its political debate under the auspices of NCWS and called for a system of dual leadership, whereby a woman would be prime minister and a man serve as president; the deputy governors in all the states would be women. (*Guardian*, July 10, 1986). I attended the Lagos symposium.

35. *New Nigerian*, April 12, 1985.

36. *Women in Nigeria Today*, 7.

37. *Ibid.*, 215.

38. Mba, chapters 4 and 7.

39. *Daily Sketch* and *Concord*, November 9, 1984.

40. An interesting incident occurred in Benin in April 1985 when two thousand Edo women marched to the *Oba*'s palace to protest various levies imposed by the Bendel state government. Their heads were uncovered, a traditional way of indicating contempt towards the measure or person against whom they were protesting. The *Oba* called for the appropriate government official; in the presence of the women, the *Oba* complained bitterly that he had neither been briefed by the state government nor consulted beforehand. To the accompaniment of the women chanting the Edo equivalent of "Long live the King," the *Oba* advised the women to disperse peacefully to avoid becoming scapegoats for the state government; the *Oba* said he would speak to the state governor on their behalf (*Guardian*, April 25, 1985).

CHAPTER 5

State, Peasantry, and Agrarian Crisis in Zaire: Does Gender Make a Difference?

CATHARINE NEWBURY

BROOKE GRUNDFEST SCHOEPF

It has become commonplace in recent years to describe Zaire's political economy in terms of crisis. The Zairian state is in crisis, observers say, for it is unable to control large parts of the economy, it fails to provide basic services to the populace, and in recent years has been rapidly losing legitimacy in the eyes of its citizens.[1] The symptoms of crisis in the economy are seen in the declining production of export crops since independence in 1960, decline of revenues from copper (the country's major mineral export and source of foreign exchange), massive foreign debt, the recurring need to reschedule debt-service payments on past loans, mismanagement, corruption, and inadequate planning.[2] The crisis is particularly evident in agriculture. While no sector of the economy thrived during the 1970s, performance in agriculture was so poor that the situation has been described as a "catastrophe" or a "disaster."[3] The state itself must bear a significant part of the blame for this dismal situation, for past state policies have hindered development in Zairian agriculture rather than promoted it.

The human dimensions of the food crisis are staggering. Although we do not hear reports of widespread famine in Zaire, many people in large towns and cities eat only once a day. In the rural areas, too, many people go hungry. The undernourished Zairian citizenry are more vulnerable to infectious diseases, intestinal parasites, and malaria, and such diseases are now reaching epidemic proportions in many areas of the country.[4]

Agrarian crisis in Africa is not, of course, limited to the single case of Zaire, but the depth and breadth of its consequences are particularly severe there. From across the continent come reports of declining per capita food production, increasing food imports, and in many areas, reduced production of export crops. Recognition of Africa's agrarian crisis is now so pervasive that a veritable explosion of studies has appeared focusing on agriculture, food production, barriers to agricultural development, and proposed solutions.[5] In the name of combatting the crisis, a whole panoply of programs is being proposed (and some are being implemented) by such multilateral institutions as the World Bank, the International Fund for Agricultural Development (IFAD), and the Food and Agriculture Organization (FAO), as well as bilateral agencies such as the United States Agency for International Development (USAID).

Some of these programs, often part of "structural adjustment" policies advocated by the World Bank and the International Monetary Fund (IMF), involve significant transfer of resources to African governments and/or their supporters. But aid of this type is far from neutral; such projects may have critical consequences for African rural producers, shaping the direction of agricultural change for years to come. The programs will also affect the capacities of states and the nature of their relationships with rural dwellers. It is important, therefore, to inquire as to the form of development the programs imply and who is going to benefit from them. Of particular concern is the impact of such programs on women, who produce 60 to 80 percent of Africa's food and also contribute to the production of cash crops for export.

In Zaire, as in most African societies, women are active in production of food crops both for home use and for sale. In fact, women are the principal food producers despite the ecological and sociocultural diversity which characterize this second largest sub-Saharan nation. Thus, increased food production must rest upon knowledge of gender roles and constraints. Yet few studies exist concerning the status of Zairian women in relation to agricultural activities, income, and family nutrition. This chapter calls attention to linkages between the effects of the national political economy, including dependency and internal class formation, and efforts of peasant women to produce food crops. It suggests that women's status in the family and community is the key to their ability to contribute to increased production efforts and to benefit from them. In light of these concerns, it is important to inquire as to how rural women's work and access to resources will be affected by the agricultural policy prescriptions now being proposed by international lenders and the extent to which women's needs and concerns are being addressed. These are questions that need to be asked, but for which as yet we have no clear-cut answers. The discussion below will outline major elements of Zaire's agrarian crisis and assess the possible ramifications for women that recent policies proposed to combat it may have.

AGRICULTURAL POLICIES

First, we need to review some of the remedies being proposed. The World Bank's agenda outlined in *Accelerated Development in Sub-Saharan Africa* (often referred to as the "Berg report" after the name of its chief author) represents a particularly influential approach. At the risk of oversimplifying and overgeneralizing, we have distilled the following elements from the World Bank study:[6]

- The crisis in Africa is primarily a crisis of production.
- Disincentives created by government policies are mainly responsible for the production crisis. Therefore, governments should intervene less in agriculture. Specifically, restrictions on agricultural prices should be lifted and marketing boards dismantled.
- A strategy for more rapid agricultural growth is needed. Emphasis should be placed on export crop production, but there should also be an effort to achieve food self-sufficiency.
- Resources should be provided to improve smallholder production and facilitate marketing, including improvement of roads and transport infrastructures. Not all smallholders would be recipients of such resources—only the more productive ones.
- Resources will also be made available for large, highly capitalized agricultural enterprises.

These guidelines from the Berg report are general and the extent to which they are implemented in a given country varies considerably, depending on the local context. Unlike many African countries where export crops constitute the main source of foreign exchange, Zaire depends heavily on the mining sector; copper, cobalt, and diamonds are a major source of state revenues. And more than a third of the Zairian population lives in urban areas.[7] Nevertheless, except for recent announcements by foreign lenders and the Zairian government that priority should be given to increased food production, agricultural policy recommendations and lending priorities in Zaire are strikingly similar to those articulated in the Berg report. The general pattern reflects current mainstream development emphasis on market forces and privatization.

Over the past decade, Zaire's leaders have sought new investments in tropical exports, such as oil palms, coffee, tea, rubber, and hardwoods, as well as inputs to major import substitution industries, including rubber, palm oil, cotton, sugar, tobacco, and pulp wood. In the 1980s, agricultural development projects supported by foreign funds have focused on improving food as well as export crop production.[8] A number of the projects are directed toward improving smallholder production, but usually also include a component allocating aid to medium- or large-sized commercial farms. Other projects concentrate on developing commercial marketing opportunities for traders in peasants' agricultural produce. In an effort to increase incentives for producers in 1982 and 1983, the Zairian government moved to decontrol agricultural prices in various regions and, over a period of several years, to abolish the parastatal marketing boards which for almost ten years had held a monopoly on purchasing such major crops as coffee, cotton, maize, and rice. By 1984 all but one marketing board (ranching) had been dismantled.[9]

Since 1983, the national currency has been allowed to float on the international market, and foreign exchange controls have ended as part of IMF-mandated reforms. New sources of agricultural credit are available to investors with collateral, and there is pressure to free agricultural inputs and machinery from import duties (the latter are only sporadically enforced). Some public agricultural resources, including research stations and former demonstration projects, have been "privatized," and private freehold landholding, termed "land reform," is growing.

Advisors believe that these initiatives will lead to increased output, capital formation, and productive reinvestment in agriculture, thereby resolving Zaire's food crisis. In theory, rising prices and improved food-crop-production should benefit peasants as well as local capitalists and multinational agro-industrial firms. But such an outcome is far from assured, given the nature of the present regime in Zaire, its political priorities and the interests of the state and commercial bourgeoisie. Two examples will serve to illustrate this point: decontrol of prices and policies designed to increase smallholder production.

PRICES, SMALLHOLDER PRODUCTION, AND THE STATE

Pressured by the international lending community, in May 1982 the Zairian government reluctantly moved to lift controls on prices for food crops in Shaba Region, the southern province where food demand is particularly high because of urbanization on the Copperbelt. The government's reluctance to decontrol food prices was based on political considerations, including pressure from employers and fear of urban unrest. Nevertheless, in 1983, decontrol of prices was extended throughout the country.[10] In less than a year, producer prices had doubled and peasants were selling more food. But then devaluation was instituted in response to IMF pressure, and a new inflationary spiral began. Two years after decontrol, peasants and observers reported that rising costs of agricultural inputs and consumer goods had outpaced receipts from increased production in all areas except the Kasai diamond fields.[11] In Shaba, official maximum prices for maize were reintroduced in 1985.[12] When price controls coupled with inflated fuel prices consequent upon devaluation eat into profits, traders may turn to other opportunities. In this case, cultivators in northern Shaba, six hundred miles from Copperbelt markets, who were part of a USAID-funded agricultural development project, were left with piles of unsold maize.

In other areas of the country, decontrol of prices does little to help peasants because traders, collaborating with local officials, are able to exercise monopsonistic control (especially where roads are in need of repair), and thus maintain unfavorable terms of trade for small-scale producers, who often receive only a fraction of the selling price in town.[13] Such conditions are dramatized in the case of the Tembo people who live in Kivu Region on the western slopes of the Mitumba Mountains.

During the past twenty-five years, peanuts and cassava produced for market have come to dominate the agricultural activities of the Tembo. Peanuts are generally regarded as a men's crop and cassava a women's crop, even though women have a major role in peanut production and husbands claim rights over the income from the cassava their wives produce. For most Tembo, the major markets for their produce are located at the paved road that reaches their area from the regional capital, Bukavu, some seventy kilometers to the southeast. Those who live far from the road (one to two days' walk) carry peanuts to the roadside markets, and such porterage is done almost exclusively by men. In areas within about three to four hours' walk to the road, cassava has also become an important marketed crop. In such areas, all the cassava and most of the peanuts are carried to market by women.[14]

In the past, some secondary, unpaved roads were in good enough condition to allow large trucks to reach smaller local markets that are two to three hours' walk from the main road. In recent years, however, roads and bridges on these secondary roads have deteriorated to such an extent that trucks can no longer use them. Even the paved road is in poor condition, pocked with potholes. Depreciation of vehicles is very rapid; therefore, only a few traders can afford to rent or purchase the large trucks needed for such transport. Most of the merchant trader/transporters who buy cassava and peanuts at the roadside markets are from areas near the regional capital and identify with ethnic groups other than that of the Tembo. These traders, relatively few in number, are able to exercise an oligopsony, setting the prices they will pay the producers. The Tembo, like other rural Zairians, are fully aware of the inequities of such conditions. As one women cassava-producer explained:

> The *commerçants* exploit us because we aren't able to get our cassava to Bukavu. We plant and harvest the cassava, but we don't have the means to transport it to town. Then, if you refuse to sell your cassava to the buyer, it will just sit and rot at home. So realizing that, you sell it to him at his price, and when he arrives in town, he gets rich, and we remain poor.[15]

Government price controls are not really very relevant in this context; lifting them has virtually no effect on the prices paid to Tembo producers. Tembo have not been quiescent about such problems: on at least two occasions during the 1970s they attempted to hold back peanuts and cassava in an effort to obtain better prices; each time the boycott was squelched through collaboration between politico-administrative officials and merchants. Local people believe that a producers' cooperative might help by making it possible for them to purchase or rent their own trucks to transport goods to market. In one Tembo area, residents have considered setting up such an organization, but they have been unable to do so because of political and financial obstacles. They have been able to establish a consumers' cooperative that sells basic necessities at prices lower than those in local shops. But shopkeepers and traders blocked establishment of a consumers' cooperative outlet at the main roadside market; consequently, the co-op could open a store only at a Catholic mission located several kilometers away.[16]

In 1982, women in Buloho, one of the Tembo areas near the road, engaged in public protest to express their dissatisfaction with the marketing conditions they faced. Their discontent focused on two key issues: the prices offered for the cassava and peanuts they sell at market, and the taxes and tolls being levied on their produce by local administrative authorities. The women petitioned the chief of Buloho Collectivity for an end to the taxes and tolls because such levies were not being used for any public purpose. Rather, the women claimed, the taxes served only to enrich the authorities:

> We don't know [what the chief does with the income from the cassava and peanut tolls]. We do know, however, that he has two houses with corrugated tin roofing. He can do a lot of things, for example, take part in selling the meat from a cow at market, or if he has a child in school at Bukavu, the family can send him a sack of cassava without his mother having done the work of drying it.[17]

Peasants are exploited by such conditions regardless of whether or not transporters are in fact making substantial profits. Traders point to multiple difficulties and expenses required to keep trucks running on deteriorating roads. Moreover, they must make payments to security forces who regularly set up blockades on roads to markets as well as to other officials who control access to licenses and supplies.[18] Few Zairians, however, would try to argue that traders in their country are destitute. Rather, popular wisdom these days asserts that "les commerçants sont comme des rois" (merchant traders are like kings), particularly in comparison to schoolteachers, whose salaries are now so low that they often do not even cover the cost of one month's supply of cassava meal for a family.[19]

As the women of Buloho perceived so clearly, "development" is to an important extent an issue of governance and who "develops" an issue of power. In Zaire's local council elections of 1982, women in Buloho helped to elect councillors (all male) who did in fact abolish the Buloho market taxes. But the energetic, politically conscious women were unable to address the real problem, nor were they capable of confronting it. This problem concerns terms of trade, as well as the broader issue of dependence on commercial crops in conditions where fields are overused for lack of fallow, soil productivity is declining, and producers are dependent on traders for prices. Moreover, the Tembo, like other rural dwellers in Zaire, experience multiple forms of exploitation that not only provide disincentives to production, but also restrict their ability to improve the conditions of production. Unequal market relations are part of the problem, but so is exploitation by the state through such extractions as taxation, bribes to officials, legal and illegal levies, and unpaid labor.[20] The following examples from the southeastern Shaba Copperbelt, extracted from diaries kept by the Schoepfs during the 1970s and early 1980s, illustrate this point:[21]

In one village a student reported that peasants consider the agricultural *moniteur* an agent of the police. Charged with agricultural surveillance, his visits result in fines. Peasants often flee when he appears in the village (1974). In 1979 an Agriculture Department official deplored this situation as a hindrance to agricultural development. Four years later, the policy was still in effect, but the official was gone (1983).

Chiefs continue to function as intermediaries in the system, profiting from the labor of prisoners put to work on their fields (1975, 1976, 1977, 1978, 1981). They sometimes direct their policemen to use corporal punishment and the practice is considered normal by officials (1976).

The wife of a chief discovered that her vegetables (produced with prison labor) were selling at 1,000 per cent markup in Lubumbashi's Kenia market (1977). Traders in the area complained of high overhead costs incurred at military checkpoints. They stressed the need to form partnerships with officials (all years). One trader reports a standing arrangement with the military commander (1976).

When examining the role of the African state in agriculture, we miss the point if we concentrate only on production and formal marketing structures. At issue is not only economics, but politics. The state, even an apparently weak one, plays an important role in shaping access to resources. And resources are crucial for agricultural development. As Berry has argued:

> If access to resources is a primary condition for development in African agriculture, it is important to understand how struggles over access are shaped, within the state and beyond it, and how they influence not only the extent of political conflict, but also the use of productive resources and the course of development.[22]

Economic life in Zaire is structured by state power in ways much more subtle and pervasive than price restrictions or even marketing boards. Despite its apparent weakness and inability to provide the services that Westerners expect of an industrialized state, the state in Zaire has continued to serve as a key vehicle for accumulation by dominant classes.[23] Several studies have shown how high officials and their relatives and clients use public resources for private profit.[24] Although the expanding second economy in Zaire may appear to be autonomous,[25] the state's role in structuring access to important resources persists. Indeed, there are indications that new infusions of aid from outside, including that for agricultural development, may be imparting renewed life to these structures of accumulation.

Elements of the politico-commercial bourgeoisie and the local petty bourgeoisie have been shifting their activities in recent years toward agricultural production and trade, with an orientation toward internal markets. Some are investing their own resources, others (mainly men) have access to subsidized credit. External funding agencies, while making some efforts to support smallholder production, have also been devoting resources to the development of large farms and marketing infrastructure for food and export crops. Such projects may well threaten the viability of smallholder production.[26] In the Zairian context, these developments signal a reorientation of accumulation by some members of the dominant classes and are already generating important changes in rural production relations. With the availability of credit and infrastructure, land is becoming a resource coveted by urban elites. "Land grabs" in various areas of the country are proceeding apace, legitimized, not uncommonly, by state policies and the state-supported legal systems,[27] but also, it appears, by foreign donors supporting large-scale agricultural modernization projects.[28] When land titles are obtained in this way, they are rarely obtained by women.

Accumulation of land frequently involves competition between ascendant locals and members of the state bourgeoisie, and such conflict provides opportunities for self-serving ethnic discourse.[29] Transformation of conflict over land into ethnic conflict is advantageous for those able to assert "traditional" claims, which in reality date only from the colonial period.[30] These are used to legitimate new appropriations. The land question is not only related to clientelist national politics. Its international aspect lies in the development finance, policy advice, and expertise supplied by Western governments giving aid to Zaire. These are linked to patronage networks in all fields, including that of agricultural development.

It is in light of these dynamic processes that we must assess the import of recent projects designed to increase production by smallholders. While encouragement of smallholder production is laudable, the programs designed to achieve this goal tend to stress provision of improved seeds, fertilizer, new techniques of planting, and use of herbicides and pesticides—all of which must be paid for by farmers from the proceeds they receive in marketing their produce. Hence in effect, such projects target "more productive" farmers, defined even if only implicitly as those who can afford to take risks with planting techniques and inputs. New technology and increased commoditization make small farmers highly vulnerable to shifts in both climatic and market conditions.[31] The latter include not only government price controls on produce, but price manipulation by traders and the general world market trend of a widening gap between manufactured inputs and prices for primary products.

The emphasis on targeting more productive farmers sounds suspiciously like the "progressive farmer" schemes of colonial states in Africa. These programs were designed to increase market production; they also had political goals. In the 1950s, as pressure for independence mounted, colonial governments sought to promote rural support by creating prosperous rural middle classes.[32] Those who favor such an approach today tend to ignore the class formation it implies and the likely effects of such an approach on women agricultural producers.[33]

The actual project proposals usually envisage expansion of cultivated areas and treat this goal as an unquestioned benefit. However, along with larger fields, the introduction of improved seed varieties, fertilizers, and pesticides increases the work load of rural women. More labor is required for weeding and processing larger yields.[34] At the same time, women's autonomy often diminishes.[35] Production decisions are made by extension agents and often conveyed through husbands. Income from improved crop sales generally goes to men. Women's crops tend to suffer, and general family welfare declines. Such projects to increase smallholder production represent increased risks and increased work for women, yet there is no guarantee that they will receive commensurate benefits. Development planners rarely target women as the recipients of credit, extension advice, and income; more commonly, project proposals refer to "farmers" (read men) "farming families," or "households." Such projects are conceived as exercises in technology transfer rather than as the form of sociocultural engineering that they in fact entail. Planners generally work within the existing, male dominated social structures, and ignore gender conflict. In the process, the status of women may actually be worsened.

Few gender-specific case studies exist for Zaire. One study, conducted in 1975 and 1976 by the Schoepfs, examined ways in which a maize-production project's neglect of the roles and status of women led to failure to meet project objectives in southeastern Shaba region. Planners had expected that men, conceived of as household heads, could direct the labor of other family members.They continued in their assumptions despite protests by women that project methods required too much of their labor and interfered with gardening and other tasks. The independence of most women, supported by their rights to land and their desire to preserve a cropping system that afforded them a steady supply of both vegetable sauce ingredients and cash with which to purchase cooking oil, salt, and fish in small amounts throughout the year, limited their collaboration in cash-crop maize production. The project extension propaganda, directed at their husbands, left the majority of women unimpressed. Only the chief's wife, who had access to the unpaid labor of prisoners, expanded her fields.[36]

Women in the study community were more able to control their nutrient intake than were the less autonomous women of neighboring groups. A comparative nutrition survey made in 1958 found that whereas most other women were nutritionally deprived, the women of the Lemba hamlet consumed a slightly greater share of proteins and other essential nutrients than men in proportion to body height and weight.[37] Rather than eating men's leftovers, as is the case in many cultures in Zaire (and elsewhere[38]), Lemba women set aside portions of meal and sauce for themselves and for the children eating with them before serving men. Where women contribute heavily to agricultural work, food processing, and preparation, such an allocation is rational in terms of energy replacement, particularly when they reproduce and nourish infants. Nevertheless, current changes attendant upon the class formation process are undermining Lemba women's relatively high status and control over resources.[39]

WOMEN, THE ECONOMY OF AFFECTION, AND THE "UNCAPTURED PEASANTRY"

What vision of development is implied in current approaches to agricultural transformation in Zaire? The agricultural development project literature continues to distinguish between "traditional" and "modern" sectors, and to assume that development involves bringing "traditional" "subsistence" farmers (or peasants) into the modern sector as labor—either as smallholders or as wage workers on large farms and plantations.[40]

One might argue that such a process represents a necessary assault of what Hyden has called "the economy of affection," which in his view constitutes an obstacle to capitalist development.[41] Hyden initially argued that peasants need to be "captured" by the state so that they will contribute to national development rather than hinder it. In a later book, Hyden follows the lead of Berg and others who favor reliance on the market and attack the supposed irrationality of government bureaucracies.[42] Such a perspective assumes that people who resort to economic exchanges in "off-the-books" networks (Marjorie Mbilinyi's term for the informal or second economy)[43] are escaping from both the state and the market. In point of fact, when peasants withdraw from formal markets, they do not necessarily revert to subsistence production, and rarely can they completely avoid the state.[44] Their strategies are better interpreted as forms of resistance, efforts to avoid further pauperization.[45] A further weakness of Hyden's concept is its uncritical assumption that control of the peasantry by other classes—even when they hide behind impersonal market mechanisms—can lead to development. These assumptions need to be questioned, particularly in the context of patriarchal gender relations which the economy of affection notion tends to obscure.[46]

We have shown elsewhere how "traditional" Zairian agrarian systems have been transformed and gender conflict exacerbated by socioeconomic changes that accompanied the introduction of colonial capitalism.[47] The result of women's subjection to male authority within the households of rural producers is compounded by the subordinate position of most peasants within the community. Development projects may pay lip service to "doing something for women," but the effects are not always as advertised.

USAID's North Shaba Project (PNS) proposed to integrate women in the development process. Actually, the women in development component never got properly started; after five years, extension efforts were effectively limited to men.[48] Increased maize production and marketing infrastructure improvements (including rebuilt roads and bridges, as well as credit for the purchase of trucks, fuel, sacks, and maize) did more to augment the profits of merchants, some of whom operate in the national political arena, than to enhance the quality of life for poor producers. In the villages, the wealthiest men's status increased as a result of their activities in the newly organized Farmers' Councils.[49] Women, who lacked power in the local social structure, became further disadvantaged as their work burdens increased. Bukaka Bonani discovered that conflict over the control of women's labor escalated in the project area.[50] Evidently many men—mainly polygynous husbands—viewed women's attempts to exercise autonomy or to control the fruits of their efforts as a threat to male prerogatives. Actually, their opposition may have been fueled by their multiple frustrations, including low producer prices in the face of high trader profits, fines and tribute extracted by the military at numerous roadblocks, and the high cost of health care and other services.

This complex project was supposed to demonstrate a replicable model for integrated rural development based on popular participation. In Zaire's environment of scarcity, fueled by what Lemarchand terms "the politics of penury,"[51] project resources enabled a few large merchants to grow richer while poor women worked harder and their young children continued to suffer from malnutrition.[52]

In the eastern highlands of Zaire, land is in short supply and men control the allocation of household land for export and food crops. Here the resources of poor households are under pressure from large farms, plantations, local elites, and ascendant classes. Women's access to land has dwindled while their labor burdens have increased. Family food supplies have suffered. In some areas where cash-crop production of coffee and quinine was widespread, one now observes cases of male producers favoring cultivation of food crops for market over export crops. However, this does not mean that rural families are better nourished because food needed for family consumption may be sold. For example, peasants in the vicinity of Bukavu, the capital of Kivu Region, sell products that have a high nutritional content, such as sorghum, and eat cheaper foods, such as cassava. Peasants engage in such transactions because they need cash for day-to-day household needs, clothing, school fees, social obligations, taxes, and tribute. Widespread malnutrition among children in this area reflects the impoverishment of the rural population. Population density, land scarcity, and soil exhaustion have been exacerbated by the continuing encroachment of large, privately-owned plantations producing export crops. People deprived of their land may obtain occasional work on the plantations but at wages too low to support them or their families.[53]

For such people, participation in off-the-books activities such as hawking, distilling home brew, digging gold, and smuggling represent both survival and resistance. It is here that gender really does make a difference. In the sphere of formal politics and the formal economy, barriers to women's active participation are substantial. Although the conditions and status of women in Zaire differ according to class position, all women in this state lack legal equality with men.[54] Moreover, most women do not have the educational background and other resources needed to compete effectively in formal state structures as presently constituted. Even those women who may possess the requisite qualifications face an array of obstacles, not the least of which is opposition from male colleagues and a pervasive ethos that lauds the sexual exploits of men while cautioning women to tend to the home and accept gracefully their subordinate status.

In a 1982 speech, President Mobutu Sese Seko emphasized his government's commitment to improving the status of Zairian women and assuring them equal rights. But he also warned that

> there will always be one head in each household. And until proof to the contrary, the head, in our country, is he who wears the pants. Our women citizens also ought to understand this, to accept it with a smile and revolutionary submission.[55]

The off-the-books sector offers a means of circumventing legal restrictions on autonomous economic activity by women—and this holds true for urban as well as rural women, wealthy as well as poor.[56] The vitality of this informal sector is a testimony to the resourcefulness and resilience of women who have contributed to its growth. Nor do the transactions and networks of this sector reflect merely a residue of "traditional" relationships. Instead, an ongoing dynamic process is occurring whereby old and new relationships are being shaped to serve the goals and needs of the participants.

Women in rural and urban areas of Zaire have been involved in the second economy for decades. Such activities have gained prominence in recent years because they have become more widespread and because their importance to family survival has increased. Because of the contraction of the formal economic sector and lack of opportunities there, men now participate in such activities in greater numbers. As Kathleen Staudt suggests, "perhaps peasants more generally are modeling themselves on women who have long taken such stances in response to the male-ordered colonial and modern states."[57]

Some participants are able to accumulate considerable wealth in the flourishing "irregular" economy.[58] Traders operating across international borders typically exchange coffee, gold, and cattle for foreign exchange or scarce consumer goods. While some authors emphasize the absence of the state in connection with this "second economy," numerous officials also are reported to be involved in smuggling, trading on their own account and, for a fee, closing their eyes to the activities of others. Plantations and ranches serve as storehouses for some of this wealth.

One should not romanticize off-the-books activities; working conditions are often harsh, with wages below those of the formal sector. Women tend to be concentrated at the lower end of the scale, in such activities as beer brewing, petty trade, and artisanal production. While not a solution to the difficulties faced by women, such off-the-books activities and survival strategies in general do permit women to gain some autonomy and provide for their families, however inadequately, in conditions of great scarcity. For a few women with family or patronage ties providing access to capital and other scarce resources, there is the possibility of accumulating substantial wealth.[59] Despite some success stories, however, income for most is limited. In sum, while allowing women to survive, informal economic sector activities do not alter the general condition of women.[60]

Indeed, success in the irregular economy can be used to scapegoat women. A front page editorial in 1986 reported the prime minister's campaign against smugglers whose activities "could jeopardize sacrifices made during the three and one half year struggle for healthy public finances and economic stabilization."[61] Instead of exposing the wealthy gold and coffee smugglers, the news story indicts

> the ever growing number of mamas in Kivu who no longer act as moral guardians but instead prefer to operate clandestinely. Just recently one woman tried to export sixty barrels of palm oil worth 100,000 Zaires ($1,538). . . . Another continues to smuggle in cigarettes.[62]

Thus, it is not clear that the apparent autonomy and the greater visibility of these activities translates into greater political influence for women, as suggested by Jane Parpart.[63] David Hirschmann has suggested that women may find ways to exercise influence in indirect ways, operating in "the interstices of power."[64] One such strategy, evident in Zaire, is women's reluctance to accept agricultural innovations which involve increased workloads without their being given access to the income from such additional labor. It is in this sense that women peasants are to a certain extent "uncaptured," as stated in a recent article by Staudt: Off-the-books activities reflect efforts by women to direct their labor into channels where they can have some control over what is produced.[65]

Many of the activities associated with the second economy are individualistic and involve private benefits. But some rural producers are also putting their energies into a growing number of grassroots organizations tending toward more collective goals which benefit the local community as a whole.[66] Participation in these groups represents a form of survival strategy that relies on solidarity from below and reflects the vitality of popular perceptions of exploitation. Some off-the-books activities and most grass-roots development initiatives in Zaire represent a particular view of development, one based on local concerns and oriented toward serving the aspirations of the majority of the rural population for improved living standards. These initiatives reflect a determination to compete for resources, an attempt by rural dwellers to limit accumulation by state structures and dominant classes which, as far as peasants can see, scarcely serve the interests of the majority.[67]

Hyden hopes that grassroots development organizations will serve to erode the economy of affection in order to serve the ends of capitalist development.[68] We hope the participants in such groups will find it possible to sustain a different view, one that nurtures solidarity out of which a more needs-oriented approach to development may be fostered. This approach would encourage production, but with priority to food crops; it would demonstrate the benefits of participatory efforts at change; and it would actively seek women's participation, addressing women's concerns as producers and family providers in their own right. Such a view is not utopian; examples of groups professing these values can be found throughout Zaire today.[69]

The future of such initiatives is uncertain, however, even though some external donors recommend aid and support to them.[70] Will the Zairian tate continue to tolerate such organizations, forms of resistance, and autonomy for peasants attempting to cope with agrarian crisis? Or, strengthened by renewed credibility in the eyes of institutions such as the IMF, will the state attempt to reassert control and try to block such activities? Even should the state decide to leave well enough alone in this dimension, state institutions promote intensified allocation of external and internal resources to large-scale capitalist agriculture. This threatens to undermine the access to land and rural labor resources on which grassroots development organizations depend. As noted above, members of the educated elite strata have been shifting their sights "homeward" to rural areas where foreign-assisted projects are building roads and bridges and creating new opportunities for organizing production and marketing. Meanwhile, landholding by villages and cooperatives is being jeopardized by "land reforms" that award private freehold tenure.[71] This process contributes to the maintenance of state power by providing resources for patron-linkages in the face of increasing scarcity.[72]

CONCLUSION

The crisis of peasant reproduction, which has worsened in many parts of Africa, is being exacerbated by changes brought about by the current class formation process, as accumulation strategies pursued by dominant classes continue to drain resources from peasant production systems. Explanations of the causes of the African food crisis are as diverse as those which attempt to account for the origins of male dominance and female subordination. Although some have proposed "naturalistic" explanations of both phenomena—ecological destruction and overpopulation for the first, biological sex differences for the second—social explanatory paradigms appear to be more powerful in both cases. They point to changing conditions of access to strategic resources.

To date, the participation of poor women in agriculture has been taken for granted by the state and development planners. Their needs have been ignored and their burdens increased. Many women have responded by fleeing intensified exploitation in agriculture and attempting to survive by means of informal or irregular activities that offer the prospect of "off-the-books" income and personal autonomy. For most, these activities provide subsistence, or less. While some successful individuals have been scapegoated, the mass roundups operated by other other governments have not taken place in Zaire.[73] However, the potential for witch-hunting remains, particularly in view of the growing AIDS epidemic in conjunction with prolonged and deepening economic crisis. AIDS is a fatal sexually transmitted disease, for which many men blame women without reflecting upon their own practice.[74]

This chapter has explored recent trends in agricultural policy in Zaire which are supposed to combat agrarian crisis by achieving increased output, capital formation, and productive reinvestment in agriculture. We have suggested that given the character of Zaire's contemporary political economy, it is unlikely that such policies will resolve Zaire's food crisis. Some local capitalists and agro-industrial firms are benefiting, but it is unlikely that positive benefits will accrue to most smallholder producers, particularly women. Rather, the conditions of many rural dwellers may actually be worsened. We see little likelihood that capitalist agricultural growth and a narrow focus on technical measures to increase production can end the agrarian crisis in Zaire, despite the optimistic projections of the lending agencies and a few scholars. The problems are political, not just economic. What is required is structural transformation which focuses on basic human needs, ensures secure access of women to land, and fosters redistribution.[75] This is essential not only for the sake of equity, but for increased food production.

In the absence of such measures, the female rural exodus, which already has led to virtually equal sex ratios in Zaire's major cities, is likely to expand. Jane Guyer has suggested that if current patterns of discriminatory agrarian change continue, Africa's rural women will increasingly provide education for their daughters so that they can escape the unrewarding drudgery of agricultural production.[76] In Zaire, rural women have seldom been able to provide education for their daughters. Nevertheless, young women continue to flee the rural areas. Without diplomas and special skills, they join the already crowded ranks of those attempting to survive through off-the-books economic endeavors. Under contemporary conditions of economic crisis, these activities are less and less viable. Consequently, many women are constrained to exchange sexual services for the means of survival. Such behavior, which in the past involved substantial health risks, now, in the presence of the AIDS epidemic, has turned into a death strategy.[77]

NOTES

This chapter is based on a paper by Catharine Newbury presented at the University of Wisconsin-Madison in 1986 and a paper by Brooke Schoepf presented at a conference on Gender Issues in Farming Research Systems and Extension, University of Florida, Gainesville, in 1986. The authors draw on research conducted in Zaire by Catharine Newbury and David Newbury between 1972 and 1975 and 1981 to 1983 and by Brooke Schoepf and Claude Schoepf from 1974 to 1979, with additional research visits by C. Schoepf in 1982 and B. Schoepf in 1981, 1983, and 1985. Newbury wishes to acknowledge funding from the National Endowment for the Humanities and support from the Centre de Recherches Universitaires du Kivu in Bukavu and the Institut de Recherche Scientifique du Zaire (formerly IRSAC). Schoepf gratefully acknowledges support from the Université Nationale du Zaire in Lubumbashi and funding from the Rockefeller Foundation, the U.S. Fulbright Program, the Tuskegee Institute, the U.S. Agency for International Development, and the U.S. Peace Corps. The authors thank the editors and participants in the Comparative Politics Discussion Group at the University of North Carolina at Chapel Hill for their comments, but bear full responsibility for the findings and interpretations presented here.

1. See Kabongo, "Déroutante Afrique ou la syncope d'un discours"; Young, "Is There a State?"; Nzongola-Ntalaja, "Bureaucracy, Elite, New Class"; Newbury, "Dead and Buried or Just Underground? The Privatization of the State in Zaire"; Young and Turner, *The Rise and Decline of the Zairian State*. Also, Gran, ed., *Zaire: The Political Economy of Underdevelopment*; Young, "Zaire: The Unending Crisis," 169–185; Kabwit, "Zaire: The Roots of the Continuing Crisis," 381–407; Nzongola-Ntalaja, ed., *The Crisis in Zaire*; Nzongola-Ntalaja, "The Continuing Struggle for National Liberation in Zaire," 595–614, and *Class Struggles and National Liberation in Africa*; Schatzberg, *Politics and Class in Zaire: Bureaucracy, Business and Beer in Lisala*; Callaghy, *The State-Society Struggle: Zaire in Comparative Perspective*.

2. See Peemans, "The Social and Economic Development of Zaire since Independence," 148–179; Gran, "An Introduction to Zaire's Permanent Development Crisis," 1–25; Callaghy, "The International Community and Zaire's Debt Crisis," and Leslie, "The World Bank and Zaire."

3. Young and Turner, *Zairian State*, 322.

4. See Jacquet, "Viens, je t'emmène de l'autre coté des nuages," 101–106. Jacquet based her analysis on summaries and excerpts of press reports from Zairian and overseas newspapers found in *Zaire Monthly* (Brussels). Widespread hunger and the spread of disease (especially malaria) among urban dwellers is confirmed by Walu Engundu, a Zairian anthropologist who has been conducting research on household survival strategies in Zaire's capital city, Kinshasa. The prevalence of AIDS is, of course, one additional facet of these conditions. See footnote 77.

5. For examples of the varying viewpoints presented in such analyses, see Bates, *Markets and States in Tropical Africa*; Barker, ed., *The Politics of Agriculture in Tropical Africa*; Dinham and Hines, eds., *Agribusiness in Africa*; Sandbrook, *The Politics of Africa's Economic Stagnation*; Abernathy,

"Reflections on a Continent in Crisis," 321–339; Shaw and Aluko, eds., *Africa Projected*; Commins et al., eds., *Africa's Agrarian Crisis: The Roots of Famine*; Ravenhill, ed., *Africa in Economic Crisis*; Berg and Whitaker, eds., *Strategies for African Development*; Hansen and McMillan, eds., *Food in Sub-Saharan Africa*; Lawrence, *World Recession*. A perceptive overview of some of these debates is provided in Lofchie's, "Africa's Agrarian Malaise," 160–187.

6. IBRD/The World Bank, *Accelerated Development in Sub-Saharan Africa*, especially Chapter 5.

7. A 1982 study estimated that 36 percent of Zairians lived in towns and cities. The number of urban dwellers has been steadily increasing in recent years as people leave the rural areas in search of jobs. Economist Intelligence Unit, *Country Profile: Zaire, Rwanda, Burundi, 1987–88*, 8. See also Government of Zaire, "Combien sommes nous? Recensement scientifique de la population."

8. See Leslie, *The World Bank and Structural Transformation*, 100–103.

9. Between 1971 and 1974, the Zairian government established eleven parastatal marketing offices. These included the Office National des Fibres Textiles (ONAFITEX), which bought cotton; the Office National de Café (ONC), with responsibility for coffee; and the Office National des Céréales (ONACER), with responsibility for maize and rice. Many food crops for local consumption (such as cassava, legumes, and peanuts) were not controlled by marketing boards. See Young and Turner, 316–322.

10. An interview with the Governor of Shaba found him in favor of limited price increases but not decontrol. B.G. Schoepf interview, 1981. See also B.G. Schoepf, "Unintended Consequences and Structural Predictability," 361–367, "The Political Economy of Agrarian Research in Zaire," 269–290.

11. B.G. Schoepf's interviews, 1985.

12. B.G. Schoepf's interview with the vice-governor of Shaba, March 1985.

13. Mahmood Mamdani's recent work on Uganda provides perceptive analysis of such processes. See his "Disaster Prevention: Defining the Problem," 92–96.

14. C. Newbury's field notes, 1982, 1983.

15. C. Newbury interview, 1982, cited in Catharine Newbury, "Women's Tax Revolt."

16. C. Newbury and D. Newbury field notes, 1974, 1982, 1983.

17. C. Newbury interview, 1982, cited in "Women's Tax Revolt," 42.

18. Between 1981 and 1983, trader/transporters traveling the 70 kilometers between Bukavu and the main roadside market among the Tembo usually encountered three to five roadblocks, depending on when the travel occurred. (C. Newbury's and D. Newbury's, field notes). In western Zaire, an observer in 1973 reported seeing eighteen roadblocks during a 300 kilometer trip between Matadi and Kinshasa, Zaire's national capital. Joseph Boute, "Demographic Trends in the Republic of Zaire," *Munger Africana Library Notes* (Dec. 1973), 20, cited in Young and Turner, 322.

19. Secondary-school teachers earned between 2,500 and 4,000 zaires per month in the 1987 school year. This was equivalent to twenty to thirty-three U.S. dollars in June 1987; by February 1988, devaluation had reduced it to

between sixteen and twenty-six dollars. The effects of devaluation were exacerbated by the inflation; consumer prices rose about 75 percent in 1987. The price of a 40 kilogram bag of imported rice rose from 2,300 zaires in October to 6,000 zaires in February.

20. The pervasiveness of corruption in Zaire has been documented by many scholars. See especially Gould, *Bureaucratic Corruption and Underdevelopment in the Third World*; Schatzberg, Young and Turner.

21. These cases are cited in Schoepf and Schoepf, "Peasants, Capitalists and the State in the Lufira Valley," 90.

22. Berry, "The Food Crisis and Agrarian Change in Africa," 67.

23. Newbury, "Privatization of the State in Zaire"; Nzongola-Ntalaja, "Bureaucracy, Elite, New Class."

24. See sources cited in note 20.

25. MacGaffey, "How to Survive and Become Rich Amidst Devastation: The Second Economy in Zaire," 351–366; "Fending-for-Yourself: The Organization of the Second Economy in Zaire," 141–156; "Economic Disengagement and Class Formation in Zaire," 171–188.

26. Schoepf, "Food Crisis and Class Formation: An Example from Shaba," 42; Peemans, "Accumulation and Underdevelopment in Zaire," 79–80, 82–83.

27. C. Newbury, "Privatization of the State in Zaire."

28. Changes in legal provisions governing access to land have facilitated and fueled this alienation of land. The new land law "means that those with power, wealth and influence are able to manipulate the system to appropriate any lands not yet conceded and titled." Schoepf and Schoepf, "Gender, Land and Hunger in Eastern Kivu, Zaire." See also Lumpungu, "Land Tenure Systems and the Agricultural Crisis in Zaire," 57–71.

29. C. Newbury, "Privatization of the State"; B.G. Schoepf, "Zaire's Rural Development'"; Schoepf and Schoepf, "Food Crisis and Agrarian Change."

30. D. Newbury, "From 'Frontier to Boundary,'" 87–98.

31. For examples of this, see B.G. Schoepf, "Food Crisis and Class Formation," 33–43, and "Food Crisis and Class Formation in Zaire." In Lawrence, 189–212.

32. Schoepf and Schoepf, "Zaire's Rural Development in Perspective," 243–257.

33. For example, the sole reference to women in the 1985 U.S. President's Agricultural Task Force to Zaire report advised that the Department of Agriculture collaborate with Zaire's Département de la Condition Féminine et de la Famille.

34. One project proposal claims that a labor surplus exists— USAID/Kinshasa Project 091.

35. Wright, "Technology, Marriage and Women's Work," 71–85; Muntemba, "Women and Agricultural Change in the Railway Region of Zambia," 83–103.

36. Schoepf and Schoepf, "Peasants, Capitalists and the State in the Lufira Valley," 89–93; B.G. Schoepf, "The 'Wild,' the 'Lazy' and the 'Matriarchal,'" and "Food Crisis and Class Formation."

37. Lambrechts and Bernier, *Enquête alimenatire et agricole.*

38. See Rosenberg, "Demographic effects of Sex Differential Nutrition"; B.G. Schoepf, field notes from Mali, 1979, 1984.

39. Palmer, "Seasonal Dimensions of Women's Roles;" Schoepf, "The 'Wild,' the 'Lazy'," and "Social Structure, Women's Status and Sex Differential Nutrition," 73–102.

40. For a critique of this approach, see Loxley, "The World Bank and the Model of Accumulation," 65–76. Critiques particularly sensitive to gender implications of such thinking include Paul, "The World Bank's Agenda for the Crises in Agriculture and Rural Development in Africa," 1–8, and Green and Allison, "The World Bank's Agenda for Accelerated Development," 60–84.

41. Hyden, *Beyond Ujamaa.*

42. Hyden, "No Shortcuts to Progress."

43. Marjorie Mbilinyi, personal communication.

44. Similar questions are raised by Geshiere, "La paysannerie africaine est-elle captivé?" 13–33, and Kasfir, "Are African Peasants Self-Sufficient?" 335–357.

45. C. Newbury, "Survival Strategies in Rural Zaire."

46. Kathleen Staudt, review of Hyden, "No Shortcuts to Progress," in *Journal of Developing Areas* 18, 4 (1984), 530–532.

47. C. Newbury, "Women's Tax Revolt" and "From Bananas to Cassava"; Schoepf and Schoepf, "Food Crisis and Agrarian Change."

48. C. Schoepf's field notes, 1981; Hardt, "Decision Making Roles."

49. Gran, *Development by People,* 73.

50. Bonani, "Une première approche des structures d'intégration de la femme," 5.

51. Lemarchand, "The Politics of Penury in Rural Zaire," 237–260.

52. B.G. Schoepf's field notes, 1985.

53. Schoepf and Schoepf, "Gender, Land, and Hunger in Eastern Kivu"; C. Newbury's field notes, 1973–74, 1982–83; Sosne, "Colonial Peasantization and Contemporary Underdevelopment," 189–210.

54. See Kalenda, "La femme zaïroise et les droits de l'homme," 363–371. In 1983, Citoyenne Ekila Liyonda (then secretary-general for women's affairs and member of the central committee of Zaire's single party, the MPR) provided slightly different interpretation of the legal status of women in Zaire. She pointed out that, in theory, Article 12 of the Zairian constitution provides for equality for all citizens, but, in practice, women do not enjoy full legal equality because of restrictive laws dating back to the colonial period. Ekila Liyonda, "Women in Zaire," *The Courier,* 78 (March/April 1983), 53. See also Adams, "Women in Zaire," 55–57.

55. Mobutu Sese Seko, speech to the Third Party Congress of the Mouvement Populaire de la Révolution (December 1982), cited in R. Beeckmans, "Afrique-Actualités: décembre 1982," *Zaire-Afrique* 172 (1983), 119.

56. For a discussion of this phenomenon in Kisangani, see MacGaffey, "Women and Class Formation in a Dependent Economy," 161–177.

57. Staudt, "Women, Development and the State," 330.

58. See Waruzi, "Peasant, State, and Rural Development in Post-Independent Zaire;" MacGaffey, "Class Relations in a Dependent Economy,"

167–177; Mukohya, "African Traders in Butembo, Eastern Zaire 1960–1980;" D. Newbury, "Historical Roots of Peasant Survival Strategies."

59. J. MacGaffey describes successful women entrepreneurs in Kisangani. See MacGaffey, "Kisangani Entrepreneurs."

60. Schwarz, "Illusion d'une émancipation," 183–212.

61. I.D. Monsa, "Le Premier Commissaire d'Etat dénonce les Fossoyeurs," *Elima* (Kinshasa), August 25, 1986, 14.

62. Monsa, "Premier Commissaire d'Etat," 14.

63. Parpart, "Women and the State in Africa," 208–230.

64. Hirschmann, "Women and Politics in Commonwealth Africa: Operating at the Interstices of Power." Paper given at the African Studies Association in 1986.

65. Staudt, "Uncaptured or Unmotivated?" 37–55.

66. See, for example, Maka, "Des paysans en marche," 521–532; C. Newbury, "Survival Strategies in Rural Zaire," especially 105 ff.; Kabwit, "The potential for Grassroots Development in Zaire."

67. C. Newbury, "Survival Strategies in Rural Zaire."

68. Hyden, *No Shortcuts to Progress.*

69. See sources cited in note 66.

70. See the recent study commissioned by Belgium's Secretary of State for Cooperation: Drachoussof, Vis and Sokal, *Approche scientifique d'une stratégie alimentaire pour le Zaire,* cited in Huybrechts, "Zaire" Economy," 1023.

71. C. Newbury, "Privatization of the State"; Schoepf and Schoepf, "Gender, Land and Hunger in Eastern Kivu, Zaire"; Lumpungu, "Land Tenure and Agricultural Crisis."

72. Willame, "Zaire: système de survie et fiction d'etat," 83–88.

73. Roundups have taken "idle" urban women and "prostitutes" to work in rural areas. For Zimbabwe, see Jacobs and Howard, "Women in Zimbabwe." For Tanzania, see Shaidi, "Tanzania: The Human Resources Deployment Act, 1983," 82–87.

74. Pepe Roberts offers an example of such a conjuncture in Ghana when women were witchhunted in the late 1920s. See Roberts, "The State and the Regulation of Marriage."

75. See Sen and Grown, *Development, Crises, and Alternative Visions,* especially Chapters 2 and 3. A plea for redistributive forms of rural development that will provide basic services to rural dwellers and thereby foster production is found in Green, "Consolidation and Accelerated Development of African Agriculture," 17–34.

76. Guyer, "Women in the Rural Economy," 32.

77. Schoepf et al., "AIDS and Society"; Schoepf, "Women, Health and Economic Crisis."

CHAPTER 6

"This Is an Unforgettable Business": Colonial State Intervention in Urban Tanzania

MARJORIE MBILINYI

Faced with crises in the reproduction of a cheap labor system, capital tries to use the state to regulate and control labor. Yet workers, particularly women and peasants, have adopted forms of resistance, some of which have been successful in the past. An example of resistance is the struggle over beer brewing in Dar es Salaam in the 1930s, which led to a confrontation between women beer brewers and the colonial government.

An analysis of British colonial discourse (1919 to 1961) reveals a particular imagery of "city" and "countryside" developed in the context of state struggles to control women and to block their movement off the farm into towns and other centers of wage employment.[1] Two phases are discernible in this colonial discourse. In the early labor-short phase of the 1920s, 1930s and 1940s, the state adopted repressive means to extract labor from the peasant economy through a migrant labor system. In the second phase, capital and the state aimed to stabilize the labor force in the context of a major capitalization drive during the second half of the 1950s. During both phases, struggles emerged over state efforts to restrict people's movements to town and to regulate and even ban off-the-book activities, sometimes even accumulation-oriented economic activities.

My analysis has used primary sources with all their immediacy of contradiction and struggle.[2] I draw from two sources in particular—a sociological survey by District Officer J. A. K. Leslie and a strategic outline for stabilizing city labor forces called *Detribalisation* by Senior Provincial Commissioner M. J. B. Molohan—for how they illustrate the way certain codes have been adopted "to express a reality which is the goal of policy."[3] Dar es Salaam, as the biggest town, with a large, floating surplus labor force, is the major focus.

CITY AND COUNTRYSIDE: FICTIONAL AND REAL

A fictionalized contrast between city and country permeated colonial commentary on the society its agents found, and the one they struggled to create and rule. In simple terms, the city was associated with non-Africans, men, adults, wage employment, and civilization; the country with Africans, women, children, subsistence and bush. According to colonial ideology, the country was home for Africans in tribal areas. The African in town was considered an alien in foreign territory who had immigrated and was in danger of being "detribalized."[4] In Tanganyikan usage, countryside referred to the peasant-based economy. Town meant sectors of capitalist wage-relations, including rural plantation enterprises which were the dominant production sector in Tanganyika.[5]

Plantations were owned by large-scale multinational companies based in Germany, Switzerland, and England and by smaller companies formed by local Asians and Europeans who were less powerful, but still taken seriously by colonial administrators. Both the plantations and the large-scale farms depended on systems of migrant labor and casual labor which provided workers at exceedingly low wages. A relatively large proportion of casual laborers were women who predominated in such labor tasks as tea plucking, coffee picking, weeding, and in grading and sorting in the agroprocessing factories which the larger companies established on their plantations and tea estates.[6] Mining was the other major industry, situated in rural locations, with social relations based on capital-labor relations.

The peasant sector contributed to the production of certain export crops, particularly cotton and later coffee, though settlers produced half the coffee up to the time of self-government. Most of the labor in peasant production was drawn from family and other household members. Casual labor was the predominant form of wage labor used by the embryonic *kulak* classes. The real significance of the peasant sector, however, was its reproduction of the entire African labor force, including petty commodity producers as well as wage laborers. The labor reserve in Tanganyika was less a geographic and administrative unit than a social reality based on peasant household production administered by Native Authorities. The viability of the migrant system depended upon the continued reproduction of the peasant sector as well as of capital-wage labor relations. Real as the division between city and countryside was, therefore, there was a symbiotic relationship between the growth of towns and other centers of wage employment and the development of petty commodity production and trade in the countryside.

The urban population of Tanganyika grew at an annual rate of 6.3 percent or more beginning in the late 1930s; by 1957, 4.1 percent of the total Tanganyikan population was urban with Dar expanding from 10,000 people in 1894 to 128,742 in 1957.[7] Although severely out-numbered at first, women comprised some 42 percent of the town population by 1956.[8]

Dar es Salaam was primarily a port town, a major market, and an administrative center; only in the 1940s did processing and other light in- dustrial investment occur. Aside from government employment and domestic service, most workers were not employed on a permanent basis. While colonial officials argued that this was the result of African preference for casual work, keeping one foot in the secondary economy of trade, casual laborers depended on the petty commodity sector to supplement their low and irregular wages.[9] At the same time, the existence of this sector provided an alternative to the wage slavery of capital-labor relations, especially the system of labor recruitment of contract workers, which workers called *manamba* ("numbers," another term for slaves). In the context of high unemployment and low wages, petty commodity production and petty trade became the major means of subsistence for most townspeople as well as for villagers. Townspeople derived a relative independence from this off-the-books sector, of which *pombe*-brewing is a good example (*pombe* is homebrew beer).

Casualization of the labor force was also capital's response to the economic crises of the 1930s and early 1950s. Casual labor was cheaper, with a lower individual wage (including no food rations) and nonexistent social wages, such as housing, sanitation, or health facilities. Casual labor was also flexible to the fluctuating labor demands of the plantations, docks, and other sites of employment.

Yet the apparent dynamism and resiliency of the off-the-books sector developed in the context of the growing impoverishment of most town dwellers. Dar es Salaam conditions were described as "misery" from the early 1930s, and a "disaster" during World War II.[10] People pawned their clothes and other personal belongings to get by, but were continuously in debt.[11] In the absence of housing regulations, housing in African zones tended to be unhygenic, contributing to high rates of disease and infant, child, and maternal mortality. This was accompanied by increased violence within and against the African community, which, according to John Iliffe, "lived in the constant presence of the the police, who questioned any African found on the streets after 10:00 p.m."[12] Racial residential patterns segregated the African population, making them more vulnerable to army and police actions and discouraging joint action among Asian, Arab, and African laborers.

Liberal critiques expressed disgust at the failure of the Township Authority to provide even "the minimum amenities for the native township," despite taxation, whereas in the European zone, officers had their "hedges cut and their drives gravelled for nothing."[13] Rather than take action, the administration condoned overcrowding and taxed proceeds. In a 1931 report on Dar conditions, for example, the municipal secretary characterized African locations as "dens of vice" and expressed a typical opposition to African profit-making:

> A vast number private [sic] residential premises in the township appear to be used as lodging houses in which a separate family is accommodated in each room as well as in every other available space, such as ends of passages, verandah, etc. The proprietors of these dens of unhygenic vice extort at least 20% per month from each unfortunate tenant and often fail to provide even such essentials as sanitary

conveniences which can be approached except with extreme discomfort. It is to my mind in every way desirable that these lodging house keepers should be compelled to disgorge to a common purpose a percentage of their gains and I strongly recommend that the Township Authority be empowered to impose a special tax upon such businesses. Private hotels and boarding houses should be similarly taxed.[14]

The Colonial authorities suppressed information about the worsening conditions in the African sectors of town. For example, when Leslie's informants insisted that they experienced hunger during certain days of every month, after their pay had run out, he dismissed their reports as "a belief" or an "exaggeration." While noting the association between hunger and unemployment, Leslie interprets this as the result of the backward, rural social relations from which workers came:

So many Africans arriving in town have hardly seen money before . . . very few indeed have used money to such an extent that they are able to calculate how long it will last and to allocate it throughout a month or a fortnight . . .

So when the country bumpkin comes into town, who used to eat and be housed free, and needed money hardly at all, he is delighted and carried away with what appear to be large sums put into his hands, and does not stop to reckon the cost of merely keeping alive until the next lot comes in.[15]

Moreover, not only does the worker have to provide for himself and his wife and children (sic, *he* provides for *her*),

there is another family, and other obligations, which are if anything more common than those to the strict family: a man's obligation to shelter and feed the members of his extended family. . . . The advent of a swarm of "locusts" as these are jocularly called, . . . though they normally bring some presents, it often happens that just when a man is at his lowest (perhaps having used his payday income to pay off debts) he is faced with the obligation to support two or three relations.[16]

This discussion obscures the objective need for popular survival strategies to combat the pauperization of Africans in towns and villages. Women were central actors in these struggles, and this centrality led to contradictory colonial imageries of African women, as shown below.

THE FICTITIOUS AFRICAN WOMAN— A SOURCE OF CONTRADICTION

Colonial authorities acknowledged that women peasants were major providers for family needs in the labor reserve. In the debate on the migrant labor system, for example, a government sociologist and expert on labor migration argued the following:

One of the most common objections to labour migration which is made both by Government officials and by missionaries is that it leads to severe hardships for the wife and children who are left at home by the labourer. It may be clear however that an Ngoni wife is less dependent on her husband than her European counterpart, and, she is able with relatively little difficulty to maintain the food supply of her home in his temporary absence. She is able to continue her relations and mutual assistance with her feminine kin and neighbours and, by the nature of the economy, and low demand, she and her children can comfortably continue with little or no money income.[17]

Women in towns, however, were consistently disapproved of. According to Molohan,

The problems presented by women in the towns who, taken away from their rural environment, and the life in which they have always been accustomed, find themselves in the towns with time on their hands and so became a liability rather than an asset.[18]

Molohan was paraphrasing Leslie's observation that workers preferred to leave wives at home because at home the wife is "an investment and an economic asset, growing enough food in normal years to feed all his family and assist him," whereas in town, with no land, she is a liability and a consumer. In reality, however, women were also producers and traders in towns. Leslie goes on to contradict himself when he describes how women "bring in quite large amounts of cash" by cooking and selling beans, cakes, sweetmeats, and fish and splitting and selling firewood. Women controlled most of the manufacturing and trade in home-brew beer, processed and prepared food, and firewood. Whereas the majority remained poor, some accumulated enough to purchase real estate and become landladies in the African side of town. About one-fifth of all titles to African-owned houses were held by women.[19]

Independent townswomen were also portrayed as immoral. Leslie devotes substantive attention to discussion of sexual relations: "free marriage," "amorality" in marital relations, the "independence of women," and "prostitution":

[O]ne of the most noticeable aspects of life in town is the license with which men and women cohabit, without the formal bonds of marriage and dowry, the uniting of two families, which is obligatory in most tribes up-country.[20]

Throughout colonial rule, the authorities actively favored, regulated, and in some places imposed the practice of bridewealth as a means of "stabilizing marriage" by enforcing women's bondage as wives in rural areas.[21] This occurred in towns as well. The colonialists probably sought to develop two different family policies for Africans, one for the working class and one for the new middle class. They preferred wives of workers to remain in the reserve, but encouraged the development of a new nuclear family culture within the emergent middle class. Prostitution was acceptable and regulated to some extent by the state in working-class neighborhoods in order to ensure provision of the services otherwise missed in places of wage employment.

In the late 1920s, for example, the Dar es Salaam Township Authority tried to license brothels and prostitutes and regulate medical inspection of prostitutes.[22] The central government was opposed, but one segment of middle-class opinion insisted that "segregation of public immoral women is necessary in the township areas."[23] He expressed horror at the presence of prostitutes in middle-class neighborhoods:

> Continuous influx of motor cars hooting and rickshaws ringing the bells and the noise produced by drunken visitors to the houses of prostitutes at late hours of the night have caused and are causing great inconvenience and annoyance to the non-native population residing in the close vicinity.

The township administrators ordered an investigation but later decided that there was no great disturbance. The official view, that prostitution was a necessary amenity in the township which provided a diversion otherwise filled by more political forms of action, was the one that dictated policy. When one of the urban-renewal programs was later established in the fifties, Leslie pointed out that "Magomeni has also its attractions for the younger element; it has a life of its own and more than its fair share of bars, clubs and call-girls."[24]

Although we know little about how prostitutes and other women viewed prostitution and its alternatives,[25] prostitution was partly based on the inferior and deteriorating position of women on the land and in the labor market. African women experienced the highest rate of unemployment and the lowest wages; they were confined primarily to the off-the-books economy. Prostitution and beer brewing provided viable and relatively lucrative incomes for many women in towns. As will be shown in the next section, state actions that targeted African women were often efforts to regulate or destroy certain branches of the off-the-books or informal economy. Sexist and racist imagery and practice were adopted to further state hegemony and capitalist profits.

THE STRUGGLE OVER BEER BREWING

The struggle over the beer market in Dar es Salaam exemplified the contradictory position of African women in colonial society. Licensing and taxing the *pombe* industry provided substantial revenue to the state. Women brewers who owned houses were taxed similarly to men. Brewing was only made illegal during the periods of food shortages or when producers had not paid for a license. The brewers in the town beer market were successful enough to maintain a staff of laborers and barmaids.

In a debate in the Legislative council in 1934, the Director of Medical Services described the business as follows:

> Of the people concerned there are 12 old lady brewers, each of whom
> has a certain amount of staff. They have their own families, and there
> is definitely a certain number of barmaids besides, who sell the liquor
> in the market. There are, of course, the backers who purchase the bars
> and employ people themselves.[26]

Their business was so lucrative that the colonial secretariat debated the possibilities of establishing a monopoly over beer brewing in Dar in the mid-
thirties.[27] The secretariat studied the organization of municipal beer halls and
beer gardens in Durban and other cities of South Africa, the Rhodesias, and
Kenya. The debate was not so much over the proposed clampdown on
African-owned business, however, but rather over the choice between
government and private ownership of a capitalist enterprise. The Secretary of
Native Affairs, Philip Mitchell, favored the creation of a monopoly on
contract to the Kenya Breweries, rather than a government enterprise. Feas-
ibility studies were carried out which, predictably, showed that the Breweries
subsidiary would be able to produce more efficiently and productively than
the petty commodity producers who controlled the beer industry. The
Township Authority would also get sound profits from the monopoly.[28]

In order to establish the bylaws required to clamp down on the women
brewers, the matter had to be taken to the Legislative Council (Leg Co.). The
problematic relationship between the executive and the legislature was made
clear in the handling of this case. For example, the District Commissioner
argued that "Government [i.e., *not* Leg Co.] should decide what it wants done
and then amend the law." On file is a contract which was written jointly with
the Tanganyika Breweries (the subsidiary of Kenya Breweries) *before* the bill
was passed in Leg Co.[29] The colonial administration had to face not only the
interests of the beer brewers in the market, but those of commercial and
capitalist enterprises other than the Tanganyika Breweries. Other non-African
spokespersons welcomed the idea of establishing a monopoly with a ban on
African brewing. However, they wanted the question of choice of enterprise
to be decided by "open" market forces.

Major Lead, a Leg Co. member, insisted that there should be a public
tender for the beer market contract. This was, in fact, contrary to the
government's original plans. He went on to call for "constitutional
safeguards" by Leg Co. to limit the power of the Township Authority to
make bylaws and the power of the governor himself "inasmuch as he could
not sanction anything which was inconsistent with existing legislation." The
Governor responded: "Would not the Honourable Member's criticism, if
accepted, prohibit the Government from every making a bye-law?"[30] Indeed!

The government manipulated classist and sexist ideologies to win its
case in Leg Co. In opening remarks on the bill, Philip Mitchell argued:

> The old women who do it now are a dreadful lot and I think merely
> dummies for a local man of evil repute. The beer contains all sorts of
> impurities. [The] obligation to brew at the beer market makes the

middle part dirty and smokey and takes space which could be used to much better purpose. Mr. Kayamba assures me that respectable native opinion strongly favors the brewery plan.[31]

The use of "respectable" middle-class "native" views to legitimize colonial policy was typical. In the second reading of the bill, Mitchell said he "took a great deal of trouble to find out what the natives themselves thought about it, especially the responsible natives, the educated men, and they were unanimously in favour of it."[32]

According to the secretariat minutes, the "real" motive for change was the monopoly's future profitability and the expectation of crushing a powerful branch of petty commodity production. However, in the presentation to Leg Co., the administrators stressed that production would be improved by more hygienic conditions: "The sale of the beer will take place under conditions which will admit of more effective supervision in the interests of orderliness and sobriety," and the profits will be used for "public purposes beneficial to the natives of the township, instead of affording substantial profit to individual native brewers."[33] Here again discourse critiques profit-making by Africans as morally bad and suspect, especially when the Africans are women, rather than a private European-owned company.

The colonial government also argued that the Brewery monopoly would improve its control over the African population. The Township Authority intended to control the hours of the beer market once the monopoly was in force. Customers would be under the supervision of the Market Master, who would regulate choice of of clientele and conditions of service. This aspect of social control was important to Leg Co. members, who believed the bill did not go far enough and should be extended to the Lupa [Goldfields] Controlled Area: "We have in the Controlled Area an increasing number of natives from our more advanced neighbouring territories, and we must take account of the influence they are bound to have on the *unsophisticated* inhabitants of the area."[34]

The administrative move to take over the beer market aroused the opposition of a sizable segment of the African population in solidarity with the beer brewers and led to organized collective resistance. The organization which took up the issue and made it a popular one was the African Commercial Association (ACA), led by Erica Fiah, presumably Mitchell's "man of evil repute." ACA successfully manipulated the press to give the issue heavy coverage which led to a lengthy and heated debate in Leg Co.'s Ninth Session. A statement was issued to the press, saying:

That this association believes the Municipal beer compound will be shortly taken over by the Government. If so it would not be fair to deprive native women of the business for which they have suffered from the beginning of the trade depression.

Also the number of persons employed in the municipal beer

compound at present can only be employed by a European firm if no profit is expected, so the preliminary measure would be to reduce the staff which means creating an unnecessary increase of unemployment in the township; this association is not satisfied with that, therefore the association would be glad if the municipal beer compound be left to continue with the brewing by the African women.[35]

The statement not only expresses solidarity with the women brewers, but also confirms awareness of the implications of capitalist transformation for producers and traders: dispossession and increased unemployment.

An even stronger statement followed in a letter to the Chief Secretary from ACA. It is reproduced in its entirety here to exemplify oppositional prose using different discourse and derived from different practice.[36]

1. I [Erica Fiah] have been directed by the African Commercial Association to bring to the notice of his Excellency the Governor the following objections to the above ordinance which is proposed to be passed at this session of the Legislative Council.

2. I may be allowed to remark that a resolution was passed at an emergency meeting of the body held yesterday embodying the objections and authorizing me to submit them to his Excellency.

Objections

(1) The whole Bill appears to have been conceived without reference to the wishes and opinions of the parties concerned viz the Natives themselves.

(2) No Native will singly be in a position to satisfy the provisions of the Bill for the manufacture of the Native Liquor and the result will be that the whole business will pass into Non-Native hands.

(3) The object of the Bill is stated to be to utilize the profits for public purposes beneficial to the Natives. It is not known what these public purposes are. So far as we are aware, there is a whole department of Native Administration which spends (sic) money for public purposes out of general revenue specially of Native Poll Tax.

(4) The net result for the law will be only to "rob Peter to pay Paul."

(5) Moreover, the Bill will throw about a hundred men and women out of employment and deprive them of their means of livelihood swelling ultimately the number of street beggars.

(6) Pombe has been an article of domestic manufacture all over the country since olden times and the Bill deprives Natives of their birthright to manufacture their own drinks.

(7) If the Government finds that Pombe is injurious to the physical, mental, moral and spiritual welfare of the African

race of the Native population, then we would welcome a
law prohibiting Pombe altogether so as to root out the
evil just as was done in the case of Tembo [palm wine].

(8)   If the Government does not see its way to close down
manufacture and sale of Pombe, then the alternative is to
supervise the same through the Health authorities and the
Township authorities like food, aerated waters, milk etc.,
for which there is already ample provision in the
Township Rules and Regulations.

(9)   The Ordinance is for Native Liquor and its manufacture, by
this can only be meant Liquor made by the Natives and
consumed by Natives. Once the manufacture passes into
non-Native hands, it is neither Native Liquor nor Native
Manufacture.

(10)   In any event, protest is hereby made against the passing
of the Bill in this session with a request that further time
be permitted for the fuller discussion of the matter as there
is no spokesman of the Natives in the Council.

3.   I beg your courtesy and kindness to bring to the august notice of
his Excellency the Governor and also to use your good offices to
see that the Bill does not become Law without giving fuller
opportunities to the Natives affected and concerned.

The African woman was portrayed as a producer in her own right, whose
struggles ought to be supported. The resolutions were produced at a
democratically organized meeting of the ACA (paragraph 2), while the
administration had acted without consulting the people concerned (objection
1). The ACA rejected passing the business from African into non-African
hands (2). The takeover was projected as another form of taxation and profit-
making, and the ostensible rationale (public purposes beneficial for the
African) was challenged (3).

Mitchell was stung by the ACA's attacks. He chose Leg Co. as his
forum to rebut its allegations—a place where neither ACA nor women beer
brewers were represented. He argued that the ACA allegation that the
company takeover of *pombe* was wrong was "a palpable absurdity."[37] He was
so provoked that he blindly contradicted earlier statements about benign work
conditions and insisted that the beer market was "exceedingly squalid and
unpleasant." In order to undermine the sympathy which ACA had evidently
aroused, he employed sarcasm:

The only people whose interests will be affected by this Bill—the
petition to which I referred said that 100 people would be thrown out
of work—are as a matter of fact 12 *old women*, and I need scarcely
say that in any arrangements that are made steps will be taken to see
that they are not left destitute. But at the same time, it seems to me
that, for all sorts of reasons, the time has come when this trade
should be brought under proper control, and I do not think, however

highly one may think of these old women—I am sure they are *most respectable citizens*—anybody would seriously suggest that an important social reform of this nature should be obstructed because admittedly some *personal profit* derived by these people will not be withdrawn from them.[38]

Once again, the administration resorted to manipulating imagery concerning "proper" codes of conduct for Africans and attacked profit-making for African women.

Your Excellency, some Honourable Members appear to be concerned about the future welfare of the old lady brewers. These old ladies have had a marvellous time for many years. They have made a lot of money. I investigated what property they had and I find that some of them own as many as four houses which they rent very profitably. Apart from that, the Township Authority does intend to employ as many of these old ladies as they can in the sale of beer, so that they will not be deprived entirely of their livelihood, and of course they have their accumulated wealth.[39]

In other words, self-employed entrepreneurs would be transformed into wage-employees, and bar girls at that—a disreputable occupation popularly perceived as prostitution. The cynical character of the entire transaction is revealed by a small parenthetical phrase that pointed out "they will still be able to work and earn money (though probably much less) under the new system."[40] The women brewers submitted a petition (which I have not been able to trace) and sent two representatives to see the secretariat officials. They spurned the offer of employment by the municipal secretary. The aim of the brewers' mission to the secretariat, according to the administrators, was to find out the official reaction to the petition. A high level of solidarity was revealed among the brewers:

From the interview with them, it seems probable that they would accept the new arrangement and the work offered, and say no more about it, but that they were not prepared to commit themselves without reference to others.[41]

Despite popular resistance, the government proceeded with its plan. However, Tanganyika Breweries failed a three-month test to see whether it could produce *pombe* acceptable to African consumers. On seventeen different trials, Africans declared the *pombe* bad.[42] The Township Authority was still prepared to give them a one-year contract as long as there were safeguards in case of failure "and provided that steps can be taken by the Administration to prevent the manufacture and distribution of *pombe* in the district within a radius of three miles from the township boundary." All these negotiations occurred *before* advertising for tender. The Breweries was then forced to reduce its bid from 80 cents to 75 cents, and was most certainly tipped that all other bids were less than the 80 cents. Among the contenders were the signatory of the ACA petition and Erica Fiah.

Illegal brewing competed with the town and brewery monopoly, and by January 1936, the Breweries wanted to withdraw from the contract. Proceeds "had fallen below expectations principally on account of the turnover being far below that anticipated. This was probably due in great measure to illicit brewing and the attendant difficulties of suppressing it."[43] Consumption dropped to half its former level. The beer was also half the usual strength. According to Kayamba, "The tenderers would not be able to provide better beer than that supplied at present unless they engaged African women to do it."[44] The government was finally forced to revoke the bylaw and return the industry to the original women beer brewers, which caused not a little embarrassment. As noted in several secretariat minutes, "This is an unforgettable business."[45]

A careful reading of all the documents indicates that the women beer brewers received community support throughout this saga, and that they persisted in what became illicit brewing. The early rejections during trial runs of the Breweries' product and the drastic reduction in consumption of the official brew are examples of widespread support for women's resistance against the state and a multinational company. Moreover, I believe that this supposedly spontaneous action was probably based on an organization of informal networks which coordinated a sustained protest. Oppositional ideology and action of this kind contributed to the development of a popular culture, which often challenged the ability of the colonial state to rule effectively, as shown in the next section.

POPULAR CULTURE

The government faced one crisis after another in Dar es Salaam in the period that followed. In addition to strike actions of the 1940s and 1950s, rising food prices and food shortages led to a generalized discontent which affected all the laboring poor. Food rationing adopted in the 1940s was continued in the 1950s because of the growing militancy of the townspeople. There was an unemployment crisis as well, which had its beginnings in the 1930s. Leslie spoke about growing criticisms of, and disregard for, "law and order"[46] and the increasing bitterness about employment, low incomes, lack of vertical mobility, squalid housing situation, and the colour bar. Indirectly, he appeared to attribute the 1950 riots to these factors.

Leslie also described what can be considered a new proletariat culture in the process of creation. He considered the "cult of the cowboy" adopted by young men to be "the African equivalent of the English teddy-boy." It consisted of a certain style of clothes ("the wide hat," jeans, and high heeled shoes) and "the idioms of tough speech, the slouch, the walk of the 'dangerous men' of the films." The "innocent form" of the cult was, to him, merely "an attitude of mind; it is the revolt of the adolescent, in age and in culture, against the authority of elders, of the established, of the superior and supercilious." In its more serious form, it was understood by authorities to be an "anti-religious movement" like the "Mabantu, which challenged the authority of the Sheiks" and the gangs which carried out "an unceasing though usually personal and defensive battle of wits with the Jumbes and Police."[47]

According to Leslie, the cult of the cowboy was "the safety valve of the dangerous mob element" of Dar es Salaam. He alleged that there were the possibilities of a flirtation with fascism, as "unformed Hitler-jungend . . . waiting for a Fuehrer to give respectability to their longing to be admired, to be feared, to have a place in the sun."[48] Sociologist Joan Vincent later repeated this image of the Dar es Salaam townsman as a lonely figure, existing within a "state of anomie" or "unattachedness," as did John Iliffe, who used phenomenological "situationalism" to conceptualize town existence: "an African's identity often varied depending on the situation in which he [sic] found himself."[49] This approach denies the possibility of class consciousness and collective action.

> Some townsmen accepted no authority at all. Probably at an early date, and certainly by the 1930s, they practised what Professor Lewis has called a culture of poverty. It was the life of the unorganized and insecure, *who took no part in town institutions* and gained nothing from them, but lived from day to day, almost permanently in debt, incapable of planning for the future. Their domestic unions were often casual, their enemies were police and authorities, their heroes were the *Wanaharamu* ("sons of sin") or smart guys of the town, their faith was application to a diviner in personal misfortune.[50]

Iliffe further pointed out that this was "not the normal pattern of life in Dar es Salaam" but that more research "in police records will show how common it was."[51]

In contrast to Iliffe's "smart guys" were "many respectable long-distance migrants" who turned to tribal elders to fill "the leadership vacuum" until the 1940s. These elders were colonial administrators at the lower echelons as well as tribal association leaders.[52] This would suggest harmony between tribal associations and the colonial administration. In reality, some associations, like the Wazaramo Union, were in constant conflict with the administration and regularly denounced the system of Native Administration.[53]

Alternatively, this "anomie" and "disorder" could be described as a new kind of order in the process of creation and a new popular culture (or cultures). This included the cowboy cult, which expressed an, albeit, macho imagery of the new proletariat. *Ngoma*, or dance groups like the women's *lelemama* societies, provided a focal point of this new popular culture. They were highly organized with a complex and hierarchical structure, and hundreds of members.[54] Women's *ngoma* groups contributed directly to the development of a new *nationalist* culture and the organization of TANU, the nationalist political organization which fought for national independence in the 1950s.[55]

TANU itself represented part of the new order. It had a strong base in Dar es Salaam, especially among those sustained by the off-the-books sector: the traders, beer brewers, and artisans. The majority of card-carrying members of TANU in the mid-1950s were women.[56] In Susan Geiger's sample of women members and leaders of TANU in the fifties, she found that all were Muslim and all but one had been active in an *ngoma* group. They were all "working women who sold *pombe* and fish and *mandazi* (doughnuts)" and were prepared "to confront and to combat regressive patriarchal norms." Most of their fathers had been wage-employed as launderers, hotel workers, and railway workers, whereas their mothers had been peasants and traders. The nationalists all spoke about the attraction TANU had for them as a movement that stressed equality between women and men.

A large portion of the "atomized" townsmen referred to by these authors, including the youth in gangs, were wage-employed in the 1930s in domestic service, brothels, petty trade, casual work, and dock work. Islam also contributed to the creation of a common culture. In Dar es Salaam, Christianity was only adopted by a minority and was associated with the emergent African middle class, what Geiger refers to as a "self-consciously separatist minority." According to Geiger, these middle-class women adopted "a cult of dependence and domesticity," although many were wage-employed teachers, nurses, and social workers. However, I believe that the issue was not religion or education so much as the development of two different kinds of class consciousness among women: a bourgeois consciousness that was mainly adopted by middle-class working women and a popular proletariat-based consciousness among working-class women, poor traders, and lumpen elements, who were all members of the laboring poor. Proletariat class consciousness cannot be understood if posed purely as a reflection of individual positions in the workplace. It also arises in the process of struggle at the site of reproduction—another workplace (the home and community). The class community emerges in everyday struggles with capital and the state. Class consciousness can, and did, embody nationalism and antisexism.

The struggle over beer brewing exemplified the power of a new class community. What linked the members of the African working-class community together, be they regular and casual workers, or traders and lumpen elements? They had a common enemy, the dominant colonial white rulers. They had a common experience of racial discrimination and racial segregation in the labor market and in residence, education, and health services, a segregation that contributed to worsening wages and incomes and deplorable living and sanitation conditions. These conditions provided a basis for joint political organization and action that overcame sex and occupational differences, linking all the members of the laboring poor together. The rulers only belatedly recognized the need for middle-class leadership within the African masses to offset the radical potential of popular culture and organizations.

In the mid-1950s, the rulers tried to promote multiracial social centers and clubs that were restricted to African middle-class women and men. European-led charity associations, such as the Tanganyika Council of Women, worked among the laboring African poor, *especially women.* Toward the end of the 1950s, on the eve of independence, the central government was forced to administer Dar es Salaam directly and to drop the system of "representative" local government under the township authority. Paternalist ideology was used to justify the usurping of power *from* the township authority. It employed an entirely different concept of the African townsmen:

> The African town dweller in Tanganyika, particularly in the older established towns, is a notoriously conservative person who has brought up to consider the District Commissioner as his "father and confessor," to whom he turns in times of trouble[57]

URBAN "INFLUX" CONTROL

A major target of administrative action became those persons who were active in the off-the-books sector, or the second economy, as it was called: the drones, spivs, prostitutes, and beer brewers. The "unstable" elements in town reportedly included casual laborers, in general, and the unemployed, especially children and youth. A deliberate policy was adopted to reduce the number of casual laborers and unemployed in town in line with the policy of stabilization of the labor force.[58] Every month, the district commissioner repatriated hundreds of boys and young men from town as "tax defaulters." The adoption of a full-scale pass system, existing in South Africa and other colonies, was considered by the secretariat, but finally rejected. Molohan pointed out that it would never work in Tanganyika, and would be too expensive "because the conditions in Tanganyika in respect of the African urban areas are so different from those pertaining in the other countries mentioned."[59]

Molohan recommended instead that the Townships (Removal of Undesirable Persons) Ordinance (Cap 104) be amended to authorize *liwalis* (local authorities, primarily Asian and Arab Muslims, appointed by the central government) and local courts, in addition to district officers, to enforce town removals. Rights to urban settlement for Africans were made more difficult by raising the period of time a person must reside in town (to forty-eight months within a five-year period) in order to be defined as "settled in a township."[60] Until 1957, the required period had only been eighteen months. To make matters worse, the law required "that the onus of proof to establish residence is on the person concerned."[61]

Such legal mechanisms *created* two categories of townspeople, the legal and the illegal. The vulnerability of the illegal group undoubtedly enhanced their willingness to accept low wages and menial work, when so required, and eased their expulsion from town, when not.

The Townships (Removal of Undesirable Persons) Ordinance (Cap 104) was originally imposed during the economic and political crisis in the early thirties.[62] It was dropped in 1944 by the Colonial Office in London due to criticisms made about its racist nature in the United Nations Trusteeship Council and by critics in England. During World War II, defense regulations provided a new opportunity to rid the towns of "undesirables." Women were specifically targeted, the rationale being that they were all prostitutes and were responsible for spreading venereal disease among the armed forces. The legitimacy of this legislation was also called into question in 1952. Provincial Commissioners, however, gave it their wholehearted support. The legislation was used not only to control the settlement and movement of prostitutes, or women so categorized, but also those persons not "gainfully employed" (i.e., people in the off-the-books sector). A deliberate policy of training and hiring was also proposed to absorb women into paid employment as domestic servants. Sexist ideology was adopted to rationalize a major shift in employment policy.

> [I]t is ludicrous that domestic service in Tanganyika should be the perquisite of the male. The territory cannot afford for much longer the luxury of locking up so many able-bodied men in this unproductive sphere of employment for which women are *far better suited and equipped*[63]

I believe that this was a conscious policy to force two family members to work for the wage of one in the context of rising unemployment and declining wages: "At current wage rates a man and his wife who are prepared to do a proper day's work should be able jointly to earn a handsome wage and in congenial surrounds."[64] This also created further economic incentives for women and men to marry or cohabit on a more regular basis. At the same time, higher urban taxes were proposed on the basis of a unitary urban local rate for women and men, without reference to race. This would increase the cost of living in town and make it less attractive for those without waged employment.

CONCLUSION

Colonial state policies toward African women were shaped by the activities and anticipated responses of women themselves. These policies were not the same for all African women. They targeted particular classes and specific occupational categories; prostitutes, beer brewers, and middle-class professionals were all treated differently. The success of state policies, provoked as they so often were by women's resistance and sometimes organized struggle, was never a foregone conclusion. As the beer brewers' struggle illustrates, women could sometimes draw on the resources and power of their entire class community in support of their efforts. We need to learn more about the kinds of issues that drew these class communities together in solidarity and in defiance of the colonial state and its capitalist interests.

It appears ironic that the colonial central government reactivated authoritarian forms of influx control and direct local government in Dar es Salaam at the very moment of transition to responsible self-government at the territorial national level. The irony is sharpened when we examine the readoption of similar influx control measures by the independent government and round-up of young people (such as the young men who were transported to the sisal plantations in the early 1980s). Similar legal and administrative mechanisms of social control were reactivated in the late 1970s and early 1980s in the state's attempt to clamp down once again on off-the-books activities. These included a special targeting of unmarried women without "gainful" employment, who were rounded up and threatened with forcible removals to their home areas.[65]

The continuity in legal and administrative measures reflects, however, continuity at the economic level. The plantation sector in Tanzania has succeeded in reasserting its own interests in regard to the foreign exchange crisis and the severe debt crisis faced by the "independent" Tanzanian state in the 1980s. The plantation sector is responsible for the largest decline in marketed crops (sisal and sugar) and export earnings.[66] It is therefore in a powerful position at the moment, especially given the state's inability to regulate and control peasant labor and produce.

The largest portion of sisal is produced by transnational corporations (TNC), with the remainder being produced by state corporations in association with TNCs. Although the sugar estates are state-owned, they were initially set up by giant TNCs and remain dependent on them for major inputs of goods and services. Sisal, tea, and sugar companies had led the demand for labor policy reform in order to ensure a cheap and regular supply of disciplined casual labor.[67] Among the barriers which capital has faced since independence are the assertion of a strong set of workers' rights and benefits, including compulsory social services. I believe that capital will not be able to resolve its labor crisis until it crushes the power of the popular class community, including the reciprocal bonds of extended kin and nonkin families, and the economic viability of the off-the-books sector. The structural adjustment programs which the IMF and World Bank now administer on behalf of Western states and TNCs are the most significant concerted steps taken by capital since African "independence" to discipline both workers and peasants and undermine the off-the-books networks of production and trade they have created. Now, as before, the success of global state policies cannot be assumed unproblematically, but neither can the success of popular resistance. The power of the colonial state is nothing compared to that of today's transnational global state system that is increasingly asserting itself financially and administratively in Tanzania and all other African nations.

NOTES

Earlier versions of this chapter were presented at the Conference of East and Central Regional Branch of International Council on Archives (ECARBICA) in Dar es Salaam in October 1984; to Karnataka University, Dharwad, India in January 1985; and to a Women's Research and Documentation Project (WRDP) seminar in Dar es Salaam. I am grateful for feedback received, and especially for the detailed comments of Karen Fields, Susan Geiger, and John Campbell.

This chapter is based on research partially funded by the Ford Foundation (Nairobi) and the WRDP in conjunction with archival and oral history research in West Bagamoyo. Most of the primary sources were found in the very helpful Tanzanian National Archives (TNA).

1. Mbilinyi, "'City' and 'Countryside' in Colonial Tanganyika" and "Runaway Wives in Colonial Tanganyika."

2. Guha, "The Prose of Counter-Insurgency."

3. Leslie, *A Survey of Dar es Salaam*; Molohan, *Detribalisation*. The quote is from Karen Fields, personal communication.

4. These ideological concepts are used in Leslie's and Molohan's works and in the primary sources listed below.

5. Mbilinyi, "Agribusiness and Casual Labor in Tanzania."

6. Bryceson and Mbilinyi, "The Changing Role of Tanzanian Women in Production"; Mbilinyi, "Agribusiness and Casual Labour in Tanzania."

7. See Mbilinyi, *This is The Big Slavery*, (forthcoming) for percentages and Sutton, "Dar es Salaam: A Sketch of a Hundred Years," 19, for figures.

8. J. A. K. Leslie.

9. *Ibid.*, 121.

10. Iliffe, *A Modern History of Tanganyika*; Depelchin, "The 'Beggar Problem' in Dar es Salaam in the 1930s."

11. J. A. K. Leslie.

12. Depelchin on hygiene; Iliffe, 389.

13. Tanzania National Archives (TNA), Secretariat Minute Papers (SMP) 26602/6-7.

14. TNA SMP 10906/I/f 35 enclosure, 50.

15. J. A. K. Leslie, 116-117.

16. *Ibid.*, 116.

17. Gulliver, *Labour Migration in a Rural Economy*, 37.

18. Molohan, para 102.

19. J. A. K. Leslie, 226.

20. Ibid., 220.

21. Mascarenhas and Mbilinyi, *Women in Tanzania*.

22. TNA SMP 10304/1.

23. TNA SMP 20887/7; editor of *The Tanganyikan Opinion*, 21.4.32.

24. J. A. K. Leslie, 165.

25. Bujra, "Women 'Entrepreneurs' of Early Nairobi" and "Postscript."

26. Dr. J. O. Shircore, TAN SMP 18883/I/179.

27. TNA SMP 26602, 18893/I.

28. 18893/I/65-66.

29. 18893/I/73-74.

30. *Ibid.*, 182-183.

31. *Ibid.*, 60A, 28.3.33.
32. *Ibid.*, 178.
33. *Ibid.*, 95-97.
34. *Ibid.*, A.B. Massie, cited, 180 (emphasis added).
35. *Ibid.*, 101.
36. *Ibid.*, signed by N. Shaaban Mbamba on behalf of the President of ACA, as is the case with all ACA correspondence, October 21, 1934. On discourse, Guha.
37. *Ibid.*, 179.
38. *Ibid.*, emphasis added.
39. *Ibid.*, Acting Provincial Commissioner (PC/EP), 180.
40. *Ibid.*, Minutes 14.11.34, 120.
41. *Ibid.*
42. *Ibid.*, Executive Officer of Township Authority to PC/EP, 16/11/34.
43. 18893/II, 191, PC/EP to Chief Secretary (CS), 26.1.36.
44. *Ibid.*, 195; 29.11.35.
45. *Ibid.*, 19.12.35.
46. Leslie, 188.
47. *Ibid.*, 112.
48. *Ibid.*, 112-113.
49. Vincent, "The Dar es Salaam Townsman" 153-154; Iliffe, 384.
50. Iliffe, 388, emphasis added.
51. *Ibid.*, 388.
52. *Ibid.*, 389.
53. *Ibid.*, 391.
54. *Ibid.*
55. Geiger, "Women in Nationalist Struggle."
56. Iliffe; Geiger.
57. Molohan, 28.
58. *Ibid.*
59. *Ibid.*, 38.
60. *Ibid.*, 39.
61. *Ibid.*
62. TNA SMP 21616.
63. Molohan, 42, my emphasis.
64. *Ibid.*, 42.
65. Kerner, "'Hard Work' and Informal Sector Trade in Tanzania."
66. Mbilinyi, "Agribusiness and Casual Labour in Tanzania."
67. United Republic of Tanzania. 1982. *The Tanzania National Agricultural Policy (Final Report).* Dar es Salaam: Task Force on National Agricultural Policy.

CHAPTER 7

Women and the State: Zambia's Development Policies and Their Impact on Women

MONICA L. MUNACHONGA

The relationship between women, the state, and the party in Zambia's development process will be examined and assessed in this chapter. We shall analyze development policies, particularly their impact on women's access to the scarce and valued material and nonmaterial resources on which personal status and power are based. In this chapter, we will also investigate women's role in the political and governmental systems or structures, particularly at high levels, in order to understand how the Zambian state helps or hinders women's development. While present circumstances suggest the presence of negative attitudes among some administrative officials, prospects for future change are not entirely dim.

WOMEN AND DEVELOPMENT IN ZAMBIA

Unequal access of men and women to agricultural training and resources has a long history in Zambia. During the colonial period, male predominance in wage labor enabled men to buy land and tools for farming. Women did much of the farming, but rarely owned the land or controlled the profits of their production. Colonial gender stereotypes, which identified men as farmers and women as wives and mothers, exacerbated this inequality by leading colonial officials to provide training and credit to male farmers.[1]

Little has changed since independence, despite official commitment to women's integration in development. Women's projects have been left to the Home Economics Section, an understaffed low-priority unit of the Department of Agriculture. The Department's field staff is comprised largely of men. In 1984, females comprised only 7.4 percent of the total 1,956 field staff.[2] This percentage and continuing patriarchal gender stereotypes explain the relative exclusion of women from most agricultural and rural development projects. Although one-third of all households in Zambia are female-headed,[3] reports show that female farmers are rarely assisted by male extension workers and that there are few production-oriented courses for their

130

benefit at Farmers' Training Centres. Moreover, many women cannot attend courses in distant areas due to domestic and familial responsibilities. For example, women farmers have been excluded from the "Train and Visit System," an extension methodology of the World Bank-sponsored "Agricultural Development Project."[4]

Furthermore, women continue to have difficulty acquiring agricultural land and sufficient credit for successful farming. A recent study indicates that very few women have managed to acquire plots independently, even in government settlement schemes. This is aggravated by legal and traditional norms that treat women as minors, economically dependent on male relatives or husbands.[5]

Widespread illiteracy among rural women hampers their development as well. Adult education and literacy campaigns are rare in rural areas.[6] Nonformal training offered to adult women by various organizations, including the Women's League, emphasizes domestic arts rather than wage-earning skills; consequently, such training does little to improve women's lives.

Even when schooling is available, girls and women receive inadequate and often inappropriate schooling. This is partially the result of historical factors. Colonial officials discouraged female education, other than basic home-economics training, to prepare women for their role as wives and mothers.[7] Some of this legacy lingers on, as education for females is considered less important than for males, particularly above the primary level. While sex ratios in primary schools are almost equal, female participation rates drop sharply at secondary school. In 1980, 11.7 percent of boys progressed to Form 5 (upper secondary school), compared to only 4.9 percent of the girls. They drop even further at the tertiary level. The University of Zambia has four males for every one female student.[8]

Training for women below the university level is still concentrated in domestic science courses (for teacher training) and secretarial courses (for vocational and technical training). Women are not prepared for industrial jobs while in primary and secondary schools. Furthermore, female students in the university are concentrated in the humanities and social sciences and thus are not prepared for technical high-paying positions in industry and government.[9]

Although broad government educational policy stresses equal opportunities between the sexes, implementation of this policy has been hampered by the negative attitudes of the largely male administrators. It is unlikely this will change as long as the bureaucracy continues to be dominated by men.[10]

WOMEN IN WAGE EMPLOYMENT

While some Zambian women have been able to attain high levels of education and hold responsible positions in the economy, most women either work in the informal economy or perform the least-skilled, worst-paid jobs. Even those women lucky enough to have waged employment (less than 15 percent)[11] suffer from discriminatory practices by employers. Salaries tend to be lower for work of equal value. Employers often refuse to provide housing for female employees, especially if they are married. Tax policies penalize working married women and incorrectly assume that household incomes are equally distributed between husband and wife.[12] Some women do not get holiday allowances, and women are forced to retire five years before men. The employment act prohibits women from most night work. The only benefit women have achieved is a ninety-day paid maternity leave,[13] and this often deters employers from hiring women.

Furthermore, the most common forms of economic activity for women, namely street vending and beer brewing, are often illegal. This greatly hampers the efforts of poor urban women to earn a living, but no attempt has been made to change the trading laws to protect or assist these women.

LAWS AND PRACTICES RELATING TO MARRIAGE

The laws and practices relating to marriage in Zambia discriminate against women as well. Zambian law recognizes the legality of unions under customary and statute law. Customary marriage law is based on African law, customs and practices, while statutory marriage law is based on British civil law. Women are disadvantaged under customary law, as they are treated as minors to their male counterparts. Marriage payments (*lobola*) give husbands considerable authority over their wives. Polygamy reinforces the double standard regarding sexual exclusiveness, and women have few rights in a divorce.

While statutory marriage rejects polygamy and undercuts the role of *lobola*, it has serious limitations. Property in marriage continues to be individually owned, giving a woman no rights to her husband's property. Customary law of succession applies to women married under statutory law as well, thus leaving widows of statutory marriages stripped of property in much the same way as women married under customary law.[14]

WOMEN AND DEVELOPMENT POLICY

Despite ostensible government support for equal opportunities and participation in the developmental process between the sexes, women's involvement in development was not addressed seriously by the Zambian government until after the launching of the United Nations Decade for Women in 1975. Until then, Zambian development plans ignored women's disadvantaged position in the political economy. Even the Third National

Development Plan (1979 to 1983) supported women's clubs as a solution to women's problems, despite their roots in the colonial past. These clubs emphasize domestic skills,provide little incentive or training for entry into waged employment, and consequently perpetuate women's subordinate position.[15]

Some improvements, however, have resulted from Zambia's participation in the United Nations Decade for Women and the influence of nongovernmental local and international agencies. The government increasingly recognizes the need to introduce development projects that stress income-generating activities, especially for disadvantaged women. But the capacity and commitment of male-dominated governments to carry out these projects remains in question. For that, we must address the issue of women's power in the state and their ability to influence the formulation and performance of government policy.

WOMEN'S STATUS AND PARTICIPATION IN STATE AND PARTY STRUCTURES

A brief description of Zambia's state organization is necessary in order to understand the nature of policy formulation, planning, and implementation processes, as well as the impact of state policies on women. Zambia has a one-party system of rule by the United National Independence Party (UNIP). The president of the nation and party, Dr. Kenneth Kaunda, appoints and heads the twenty-five-member Central Committee, a body with far-reaching powers. It has full authority for programming and implementing party policies and determines candidates for election at all levels of the party organization.

In Zambia, the party and the state are merged and are controlled by the same person. As head of the party, the president/chief executive controls all other state structures, including the cabinet and the legislature. Under the 1973 Constitution, the party is supreme, and it continues to exercise effective control over the bureaucracy (i.e., government and parastatal administrative structures). This is achieved by the appointment of bureaucrats who support the party's ideology and policies.

Despite the one-party system and the president's considerable executive powers, President Kaunda takes into account the views of his colleagues. As a result, membership and influence in the party and government institutions can provide leverage over presidential policy.[16] Consequently, it is important to understand the position of women in the party and the state.

During the preindependence liberation struggle, women played an important role in the nationalist parties. UNIP women established a Women's Brigade which was "a specialized wing of the United National Independence Party responsible for mobilizing, organizing and educating womenfolk on the revolution."[17] Although supposedly assigned an auxiliary political role, the Brigade leaders were often in the forefront of political conflict. Women helped fight for political independence by the "felling of trees to block roads making them impassable to the enemy, preparing food for freedom fighters in the fields, staging half-nude demonstrations, taking part in civil disobedience".[18] They also picketed beer halls in support of their male counterparts. Women were motivated to fight with men by their desire to achieve freedom and because they recognized the need to end the social injustice which accompanied colonial rule. This motivation was undoubtedly spurred on by the sexist nature of colonial rule, which exploited them both as Africans and as women.[19]

Political activism did not translate into political positions for most Zambian women after independence. Despite formal equality, most women have chosen to remain in the background of political life. The table included in this chapter reflects this disparity.

The reasons for this pattern are numerous, but high rates of illiteracy and limited educational and employment opportunities no doubt contribute to it. The widespread belief that women should be primarily wives and mothers discourages women from entering the political arena as well. During the liberation struggle, female political organizers were accused of neglecting their families; even today most men and women agree that politics fall within the men's spheres of activity. This attitude is reflected in and reinforced by state institutions, such as the media and the schools. Zambian school textbooks portray women as creatures of the domestic sphere.[20] These social and cultural norms, along with economic and educational subordination, conspire to reduce female participation in key political and state machineries such as parliament and the Central Committee.

The few women in parliament face a number of problems. Underrepresentation restricts their capacity to affect legislative change. Moreover, female MPs often lack the necessary knowledge, tactics, and sophistication needed for lobbying support in matters that affect them and in which a number of male MPs might be sympathetic to the women's cause. Thus, small numbers, inexperience, and societal norms encouraging deference to men reduce the effectiveness of the few female parliamentarians.[21]

Has the Women's Brigade in the Party provided an alternative source of influence within government? After independence, the Women's Brigade introduced new objectives in order to help consolidate independence and promote economic development. Changes in the political environment, from a multiparty system to a one-party participatory democracy in 1973, led the Brigade to become more broad-based in order to make the Party's presence felt in all corners of Zambia. In 1975, President Kaunda lauded the Brigade "as a revolutionary force in Zambia's development,"[22] and supported the decision to grant the Executive Secretary of the Brigade, now known as the Women's League, formal representation on the Central Committee.[23] That same year,

Distribution of Top Party and Government Posts by Sex

Position	1974 F	1974 M	1975 F	1975 M	1976 F	1976 M	1977 F	1977 M	1978 F	1978 M	1979 F	1979 M	1980 F	1980 M	1981 F	1981 M	1982 F	1982 M	1983 F	1983 M	1984 F	1984 M
Member of Central Committee	3	22	2	20	3	21	3	22	3	21	2	20	2	22	2	23	2	23	2	23		
Cabinet Minister	1	22	1	20	0	23	0	25	0	26	0	16	0	17	0	18	0	20	0	20		
Minister of State	2	11	2	11	1	14	1	13	1	14	3	13	3	20	3	19	5	17	5	17		
Member of Parliament*	6	129	4	109	3	128	4	128	7	128	8	111	6	127	8	120	6	103	6	109		
Provincial Political Secretary	0	0	1	9	2	9	1	10	2	9	3	14	4	14	4	14	4	18	4	18		
District Governor	2	65	2	61	1	58	2	60	2	66	2	68	2	67	2	67	1	67	1	92		
District Political Secretary (Regional Officials)	52	203	49	108	46	105	54	102	53	88	51	86	59	103	57	98	52	94	58	98		
Ambassador**	1	20	2	24	2	22	—	—	—	—	—	—	1	9	0	28	—	—	0	24		

* (a) Total female and male parliamentarians include women cabinet ministers and ministers of state.
   (b) The total number of parliamentarians is supposed to be 135, but due to vacancies and absenteeisms during National Assembly sessions, the data shown here show those members who were present.

** Statistics of 1977, 1978, 1979 and 1982 could not be obtained.

Source: Compiled from Statistics available at the UNIP Research Bureau.

the Women's League drew up an ambitious Ten Year Programme of Action, which coincided with the UN Decade for Women, emphasizing equality, development, and peace.

In 1979, the Women's League established its own constitution and thus became a legal entity. Its aims and objectives were to be set within the Party's "socialistic objectives and the Philosophy of Humanism," with a broad concern for all aspects of development. Constitutional provisions were also made for Women's League membership in the general, provincial and district conferences and at the national, provincial, and district councils of the party.[24] Thus the Women's League is represented at all levels of the Party.

The Women's League has successfully fought for women's issues to be represented directly on the Central Committee of UNIP. In 1984, a Women's Affairs Committee was set up as one of the subcommittees of the Central Committee. Previously, women's issues had been represented through the Elections and Publicity Sub-Committee (1971-1973) and the Political and Legal Sub-Committees (1973-1983). The Women's Affairs Committee

> was the result of over ten years of bargaining and representations. Resolution after Resolution at various Women's Conferences and National Councils were passed urging the Party and its Government to create a Women's Department within the Office of the Prime Minister or a Ministry of Women's Affairs for that matter.[25]

The significance of the creation of the Women's Affairs Committee lies in the fact that women now have direct representation on the Central Committee.[26] Women now have full-time representation for policymaking on all aspects of life, including those concerning women. The Women's Affairs Committee includes permanent secretaries from ministries with departments/sections dealing with women's issues (i.e., Ministries of Agriculture and Water Development, Labor and Social Services, Cooperatives, Health and General Education, as well as Ministers of Finance and Development Planning, and Foreign Affairs). It also includes representatives of some nongovernmental women's organizations.

At the present time, the Women's Affairs and the Youth and Sport Sub-Committees are chaired by women.[27] Two women head provinces, which gives them power and authority over both sexes in provincial government and party administration. All four of these women are currently members of the Central Committee.

The Cabinet rejected the League's suggestion for a Ministry of Women,[28] but compromised by establishing a Women's Unit in 1984. This Unit is located in the National Commission for Development Planning, and coordinates, monitors, and evaluates women's projects. However, like the Home Economics Section in the Department of Agriculture, the Women's Unit in the National Commission for Development Planning (NCDP) is assigned low status and consequently suffers from inadequate financial allocations and staffing. Both the Women's Affairs Planning Committee at

NCDP and donor agencies like Norwegian Aid and Development (NORAD) (in their Plan of Action for Assisting Women in Zambia) recommend the need to strengthen the Unit by appointing a person of high rank with experience in women-in-development issues.

WOMEN AND STATE POLICY

The impact of these organizations on state policy toward women is difficult to evaluate. The integration of both the Women's League and the Women's Affairs Committee within the Party is certainly unique to the region.[29] Some direct benefits to women have resulted from this structure. The women's unit has successfully argued for the inclusion of a chapter on Women in Development in the Fourth National Development Plan. Influenced by the Women's League and the Women's Affairs Committee, the Party has become increasingly active in assisting women to improve their living standards. The Ten Year Programme of Action emphasizes assistance to rural women in the spheres of health, education, housing, and water supply. A second program of action (1985 to 1995) has been drawn up, stressing among other things, women's development in education (through literacy campaigns), political education, and assistance to women food producers.[30]

The Women's Affairs Committee has made some important policy recommendations, but it depends upon sectoral ministries to implement them; and implementation has not always followed. Indeed, in 1986 only two of the five ad hoc committees set up by the committee were headed by women, and the two female heads were closely tied to President Kaunda.[31]

Despite pressure from women's organizations both inside and outside the Party, legislative changes to improve the status of women have been slow or nonexistent. The Zambian Constitution promises women protection against discrimination (article 13[a]), and Zambia was one of the original signatory parties to the November 1967 United Nations Declaration on the Elimination of Discrimination against Women. However, in order for this article to be enforceable, a government had to ratify the United Nations Convention on the Elimination of All Forms of Discrimination Against Women by March 1980. Zambia did so only in February 1985 "in spite of the fact that the Women's League, among others, had been calling for ratification for years."[32]

Although the 1970 conference on women's rights in Zambia resolved that the government should change the marriage law in favor of a unified system, nothing has happened.[33] And since 1976, efforts to introduce legislation on succession to protect widows have failed. The proposed system of sharing a man's property (i.e., 50 percent to his children, 25 percent to his widow and 25 percent to his dependent relatives) received little support from influential people such as Members of Parliament and senior civil servants. The proposed law of succession has not been debated in parliament since early 1983 when it was rejected. The MPs seem more concerned with incorporating polygyny into the Marriage Act.[34]

The distribution of a man's estate has been changed since 1983 as follows: 50 percent to children; 20 percent to widow(s); 20 percent to parents of the deceased, and 10 percent to dependent relatives. Nevertheless, the importance of the proposed legislation to women is reflected in the fact that the women-run Non-Governmental Organization Coordinating Committee has had the proposed legislation translated into major local languages for purposes of educating the public, particularly poor women in both rural and urban areas. But despite this pressure, as recently as March 1987, the Minister of Legal Affairs and Attorney General promised a seminar run by the Zambian Association of Research on Development (ZARD) that the revised proposed law of succession would be brought to Parliament within two weeks of the seminar. Nothing has happened to date (i.e., January 1989).

All this suggests that women in Zambia still have little political power and influence in decisionmaking compared with men. They also have limited economic power both in the society at large and within the family. The low level of women's participation, particularly at high levels of national decisionmaking, implies that women's interests are not only subordinated to those of men, but also that women are only marginally integrated into development.

FORCES FOR CHANGE

A recent report by the Women's League suggests that a number of constraints limit the League's effectiveness as a lobby for women's issues. Some of these are general problems and have been discussed, i.e., the high rate of illiteracy, the double burden of reproductive and productive labor, limited access to economic resources, social attitudes emphasizing women's primary role as housewife/mother, and male dominance at the policy implementation level. Other problems impede change. Women often do not know their legal rights, and so do not fight for them. When they do, lobbying is hampered by the paucity of available women in decisionmaking positions (not all of whom sympathize with women's concerns),[35] and the small number of female legal practitioners in Zambia who might prosecute women's cases. Between 1965 and 1984, for example, only fifty females were admitted to the bar compared to 501 males. Female legal practitioners comprised only 9.1 percent of the total (551) during this period. Of the fifty female legal practitioners, only two are High Court Judges, and seven are Magistrates.[36]

Another more serious problem is that the league is dominated by less-educated urban women who have often displayed little sympathy for educated, especially single, urban women. During the colonial period, the Brigade was led by the better-off urban elite, such as miners' wives of the Copperbelt.

Today League leaders continue to be largely petty traders and urban dwellers who gain much of their prestige from being wives of UNIP men. These women have supported government attempts to control educated, single urban women—even when that control takes the form of labeling them as prostitutes and barring them from public places without a male escort.[37]

League leaders have joined UNIP officials in their efforts to blame economic decline and failed development on these women, who are supposedly destroying the family, causing moral decay, and undermining traditional values.[38] This attack may arise, at least in part, out of feelings of insecurity, particularly on the part of those women leaders with little education and/or skills necessary for effective competition in a male-dominated society. More research is needed to fully understand this matter. Meanwhile, these tensions continue to undermine solidarity among urban women and may well explain the League's declining membership in urban centers as well.[39]

League support in the rural areas has also declined. League leaders at the district level, called "Mama Regionals," have little to offer rural women. Always the last to benefit from shrinking party funds and usually without transport, the Mama Regionals lack the resources to fulfill often well-intentioned plans for rural women's development. They are left calling for more food production from already overburdened women, while offering nothing more substantial than an occasional "leadership" course on humanist principles.[40] Not surprisingly, the Women's League plays little role in the lives of most rural women.

However, some forces for change are emerging in Zambia. The UN Decade for Women publicized women's issues and legitmized them as an international concern. The Forward Looking Strategies formulated at the Nairobi Meeting in 1985 continue to provide leverage for organizations, such as the International Association for the Advancement of Women in Africa (ASAWA), which was launched at the Non-Governmental Organizations' (NGO) Forum in Nairobi. ASAWA has taken root in Zambia, with full support of the Women's League and the Party. While still relatively small, ASAWA has provided an organization for progressive women concerned with mobilizing change at the grassroots level. The Association is currently investigating the establishment of cooperatives and credit unions for women.[41] These activities offer a bridge between middle-class and poor urban women, and could provide the basis for cooperative action in the future.

Some of the more educated urban women are forming their own organizations as well, which provide a platform for women who are uncomfortable in the League. Some of these, such as the Zambian Association of Research and Development (ZARD), promote women's development by investigating the conditions of women's lives. Others, such as the YWCA, the Zambian Alliance of Women, and the Catholic Women's League, sponsor development projects for poor women and have been acknowledged as progressive forces by the government. Others, such as the International Federation of Business and Professional Women and Media, enable women's occupational groups to lobby the government for change. These organizations are fairly small and somewhat isolated from most women. They are not going to mobilize a broad women's coalition, but they are pressure groups with the potential to play an important role in the creation of new strategies to improve women's lives.[42]

Women's issues are also being raised by foreign aid donors who are responding to international concerns about women and development. These agencies, along with local women's groups, are bringing new pressures to bear on the Zambian government. Some policy and personnel changes seem to be occurring as a result. A number of WID experts have been placed in important ministries, including the Ministry of Planning, encouraging their ministries to be sensitive to women's issues. This is encouraging, but further action is required before the prospects for change can be evaluated.[43]

CONCLUSION

While women's opportunities have improved since independence, women still trail well behind men in their access to society's material and nonmaterial resources. Some laws, especially regarding marriage and inheritance, openly discriminate against women; others ostensibly protect women, but are rarely enforced.

Zambian women have found it difficult to obtain desired changes in policies, legislation, and practices that hinder their progress. This is no doubt partly due to women's minority position at the levels of national decision-making, policy formulation, planning, and implementation. Change has also been impeded by social attitudes that assign women the roles of wife and mother and advocate male dominance in the public sphere.

Discrepancies between formal support for women's development and actual practice will not disappear easily, because the attitudes underpinning this reality are not amenable to legislation. They can only be changed by long-term political education, which will require coordinated and concerted campaigns by Zambian women, and a new unity of purpose. This is a tall order, but many ingredients for change are in place. Vocal, educated young women are pressing for change. The economic crisis is forcing urban and rural women to search for new answers. The international women's movement is keeping women's issues in the public eye. Thus both internal and external forces are conspiring to raise the consciousness of Zambian women. Whether this can be translated into effective action remains to be seen.

NOTES

1. Muntemba, "Women and Agricultural Change."

2. Government of the Republic of Zambia (GRZ), Women's Affairs Planning Committee at National Committee of Development Planning (NCDP), 1986. *Report on the Sub-Committee on "Women in Agriculture and Rural Development."*

3. GRZ, *1980 Census of Population and Housing in Zambia.*

4. Zambia Association of Research and Development (ZARD), *Eastern Province Agricultural Development Project, Mid-Term Report*, 1985; *Southern Province Agricultural Development Project, Mid-Term Report*, 1985.

5. Women's League. 1985. *Report to World Conference of the United Nations Decade for Women: Equality, Development and Peace.* Nairobi, Kenya (July 15-26). The study is an ongoing investigation into women's access to agricultural land. The author is a member of the research team.

6. Keller, "Development for Rural Zambian Women"; GRZ, *Report of the Women's Affairs Planning Sub-Committee on Women in Agriculture and Rural Development, 1985.*

7. In 1963, female students comprised 21.1 percent of Standard IV. This percentage dropped to 13 percent in Standard VI and 10.9 percent in Form II. Only 8 percent of the students who earned a school certificate were female. Hurlich, *Women in Zambia*, 79.

8. Achola, "Where have the women gone?"; GRZ, Ministry of Education, *Educational Statistics*, 1980; GRZ, Women's Affairs Planning Committee at NCDP. 1986. *Report of the Sub-Committee on "Women's Participation in Education and Training."*

9. Tembo, *Sex Biases in Zambian Textbooks*; Women's League, *Report to World Conference*; Bardouille, "University of Zambia Students' Career Expectations; Sanyal et al., *Higher Education.*

10. GRZ, *Zambian Manpower Report*, 1969:34.

11. Akerele, *Women Workers.*

12. Munachonga, "Conjugal Relations," Chapter 3.

13. Zambia, Women's League, *Report to World Conferences*, 57-59.

14. Morgan, *Sisterhood*, 739.

15. Muntemba, "Women and Agricultural Change," 93.

16. Ollawa, *Participatory Democracy in Zambia.*

17. Sikaneta, "Analysis of the Women's League of Zambia."

18. *Ibid.*

19. Harris-Jones, *Freedom and Labour*, 65; *UN/ECA/FAO Economic Survey Mission Report, 1964.*

20. Harris-Jones; Tembo, *Survey on Sex Biases.*

21. Interview with the director, Law Development Commission, Lusaka, March 1983.

22. Sikaneta.

23. Hurlich.

24. Hurlich, 23; Sikaneta, 5-7.

25. Sikaneta, 10.

26. Other Sub-Committees of the Central Committee are: Political and

Legal, Economic and Finance, Social and Cultural, Elections and Publicity, Appointments and Disciplinary, and Youth and Sport.

27. Interview with the Secretary for Administration, Lusaka.

28. The cabinet argued that the creation of a specific structure for women would violate the policy of humanism, with its emphasis on equal opportunities for all. Hurlich.

29. For comparison with other countries in the region, see *Report of the Sub-Regional Workshop for SADCC Member States on Women and Development*. Harare, Zimbabwe, April 1986.

30. ZARD, *Women's Rights in Zambia*; Zambia, Women's League Programme of Action, 1985-1995.

31. *Times of Zambia*, February 18, 1986. Cited in Geisler, "Sisters under the Skin," 59.

32. *Women's League Report*, 1955.

33. Schuster, *New Women of Lusaka*; Munachonga, "Conjugal Relations."

34. GRZ, Law Development Commission. 1982. *Report on Law of Succession*; Interview with the director, Law Development Commission, Lusaka, March 1983.

35. Mrs. B.C. Kankasa, one of the first female MPs, is a vehement opponent of women's reproductive rights. Geisler, 50.

36. *Women's League Report*, 1985.

37. Mrs. Kankasa has even proposed that the police "round up single women found on the streets after dark, and called for stiffer penalties of up to six-months imprisonment for those women who were found 'loitering.'" Geisler, 52-53.

38. *Ibid*. 48.

39. In 1986, not more than 3 percent of the women in the Copperbelt Province belonged to the League. *Times of Zambia*, January 6, 1986. See Geisler, 47.

40. Geisler, 54-55.

41. The International Association for the Advancement of Women in Africa (ASAWA), *Report on the Proceedings of the Workshop of Women's Effective Participation in Agricultural Production and Food Processing*, held at Lusaka, October 15-November 1, 1985.

42. Geisler, 56-61; Keller, *The Integration of Zambian Women in Development*.

43. Keller, *Integration*; Dr. Bonnie Keller, a Women in Development (WID) expert, is in the Ministry of Planning representing women's issues; a Zambian woman works with her.

CHAPTER 8

The Black Market and Women Traders in Lusaka, Zambia

KAREN TRANBERG HANSEN

Zambian newspapers often feature stories with dramatic photographs of women traders being chased off city streets by mounted police or youth patrols and of women traders marching to or demonstrating at party offices, complaining of harassment and price hikes. Variations on such stories appear in cities across the Third World, not only in news media but also in studies by social scientists. They depict the encounter between women traders and agents of the state in antagonistic terms: it's women *versus* the state.

It is important, however, to qualify the tendency to construe the relationship between women traders and their state in reactive terms, which portrays the state as a monolithic entity and women as a generic category, and is a simplistic account of the causal relationship between these factors. Marx's notion of the state as resting on civil society whose class composition it reflects exemplifies this double problematic. Marxist-influenced scholarship has sought to modify this conception by investigating the relationship between the state and its constituent elements,[1] sometimes including gender relations.[2] The state comprises administrative, legal, and coercive apparatuses and their changing and complex relationships. Their effects on distinct social segments are highly variable in historical terms and often differ from one country to the next. In their turn, a society's segments relate to the state's structure in diverse and changing ways. If we acknowledge, with Poulantzas,[3] that state apparatuses are full of conflict and struggle, we might also recognize that not all state agency is located within state apparatuses. The state expresses itself in other contexts, such as in the relationship between women and men in private households. Causality arises from the changes in women's household development cycles and the cultural practices that shape them. State policy certainly sets limits, but within those limits, women make their distinct life histories—even in trading.

This chapter analyzes changes in state policy concerning urban marketing and trade and women's participation in small-scale trade and marketing in the low-income periurban township of Lusaka, Zambia's capital. I use my findings to explore the need to disaggregate the generic experience of one population segment, namely women who live in a low-income township. I therefore investigate how state agencies on the one hand shape and on the other hand are acted on in diverse ways by women of distinct age groups in different marital situations.

My research, conducted in 1971, 1981, 1984, and 1985, is based on a sample of one hundred households. During that time, the Zambian state changed in many ways, including the policy apparatus that structured small-scale marketing. In the late 1970s, formerly restrictive yet tolerant policies concerning marketing tightened and created a phenomenon known in Zambia as the black market. Herein, I first survey changes in state policy concerning small-scale urban marketing during the colonial and postcolonial periods. I then account for the appearance of the black market, and describe more recent policy shifts in the wake of belt-tightening economic reforms in Zambia by the International Monetary Fund. My research setting is then described, and I trace women's changing market participation and household histories in relation to market/state policy shifts during the period. I contrast the experience of these women in marketing and trade to that of younger women. Finally, I return to the question of causal dynamics in the relationships between the state, women traders of different ages, and marital backgrounds, and the gender dynamics in low-income households.

STATE POLICY ON SMALL-SCALE TRADE
AND MARKETING IN URBAN ZAMBIA

The nexus of small-scale trade and marketing in Lusaka is a result of the encounter between male African migrant workers, the colonial state, and the dominant capitalist interests of the mining companies. The state and capital sought to operate cheaply while making profits by treating African workers as units of labor receiving substandard wages and housing. Once their work contracts were completed, they were expected to return to the rural areas to join their wives and families.[4] Not all of them did so, and from the early decades of this century, squatter housing evolved in Lusaka. In spite of regulations preventing migration to towns, many women also left their villages; some were wives of migrant workers, while others were single and migrated on their own. Some found shelter and made a living in squatter areas, where a variety of trading and service activities arose, catering for the needs of a low-paid, overwhelmingly male, labor force.[5]

Colonial authorities ignored, or rather tolerated, these settlements. Squatters made a living on their own terms and could be readily recruited for wage labor once the need arose. Their populations comprised about 22 percent of Lusaka's total population in 1957.[6] Authorities also turned a blind eye to the economic activities pursued by some of the squatters and others as well.

Who participated, what was produced, and what circulated within this domain of activity was conditioned by four sets of factors:

1. The administrative and legal control system *de jure* used race and *de facto* gender to structure the market and give Africans the least desirable work, housing, and political participation. It also influenced what they could sell, when, and where to market it.[7]

2. The structure of production in the overall economy, which hinged on the mining of copper for export, discouraged local manufacturing in favor of imports from South Africa, Southern Rhodesia, and the United Kingdom.[8]

3. Consumption styles were gradually instilled in Africans as a result of their encounter with the commodity market; imported household goods, European-style clothing, and fabrics soon replaced traditional products.[9]

4. Cultural practices among the region's different ethnic groups and their hierarchically, gender- and age-based divisions of labor and authority—rural women's subordinate, yet autonomous, productive roles—were transformed in the cities, because of their households' new dependence on economic activity shaped by a profit-oriented capitalist market that exploited men's labor power in return for low wages.

The relationships between these factors contained many contradictions. Women were only welcomed as wage laborers in such gender-typed jobs as nursing and teaching when the postwar economic boom created a labor scarcity across all sectors of the economy. At that time, they had already begun to pursue income-generating activity of their own accord. In spite of the demands of married life as culturally defined in most ethnic groups in Zambia, which construe women as mothers and wives first, married women found ways of contributing to strained household budgets, as did single women and heads of households concerned to make a living. They worked primarily in marketing and small-scale trade in spite of the rules and regulations aimed to curtail such activity. Urban women monopolized the sale of home-brewed beer and alcohol, sometimes coupled with sexual services.[10] They also sold produce and ready-made food in their neighborhoods, and they gradually entered market trading. A 1954 study of Lusaka's main African market showed that one-fifth of the market vendors were women.[11] By 1959, their participation had increased to one-third.[12] They clustered in the least-profitable trade: selling fruits and vegetables. Most of them were married to market vendors, but some were single heads of households. Studies from the Copperbelt supplement these findings.[13]

The first of these four sets of factors changed upon independence in 1964 when the rules and regulations that had structured the migrant labor system and the migrants' access to housing and work by race were eliminated. But the new men in power did not consider gender a critical factor, and except for a tiny well-educated segment, women did not get noticeably better access to wage employment after independence.[14] Many of the colonial era's regulations regarding trade and marketing remained in effect. The sale of home-brewed beer and of goods from homes, yards, and streets without a license continue to be illegal. Migration to urban areas increased as many people left their villages, anticipating new work opportunities in towns. By the early 1970s, this process had grown to such an extent that half of the country's population had become urban.

Regarding the second set of factors concerning the economy, development plans conceived in the wake of independence were aimed at diversifying the economy. Although the local manufacturing sector grew slightly,[15] copper remained king, and the manufacturing firms were often the import substitution of luxury goods for the better-situated segments of society.[16] After the creation of a one-party system in 1973, the state increasingly became involved in running the economy, taking over the controlling interests in the mines, and nationalizing much private business in the form of parastatal companies. Declining export revenues from the sale of copper in the early mid-1970s through the present placed new pressures on the cities' economies and their housing stock. Wage employment stagnated, forcing increasing numbers of people to make a living by other means. Since then, the economy has increasingly been tided over with foreign aid and loans.[17]

The consumption pattern favoring European-style goods and nonlocal commodities still holds sway and continues to influence what is bought and sold in Lusaka's markets. For political reasons, southern import routes were closed after independence, and foreign goods were still available—more than before independence—from the United Kingdom, Southeast Asia, the United States and elsewhere.[18] Southern goods became available again, at least for those with money to buy, in 1978 when the border with Rhodesia, now Zimbabwe, was reopened to ensure adequate supplies of maize and fertilizer, as well as for copper export purposes.

The men in power, as well as within households, believed the cultural practices that prop up a gender-based division of labor in the marketplace and the home were not to be questioned. The depressed economy made making a living an uphill battle in which men and women of different classes take different interests. Poor women with few marketable skills have few employment options. Their chief wage-labor opportunity is domestic service, to which they turn only as a last resort when their family experiences a financial crisis. The wages are poor, and work conditions undesirable. Domestic service not only conflicts with the demands of married life, but it also erodes the limited autonomy women are establishing in their own households. They prefer economic activities they can undertake in their homes, yards, neighborhoods, or nearby markets. In Zambia, such work involves buying and selling consumer items, the vast majority of which, including basic-staple maize meal, are of nonlocal origin.[19]

THE BLACK MARKET

Changing modalities of legal control of trade and marketing, fluctuations in the availability of goods, and evolving household dynamics form the context within which women traders operate on a small scale. I will discuss the first two elements, turning to household dynamics in a subsequent section.

Women's chief items of trade were charcoal, fruits, vegetables, dried fish, prepared goods (including home-brewed beer and distilled alcohol), cooking oil, secondhand clothing, and handwork. Depending on product availability, some women also sold salt, sugar, rice, soap, detergent, and candles. They purchased most of these items in the heart of the city as and when they were available, and transported them to their periurban township on buses or taxis they shared with others.

Except for charcoal and secondhand clothing, most of the above-named items have been intermittently in short supply since the late 1970s. Recurring shortages of basic commodities have made the term "black market" part of the ongoing debate concerning the struggle for jobs and means of living. Although it is difficult to establish precisely when a black market in essential commodities became firmly established in Zambia,[20] one observer suggests that it reached its peak in 1979, "when a combination of a poor harvest of the principal food crop, maize, coupled with previous low foreign exchange earnings from the principal export, copper, resulted in severe shortages of commodities and immediate inputs for industry as most available resources were employed in the import of maize to avert starvation."[21] Soap, detergent, candles, cooking oil, and bread are among the items that are frequently scarce and, therefore, black-marketed.

The growth of the black market is fueled by local, as well as new external, economic forces. Under pressure from the IMF (International Monetary Fund), the state in December 1982 decontrolled prices, except for mealie-meal, candles, and wheat products. It began subsequently to phase out subsidies, placed a ceiling on wages, and reduced employment in the public sector and in the mines. Several devaluations, runaway inflation, and declining revenues from copper exports turned the frequent shortages into almost constant ones, and increased the scope of black marketing. The term black marketing as known in Zambia in the mid-1980s no longer refers to just selling essential commodities in short supply in the legal retail outlets.[22] It now commonly refers to any illegal marketing activity. Black marketing encompasses unlicensed vending in streets, yards, and homes, including the sale of individual cigarettes by young men commonly referred to as *michanga* boys; it also encompasses the trading activities of the women in my study, except for those who pay a fee to trade in the township's markets. I use black marketing in this inclusive sense.

While the state's intrusiveness in the economy, including small-scale marketing and trade, theoretically forecloses some opportunities, it indirectly opens up a range of others. Conflicts between the state's apparatuses (in this case, the administrative and coercive ones that enforce rules and regulations) provide a loophole for economic opportunity. In a conceptual sense, women traders who grasp this opportunity do not disengage from the state or operate outside it, as some observers have suggested.[23] Such observations must be demonstrated in a historical sense and specified in relation to their local politicoeconomic and sociocultural contexts. In the Zambian case, women's economic activities are prompted in part by state agencies that unsuccessfully seek to regulate marketing activity, leaving it distorted. Small-scale trade and marketing are facilitated by state ineffectiveness, operating in spite of the state's attempt to intrude. Such activities, though small in scale and mostly uncounted in official economic statistics, are made possible due to the loopholes in state policies and imperfections in the economy. They are the products of a market economy that is managed, however imperfectly, by the state. In urban Zambia, these activities are oriented entirely toward survival in that market economy.[24]

In spite of the restrictive regulatory framework, many women benefit directly from buying and reselling, providing needed commodities in their neighborhoods and contributing to their welfare as well as that of their household. They make basic necessities available, enabling township residents to purchase household requirements without traveling downtown in search of scarce commodities for which they have to wait for hours.

These women traders and small-scale marketers obtain their commodities from several sources. They buy fruit and vegetables from three downtown open-air markets, served by periurban truck farmers. Cooking oil, salt, sugar, soap, and detergent are purchased from state shops and private retailers, all at official prices. Some of these commodities are occasionally obtained through friends and relatives who have retail licenses to purchase from the National Wholesale Corporation. Some women with friends or relatives in neighboring countries travel widely to obtain items of clothing and apparel. Such long-distance trade fluctuates and changes regional focus, depending on the availability of foreign exchange. Food commodities are usually bought in bulk and broken down into tiny units for sale. In all resale transactions, the original price is marked up several times.

The December 1982 price decontrol coupled with recurring scarcities, a series of steep price hikes of basic consumer goods, stagnant wages, and growing unemployment made black marketing rampant.[25] The police staged several highly visible actions to curtail it. Mounted police harassed women street vendors, confiscating or destroying their wares. Armed paramilitary destroyed commodities and brought black marketers to the police station. The party's youth branch was employed in many street clearances, sometimes beating up women traders. Several urban and district councils sought to invoke the Markets Act to formulate uniform prices for essential commodities sold in their markets and to establish a system of inspection of weights and scales. Labor unions and the public called for the reintroduction of price controls.[26] Contradictory attitudes between state agents of different levels regarding price policy had no effect on the situation. Black marketing continued.

The police, already stretched thin, were aided by vigilante patrols deployed to catch thieves and remove street vendors, black marketeers, foreign-exchange dealers, and ivory and diamond sellers. Vigilante groups were granted legal powers to arrest suspects and hand them over to the police in 1985.[27] In spite of intensified harassment "to get rid of these men and women who are exploiting the masses by buying goods in bulk and selling them at high prices," black marketeers usually reappear.[28]

WOMEN'S SMALL-SCALE TRADING AND MARKETING IN A PERIURBAN TOWNSHIP

The women I studied between 1971 and 1972 lived in Mtendere, a township on the outskirts of Lusaka. The settlement was opened in 1967 as a site- and service-resettlement scheme, but its planned services had been discontinued; it held squatter status at the time of my work.[29] Of Lusaka's total population of some 250,000 in 1971, about one-third were squatters. Mtendere had 10,000 inhabitants. With no school or clinic, residents had to rely on town-based facilities and were served by a few poorly stocked grocery shops, several liquor stores, bars, and taverns. No butcher shop existed. A small market, operated by the Zambia Marketeers Cooperative, required a party membership card and payment of a daily fee by customers.

Although my sample survey of one hundred households cannot represent all of Lusaka in a statistical sense, the range of activities it described is found throughout Lusaka's low-income areas.[30] Perhaps due to Lusaka's geographical location, ethnic groups from the eastern part of the country comprised about half of my sample. Most of these groups are matrilineal. Some foreign nationals lived there as well, mostly from Malawi, followed by Zimbabwe and South Africa. Most of the Malawians came from matrilineal societies, whereas those from the south were patrilineal. Few of the residents were new urbanites. Twenty-five percent had lived in Lusaka for more than ten years, the remainder having spent an average of seven years in the city. Several had lived in other urban areas before coming to Lusaka.

In 1971, most of the women were married, some for the first time, while others remarried after a divorce or death of a spouse. Two of the marriages were polygynous. Two households were headed by women who received support for themselves and their children from consorts. The average age of the women was twenty-seven, but more than one-third were older. They had an average of four living children. More than half of the total sample population consisted of children below fourteen, slightly more than half of the children over the age of fourteen had left the settlement. In a quarter of all the households, additional residents were present, mostly relatives who were newly arrived from the countryside in search for jobs or children attending school. There were also rural visitors.

Fifty-two of the women had never gone to school, whereas twenty-nine of their husbands had not. The women who had attended school averaged four years, compared to five for their husbands. None of the women were wage-employed in 1971. Only two husbands made no income. A quarter of the husbands were wage-employed in construction and related industries, and approximately another quarter worked as domestic servants in private households or in the field of food service in institutions. The remainder were either self-employed or low-level white-collar workers. The fourteen men who were self-employed within the settlement operated small market stalls, hawked clothes or produce, repaired cars, and built houses. The men had a lower average monthly income than the amount estimated for expenditures on food in an urban budget survey (Republic of Zambia 1969) of low-income households of similar size.[31]

More crucial than the actual level of income is the question of how much money husbands allocated to wives and for what purposes. My study of household budgeting[32] showed that while eighteen wives claimed to be in charge of their husbands' wages, the majority of my informants depended on their husbands for a monthly allowance. Half of the wives in the study received ration money to purchase food and clothing. Twenty received a small allowance from their husbands, who bought the main staples; five received no money at all.

Most of these women could not meet the monthly consumption needs of their dependents, not to mention expenses on school clothes or those resulting from the arrival of visitors from the countryside. Many wanted to work, but knew that they had few wage-labor opportunities due to their limited education and the oversupply of male labor.[33] While some felt that their husbands might prevent them from working, others had seized economic opportunities locally.

Less than one-third of these women had devised ways of making money. Thirteen of them worked full time from their homes, yards, or streets, selling home-brewed beer or distilled alcohol, fruit, vegetables, dried fish, cooking oil, ready-made food, charcoal, kerosene and secondhand clothing. Eleven women undertook similar activities intermittently, and also did such handwork as sewing, embroidery, knitting, and crocheting. A few had traded previously but stopped doing so in 1971. Their resources, except for charcoal and secondhand clothing, were bought at downtown markets. They purchased charcoal from persons who burned it in the countryside; in two cases, a relative was the middleman. Secondhand clothing was bought "in the yards," i.e., at expatriate residences.

The women who marketed and traded were older, had more children, and were less educated than other women, and more of them had unskilled workers as husbands. From their perspective, work was synonymous with trade and marketing. The proceeds of these productive activities were used principally for securing their own wellbeing and that of their children. These women worked in spite of official harassment which, in 1971, mostly involved brewers and distillers who were sometimes apprehended and arrested or released after paying fines. This trade was the women's most profitable activity in 1971.

On my return in 1981, I found that this settlement no longer had squatter status. Its population of 20,000 had doubled, as had that of Lusaka, which then had a population of 500,000 (half of whom were squatters). Residents lived on approximately the same number of plots as in 1971, and the population increase was housed in extensions and subdivisions of existing units. A clinic and a school had been built, as had several shops (all poorly stocked), many more bars and taverns, and butcheries, most of them illegal. I identified ninety of the original one hundred plots on which I had interviewed householders in 1971[34] and found forty-six of them living in the very same place. I traced the whereabouts of twenty-two households that had moved to other locations in Lusaka or to other towns; a handful had returned to the villages. The households included ones in which a spouse had died or a divorce had taken place. I was unable to locate the rest of the original households; some of their houses were said to have been sold, but no further information was available about the former inhabitants. Those I did trace often rented their houses to nonrelated persons and had a relative collect the rent. In a few cases, relatives lived in the previous residents' houses.

The persons I could trace in 1981 represented a cross section of the original sample in terms of age, averaging thirty-seven years, with fifteen being forty-five years of age or older. Most had remained married to the same husbands, while two women lived as single heads of households. The major marital change had been the addition of spouses. In 1981, there were ten cases of polygyny, as compared to two cases in 1971.[35] Most of the men who were married polygynously were unskilled workers; several held office in the local party branch.

More children had been born, while others had left home. These households grew in diverse ways. Relatives were living in about one-third of these forty-six houses and included married offspring with children and spouses, unmarried daughters with children, householders' younger siblings (sometimes with families), or aged parents brought to town from the countryside. In slightly less than one-fourth of these households, one or more children lived at home after "failing" grade seven. In other homes, relatives depended on the households for food and occasional financial handouts; in other cases, it was a relative who contributed cash or services to the household.

During the ten-year interval between these two studies, the economy stagnated and wage employment declined. Yet, in about half these households, the husbands worked for the same employers as in 1971. These were predominantly public-sector employers, but they included a few long-established private firms. In most of the remaining cases, husbands did the same types of jobs as in 1971, but had different employers. The shift had taken place from private to public-sector employment. The only type of occupational change was from wage to self-employment (bricklayers who set themselves up in the township or men who, after holding many jobs, sought to establish themselves locally in trade).

As in 1971, the wives' housekeeping allowances barely covered the needs of these expanding urban households. In 1981, only eight wives made no money. Eight were now wage-employed, working as domestic servants, hospital attendants, or cleaners. The rest were involved in trade, seven in the settlement's market, the others from homes, yards, and streets. Their trading included the same items as in 1971, but more women knitted and crocheted in 1981, using yarn and needles purchased abroad (they were unavailable locally). They sold their handwork off and on. Some periodically sold such scarce goods as salt, sugar, and rice. Occasionally, items brought to town by rural relatives were sold from homes and yards (mostly dried fish, vegetables and fruit). Rural visitors would return to their villages with such scarce items as cooking oil, soap, and detergent (sometimes clothing, which was sold on commission for an urban relative). These activities were common trading practices in the township. Since most people operated without licenses, the extent of black marketing was enormous. Tips on how to organize a black market activity were widely shared as were the "tricks of the trade" (advance warning in cases of police clampdowns and evasive practices to avoid confiscation or destruction of goods).

Some women's range of trading activity had expanded to include items of apparel, the most popular of which were shoes, handbags, clothing and watches. These items were obtained on shopping trips some women undertook, in groups of two or three, to neighboring countries to buy commodities, including food staples in short supply or of poor quality in Zambia. This type of long-distance trade had developed after Zimbabwe gained independence in 1980, but also included Botswana, Swaziland, Malawi and Zaire.[36] To undertake such trade, women had to be familiar with travel and ways to avoid customs inspection. They had to use time, which prevented them from doing their usual tasks. Capital, in the form of foreign exchange, is a must, as is a social network that provides information about where to shop and a place to sleep. It was a risky business, but a profitable one. Such goods resold in 1981 with as much as a 200 percent profit.

Four of the eight women who did not work in 1981, did so in 1971. They had all brewed and sold beer. They had been unwilling or unable to shoulder the risks of illegal brewing in the face of occasional police sweeps, followed by fines or arrest. Competition had also increased, as several more licensed beer halls had opened after 1971. In three of these households, subletting rooms to tenants provided an additional source of income. Although subletting is illegal in Zambia, several houses had been extended for this purpose, thus providing a black market in housing. (The township administration is supposed to prevent this practice. Its toleration of subletting is an example of the arbitrary enforcement of state-level policy by a local administrative agency.)

By 1984, only thirty-four of the original households were available. Between 1981 and 1984, twelve households dissolved in a variety of ways, including (in order of priority) transfers to other towns, return to the villages, and death. Relatives lived on a few of the original plots. I was unable to trace the whereabouts of three households that were polygynous in 1981. Among the reasons given for this dissolution of other households was divorce. Of the thirty-four households who had remained, six were polygynous in 1984. In one of the polygynous households, a co-wife had left in 1981. Three households were now headed by women. One case involved the death of a husband; another, a divorce. In one case, a husband returned to the village, leaving his wife behind in Lusaka since she was unwilling to accompany him. The rest of the women lived with the same spouses.

Between 1984 and 1985, the dissolution processes touched additional households. The sample was now comprised of twenty-nine households. Three, including a polygynous household, had moved to other townships in Lusaka, one to a periurban rural settlement. One householder had died. In all cases, relatives now resided on the plots. Between 1984 and 1985, one woman had divorced her husband and now headed a large household of unmarried daughters and their children. The rest of the women lived with the same husbands as they had in 1971.

By 1985, Lusaka had grown to some 750,000. The township was spilling beyond its only expandable boundary. I estimate conservatively that its population might have increased to about 30,000. Few of the women had had additional children, but most of their homes housed married or unmarried dependents with offspring.

The economic activities the women pursued in 1984 and 1985 were largely the same as in 1981. The brewers and distillers in this group persisted in their activities. A small group of women, almost the same number as in 1981, made no income. A few more had begun to trade, and some of the previous traders now operated from the township's markets. Between 1984 and 1985, a second market had opened. A couple of domestic servants had become cleaners in institutions. Long-distance trade, however, almost ceased in 1984 due to import restrictions and drastic cuts in foreign-exchange allowances. In 1985, a revival was taking place in this trade, but with a change in regional focus. Some women now traveled to areas immediately beyond the borders of Malawi and Zaire, where, unlike Zimbabwe and the south, sellers still would accept Zambian currency. They brought back printed cloth, items of clothing from both countries, and rice from Malawi, a commodity in shortage in Zambia.

While more women were making a living without being wage-employed, their husbands had not experienced major employment changes. A couple of husbands had retired from the labor force and were supported by their wives and/or with the help of adult children. The remainder worked in low-income jobs, mostly in the public sector, in the types of activities that have been Lusaka's mainstay regardless of economic ups and downs: service, distribution, and administration. A few men were self-employed in the township. More wives had taken on work than in 1971, and several cited the rising cost of living as the reason they took on cleaning or domestic service jobs after the mid-1970s. For the same reason, more women said they had begun to sell in the market or intermittently from homes and yards. None of the women who had continued to trade since 1971 had been able to set up a shop or some larger enterprise. At most, between 1981 and 1985, they switched from home- or yard-based vending to trading in the market. Then as now, they spent most of their earnings on food and daily necessities for themselves and their children.

It thus seems that the households remaining in the township through 1985 had weathered the economic deterioration in no small degree due to the women's work efforts. In spite of harassment by police and party youth and being maligned in the press, the small-scale work efforts by these low-income women contributed that little bit that critically affects their households' ability to survive. This assessment, however, glosses over the direction of causality and interprets women's activity merely as a response to a depressed economic situation. To qualify this, I now take a closer look at women's household situation, specifically their changing relationship to husbands and children.

HOUSEHOLDS, DEVELOPMENT CYCLES, AND WOMEN'S CHANGING DESIGNS ON LIFE

The stagnation in mining and manufacturing and the growing involvement of their state in the economy from the early 1970s to the mid-1980s have entailed three changes in the way persons in this study make a living. Increasing numbers look to the public sector for wage employment; marriage is not what it used to be, since husbands are unable or unwilling to support wives and children; and the lower level of Lusaka's trading markets, streets, and yards has become glutted with women traders. The relationships between these changes are complex, and their effects on individuals are compounded over time.

Age and marital status are critical factors to consider. My own work and the findings of others[37] show that women who trade and market are neither young girls just from the countryside nor newlyweds. They tend to be middle-aged married women who are close to or beyond their childbearing years. They can also be single heads of households, either widows, divorcées, or women who support their children without a husband. Lusaka's world of market trade thus exhibits a discernible division of labor by sex, age, and, to some extent, marital status.

The women traders I met in 1971 were not newly married. In a supporting sample I drew in 1981 from households established after the 1971 survey, recently married wives with no children, or young ones, hardly engaged in these sorts of trades; the younger wives had not done so in my initial 1971 sample. Included in my 1981 study was a survey conducted in the township's market which focused on the gender division of labor in commodity specialization. Women dominated in the fruit, vegetable, and dried-fish trade; among them were many middle-aged and single heads of households. I made similar observations concerning age and marital status in relation to trade and marketing in a supporting sample I undertook in 1984. Some young wives said their husbands discouraged them from working. These women were better educated than those I first interviewed in 1971, and they had different aspirations. Speaking of white-collar jobs in government offices, some of them said they had "no sense," meaning no skill, to apply for such jobs or for marketing and trade. Such skills may, of course, be acquired, but it will take another five to ten years before we may know whether the working experiences of women in these samples will differ significantly.

Meanwhile, my observations concerning age and marital status in regard to marketing and trade must be discussed in relation to the household development cycle and the changing expectations spouses have about one another. Once children arrive, the urban wife is expected to provide their food and daily maintenance. She may receive an allowance from her husband's earnings for this purpose. But her allowance is rarely sufficient to provide children with school uniforms, school shoes, and other necessities. My studies show that many small-scale traders who were mothers of schoolchildren used their earnings to cover their own daily needs and those of their growing children, at least through 1985. The money-allocation system between the spouses depends entirely on the husband's goodwill. The urban wife has no assurance of her husband's support, and no security for daily needs or provision for her children's education.

Over the stages of the household development cycle, women and men hold different, and changing, views as to who engages in work and how earnings are to be spent. They use money and networks for different ends. The allocation pattern of household allowances just described changed for many women at the end or beyond their childbearing years. My 1981 market survey offered intriguing evidence that such women devised ways to conceal part or all of their earnings from their husbands. A couple of cases involved women who commuted by bus to market stalls they registered in the name of a lineal female relative. They put some of their earnings into a bank account bearing that relative's name. One of them bought cattle, which she kept at her sister's home in the country.

Such practices enable women to hold on to part of their earnings in case of death or divorce. Middle-aged married women who are almost beyond their childbearing years may be more concerned with having their own money than women at other life stages and in different marriage situations and are concerned with benefits they can receive by engaging in an economic activity. This is so because customary practices, in many cases, continue to shape women's rights in an economic setting otherwise structured by forces that seem unrelated to custom. In matrilineal systems, children trace descent from their mother. Difficulties readily arise about the dissolution of property after a husband's death. In this situation, the husband's matrilineal relatives may descend on the urban household, grabbing all it contains, sometimes claiming the house and thus ignoring that the amassed property was a result of the work of both husband and wife. Cases of widows and children left destitute in this way reach Zambian newspapers from time to time. I came across several in my research. Not all cases are so extreme that the widow is left with nothing, but the fact that they do occur shows that the urban wife from a matrilineal group need not expect security in her old age.[38] This does not mean that matrilineal succession practices persist unchanged, but that the way they operate has been altered by the vicissitudes of urban living.[39] Today, few widows allow themselves to be "inherited" by a man from the husband's lineage. Widows without their own lineal kin to rely on for support are especially vulnerable, more so when they are left with children. To make a living, they have few other economic avenues to pursue than small-scale trade.

In addition to the possibility of a spouse's death, there is the prospect of divorce. Barring death or divorce, men of all ages and classes in Zambia are often involved with several women.[40] The relationship between wives and husbands is potentially fraught with tensions. On the one hand, the wife wishes to secure support from her husband, yet, on the other hand, she does not trust him. Only a portion of men's disposable means reach their own households. The urban, middle-aged married woman whose children are grown may therefore be more concerned about having her own income that is not spent on household necessities than a younger woman. The older the children, the less likely a husband's whims will threaten his wife's independent activity. Over the course of her life, the urban wife in Zambia thus takes more rights to herself.[41] As children leave home and/or begin to work, she and her husband operate more autonomously; women's designs increasingly become focused on how to secure a living without having a spouse to depend on or be troubled by.

CONCLUSION

Economic intervention by the Zambian state in matters of marketing and trade has left loopholes for women's black marketing because the changeable set of state apparatuses constructed to administer and coerce it are ineffectively and ambiguously applied. The structural crisis in the economy and the tensions which arise cause a struggle on two fronts: access to state apparatuses, and age- and gender-based autonomy within households. The specific nature of this struggle depends on which state apparatus we study in relation to a specific population segment, when, and where.

My argument concerning state policy in regard to lower-class women and their involvement in marketing and trade in a township on Lusaka's outskirts over a fourteen-year period revolves around the direction of causality. It qualifies the idea of state intrusiveness, casting doubt as to the extent to which the state may be said to determine action. Much recent Marxist writing has been preoccupied with the state's role in the economy or with the oppressiveness of the state. This leaves questions of human action unproblematized and fails theoretically to account for the role of noneconomic relations. Agreeing with Azarya and Chazan that "one could question . . . whether the state is really the critical reference,"[42] I advocate an approach that accounts for the interactive roles of state policy and local cultural practices. The capitalist market and its structures, which have created a black market in Zambia, are only a way station through which commodities and services, linking providers and users, flow. Beyond these relations are social processes that determine who does what work, the work regime, and how the fruits of the work are allocated. In a descriptive sense, the individuals affected by these processes comprise urban households regardless of their nature. The causality I call for emerges from the unfolding of household dynamics, and it affects the way both sexes of different ages carve out some means of a living within an overall economic context that severely limits their opportunities.

Women's activities in the black market in the township I studied seem at first glance to be shaped by the pressures on Lusaka's housing stock and the limits of its wage labor, the erratic availability of basic consumer goods, and the need to supplement household income. Yet they are also textured by social and cultural practices. These differ in terms of ethnic backgrounds. However, regardless of ethnicity, an intergenerational and gender-based hierarchy of authority prevail. Across class, relationships between men and women are largely authoritarian and asymmetric.[43] This dimension is likely to have been shaped by men's greater exposure to urban wage labor, both past and present. Although matriliny everywhere is in the throes of change and observers differ in predicting the outcome,[44] matriliny still provides an ideology that at certain stages of the household development cycle can curtail sharing and promote separate responsibility. The tensions implied in this ideology are difficult to contain in Zambia's depressed economy. They are fought over by women and men in private households, and result, as I have shown here, in persistent attempts by women past childbearing to secure some economic means in their own right. Women's small-scale trade and marketing activities arise out of gender dynamics built into the operation of both the state and the households of which they are members. Regardless of police harassment, vigilante patrols, and men's objections, Zambian women such as those I studied have their own designs on life and are working to redraw a restrictive gender boundary behind which the collusion of man and the state have for a long time sought to keep them in their homes as dutiful wives and mothers.

NOTES

This is a revised version of a paper presented at the Annual Meeting of the American Anthropological Association in 1986. I am grateful for helpful comments from Henry Antkiewicz, Florence Babb, and this book's editors, and for research grants from the University of Minnesota, the McMillan Fund, the U.S. National Science Foundation and Northwestern University.

1. Evans, Rueschemeyer, and Skocpol, *Bringing the State Back In*; Giddens, *The Nation-State and Violence*.

2. Parpart, "Women and the State"; Rapp, "Gender and Class"; Staudt, "The State and Gender in Colonial Africa."

3. Poulantzas, *State, Power, Socialism*.

4. Heisler, *Urbanisation*.

5. Hansen, "Lusaka's Squatters."

6. Martin, "Housing in Lusaka," 74.

7. Heisler's *Urbanisation* describes the administrative system that structured the colonial migrant-labor system. A series of ordinances passed in the late 1920s on "Employment of Natives," "Native Registration," "Vagrancy," "Natives and Private Estates," "Townships," "Municipal Corporations," "Public Health," and "Native Beer" shaped urban African activity.

8. Baldwin, *Economic Development and Export Growth*.

9. Roberts, *Zambia*, 178; Mitchell's *Kalela Dance* is one of several studies from the colonial period that drew attention to black Africans' preoccupation with Western-style clothing.

10. Wilson, *Economics of Detribalization in Northern Rhodesia*, I, 66. Wilson did not distinguish between prostitution and temporary living arrangements as economic activities for women.

11. Nyirenda, "African Market Vendors," 37.

12. Miracle, "Structures of African Commerce."

13. Chauncey, "Locus of Reproduction"; Parpart, "Class and Gender."

14. Schuster, *New Women of Lusaka*; Hansen, "When Sex Becomes a Critical Variable."

15. As a percentage of GNP, manufacturing grew form a low of 6.7 in 1965 to 13.0 in 1975. Bhagavan, *Zambia*, 52.

16. *Ibid.*; Seidman, "Distorted Growth."

17. Gertzel, Baylies, Szeftel, *The One Party State in Zambia*; Southall, "Class Formation."

18. Bhagavan; Young, *Industrial Diversification in Zambia*.

19. Although the number of people engaged in marketing and trade has expanded enormously since independence, it is not as diversified or rich as that of West Africa. For a discussion, see King, *The African Artisan* 62, 203.

The Zambian situation seems more comparable to South Africa, where most of this activity revolves around trade rather than the manufacture of articles. Dewar and Watson, "Urbanization," 132; Maasdorp, "Informal Housing," 162; Hansen, "Household Work."

20. The term "black market" was not part of the economic discourse in Zambia during my first period of field research in 1971 and 1972.

21. Fundanga, "Urban Poor in Lusaka," 153.

22. Fundanga identifies illegal financial activities in Zambia in at least three other major areas: (1) illegal currency transactions which may run into tens of millions of Kwacha each year; (2) illegal trading and large-scale smuggling (emeralds, for example) until the recent establishment of the Gem Trading Authority. Emerald smuggling alone amounted to over K30 million annually in recent years; and (3) organized large-scale crime, such as car theft and armed robbery, especially on the Copperbelt. One U.S. dollar cost approximately K1.80 in 1981. After numerous devaluations and the establishment in late 1955 of an auctioning system, one U.S. dollar cost K13.48 in November 1986. Fundanga, 152.

23. Parpart, "Women and the State."

24. Hansen, "The Urban Informal Sector."

25. Between December 1982 and September 1985, the price of a fifty-kilogram bag of mealie meal, the urban staple, almost tripled, from K11.72 to K28.77, as did a five-liter tin of cooking oil (from K8.42 to K25.77); the price of bread doubled and that of sugar tripled. (Republic of Zambia [GRZ], *Monthly Statistics*, 10–12: 46). Between 1983 and 1984, the consumer price index for the low-income group shot up at its highest rate ever: 23.6 percent (*Times of Zambia*, March 6, 1985:4). It increased by close to 40 percent between 1984 and 1985 (GRZ, *Monthly Statistics*, 10–12:41). The index number grew from 75.1 to 513.3 between 1971 and 1985, an increase of nearly 700 percent.

26. *Times of Zambia*, June 9, 1984:1 and January 24, 1984:4; *Zambia Daily Mail*, February 1, 1984:1; *Times of Zambia*, May 15, 1984.

27. Through the Zambia Police (Amendment) Act, 1986. *Times of Zambia*, May 27, 1986:5.

28. *Times of Zambia*, January 21, 1984.

29. Mtendere functioned as a squatter settlement until 1972, when the government changed its hostile attitude toward squatting and initiated a program to upgrade some of Lusaka's oldest squatter settlements with World Bank funding.

30. Jules-Rosette, *Symbols of Change*; Todd and Shaw, "The Informal Sector."

31. GRZ, *Urban Budget Survey*.

32. Hansen, "Married Women."

33. Hansen, "The Urban Informal Sector."

34. Some of the ten "missing" plots may have disappeared over the intervening years due to regulation of roads and common areas in the settlement.

35. These were cases of polygyny that were publicly recognized. In addition, several wives told me that their husbands had wives "on the side." In other cases, I learned about such a practice not from the wife herself, but from her neighbors.

36. Pottier, "Defunct Labour Reserve?" (1983) discusses how a rural society near the Tanzanian border was involved in such trade toward the latter 1970s.

37. Beveridge and Oberschall, *African Businessmen*, 87; Oberschall, "Lusaka Market Vendors," 114–120; Todd and Shaw, 420–421.

38. The long-drawn debate over changes in the succession laws in Zambia are central to the struggle between women and men on the one hand and between them and the state on the other. For a discussion, see Mvuga, "Reform in the Law."

39. If matrilineal succession practices are shifting toward patriliny, "grabbing" may in part be attributed to such a shift. Technically, in this case the children would be cared for by the husband's kin; only the widow would be left destitute. This does not always happen, but Zambians definitely speak of "grabbing" in the language of matriliny.

40. This phenomenon is not unique to Zambia. Similar observations have been made across urban Africa. Oppong, "From Love to Institution"; Nelson, "Female Centered Families."

41. Hansen, "Negotiating Sex." Poewe noted the same for rural Luapula: "Most of these women are quiescent in their ideological pronouncements during their reproductive years, when they have much to gain from productive husbands, only to become vocal and independent of their spouses as their children grow up." "Matriliny in the Throes of Change," 354.

42. Azarya and Chazan, "Disengagement from the State," 129.

43. Keller, "Marriage and Medicine" and "Marriage by Elopement"; Schuster, *New Women of Lusaka*. Epstein made similar observations in his study of Ndola on the Copperbelt in the mid-1950s. *Urbanization*, 75–79.

44. Colson, "The Resilience of Matriliny"; Lancaster, "Women, Horticulture and Society" and "Battle of the Sexes"; Poewe, "Matriliny" and "Matrilineal Ideology."

CHAPTER 9

Zimbabwe: State, Class, and Gendered Models of Land Resettlement

SUSAN JACOBS

This chapter discusses the interrelationships between state policies, gender relations, and some aspects of class relations in Zimbabwe. It gives an overview of some macrolevel state policies regarding women and then explores certain policies of the government's land resettlement program and its effects on women. The two models of resettlement—individual family farming and production cooperatives—are discussed in relation to the class "nature" of the state, as well as with regard to gender relations. In all of the above cases, I argue that the effects of state policies and class factors have been contradictory for women.

By contradictory, I mean that some policies, be they operative at macro/national or micro levels, are seen and experienced by women as beneficial to their gender positions, whereas other policies are seen as detrimental. Some policies may be both beneficial and detrimental at the same time. The terms "betterment," "detrimental," "positive," and "negative" are used here in the sense of rendering women better or worse off materially, rendering them more or less subordinate to men, and/or rendering them more or less able to act autonomously.

Gender relations, like other types of relationships, can be activated or affect people at different levels, both individually or collectively. Thus, the contradictions mentioned which affect Zimbabwean women can be activated and enacted broadly by state policy, with its direct or indirect consequences; at the level of class action;[1] at the level of smaller collectivities (e.g., men in a particular village); and at the individual or household level. Both class and gender interests may be expressed by state policies and the collective or individual actions of men and/or women.

The actions referred to in this chapter are mainly those of men. As Folbre[2] has argued, patriarchal relationships have had a long history in Zimbabwe and have constrained the arenas in which women can exert their power and influence. However, this is not to imply that women merely accept the consequences of others' actions; they also act and have strategies of resistance.[3] That such resistance is not dealt with at length here does not imply that women are passive.

STATE AND CLASS

The state is seen here as "an institutional expression of class relations."[4] However, in discussing the Zimbabwean state, the problem is to locate which class rules. The economy in Zimbabwe is dominated by large, transnational corporations, particularly in agriculture, mining, and finance.[5] However, it is commonly agreed that the dominant class in Africa (politically and ideologically) cannot be international capital because of its lack of internal representation.[6] National capital in Zimbabwe is still largely white-owned and has some leverage, but the national bourgeoisie cannot be considered a strong force. In any case, it was politically defeated with the independence struggle. Zimbabwe's small black sector is also weak,[7] although its position is strengthening.

Since independence in 1980, political power has been held by the Zimbabwe African National Union (ZANU), which spearheaded the guerrilla struggle that led eventually to a negotiated settlement in which the majority black population gained political representation. Higher state officials and ministers in ZANU can be considered a governing "class" or, more properly, a governing stratum. Although some individuals are wealthy, they have no substantial economic base of their own; their power lies almost exclusively in state control. The governing stratum in Zimbabwe, then, is as yet part of the petty bourgeoisie[8] rather than the bourgeoisie. The latter is either located outside the country or forms a hostile enclave with little political power within the country. A disjuncture exists, then, between those holding state power and the classes holding economic resources. The governing group is in a fundamentally weak position because it lacks economic control. Since it is concerned with maintaining national capital and not frightening off international capital, the space it has to secure its own material position, should it attempt to do so, is a narrow one. In the absence of a growing economy, any such move could necessitate increased exploitation.

Because of its weak position, the ruling stratum faces problems of legitimation.[9] It has coped with these by appealing to a broad base. In practice, however, benefits from the state have been differential. Although the state has succeeded in aiding the peasantry, it has done less for the urban working classes.[10] In order to build its appeal, the ruling group has constructed an ideology hostile to international capital, including socialist and nationalist rhetoric and appeals to African "tradition." It has been fairly successful in this effort; the government has for some time enjoyed popularity in Shona-speaking areas. Since the recent Unity accord, this support is more nationally based. This is no doubt largely due to ideological appeals, and its welfarist reforms, most notably in primary education and health care. However, these have not generally been of a socialist nature in the sense of any mass, collective appropriation of or control over production, distribution, or decisionmaking. Despite its successful management of legitimation, the ruling stratum's precarious class position remains, and inclines it to vacillating and contradictory behavior.[11]

WOMEN AND STATE POLICIES

Does an analysis of the overall character of the state have any particular implications for women and gender relations?

The governing stratum is influenced in its beliefs about society and women's place in it, from several directions. Three sources of belief have been particularly important. One, deriving from precolonial society, stresses women's role in biological reproduction and the social reproduction of the lineage. A second derives from a version of Marxism in which women's subordination is conceptualized as stemming directly from capitalism and/or colonialism and in which the key to female emancipation lies almost solely in bringing women into production on an equal basis with men.[12] A third and Western model of the nuclear family with women as mother and partner (albeit a subordinate one) has also been influential. None of these models offers a critique of the family or of women's subordinate position in (most) households. It is likely that there is no one dominant ideology within ZANU and the postindependence government it formed. Rather, several conflicting ideologies exist that influence policy.

Ideology—seen here as a set of structured beliefs and practices—is a central component of gender relations. I argue that neither state policies in general nor particular changes (such as land redistribution) can be analyzed adequately outside the context of gender relations. The petty bourgeoisie, of which the governing stratum forms a part, is gendered, as are other classes, so that one may inquire as to how its policies relate to its gender and class natures.[13]

Both gender-specific and gender-neutral policies will be used to discuss the contradictory effects of policies toward women. Before examining the land resettlement program, which is ostensibly gender-neutral, I will place it in the wider context of the historical and legal framework of gender relations and of state policies, first in tribal and colonial societies and then since independence.

HISTORICAL SKETCH OF GENDER
RELATIONS, PREINDEPENDENCE

British colonial authorities tended to not legislate directly in most matters concerning women, a concept in line with their policies of indirect rule and of leaving African institutions "intact," while at the same time altering their structural bases.

The agrarian history of Rhodesia has been well documented elsewhere.[14] Here I wish only to make a few relevant points concerning this history. The colonial occupation of Zimbabwe began in the 1890s. After it was realized that the country would not constitute a second "Rand," the colonial and settler state was concerned with promoting white farming interests and obtaining labor from the African population. Prior to colonial times, tribes of Shona peoples (the largest group) engaged in shifting cultivation and cattle herding; Ndebele peoples (the second most numerous) concentrated more on herding and raiding. With the occupation, an enforced racial division of land created Reserves (later called Tribal Trust Lands, or TTLs, and now known as Communal Areas, or CAs) that eventually became barren and overcrowded. Black men were forced or persuaded out of the reserved areas to engage in migrant labor in towns, mines, and commercial farms, leaving women, children, and elderly men behind to engage in subsistence agriculture. Throughout Rhodesian history, competition from a black petty bourgeoisie, let alone a black bourgeoisie, was greatly feared by white settlers, and the development of these classes was for the most part successfully blocked.

There was only one unsuccessful attempt to reform this system under the 1950s Todd government.[15] Today, the reserve system continues, although there no longer exists any legal racial reservation of land: 57 percent of the Zimbabwean population lives in Communal Areas.[16] Of this population, 82 percent consists of women and children under the age of fourteen.[17]

The "worker-peasantry"[18] established in Rhodesia was almost entirely male. Very few formal wage-labor opportunities were available to women. The first opportunities Zimbabwean women had to earn cash were as prostitutes; mine owners and the state connived to encourage prostitution on mine sites so that families would not live in the compounds.[19]

For women, urban life is still associated with prostitution. Even such jobs as domestic work, which is often associated with female labor, are dominated by men in Zimbabwe. Weinrich gives the following figures for employment of women in the Rhodesian labor force in 1974 (probably the high point for women): 5 percent, manufacturing; 3 percent, teachers; 9 percent, various services; 16 percent, domestics; and nearly 65 percent in commercial agriculture.[20] The last category of women constituted 23 percent of the agricultural workers in 1973; these women work for exceedingly low wages, are most commonly wives of male agricultural workers, and are often employed on a casual basis.[21] Women were largely excluded from the working class and from the small black petty bourgeoisie.

It is often difficult to document the reasons why exclusion of a group occurs because, by its nature, exclusion is not seen; it simply need not be discussed. Women's relative exclusion from wage labor is likely to have been less a deliberate strategy than a congruence between the interests of African men, who collectively gained a good deal of power in the process, and white colonial officials' ideas about women's place in the home.

Women's minimal participation in waged work means that the peasantry (mainly poorer rural producers dependent upon remittances) is largely female. However, in spite of the importance of their agricultural labor, married women are not usually empowered to make decisions concerning agricultural production because of the continued strength of male authority.[22]

There is much debate today in Zimbabwe about whether women's lack of social power stems from colonial or precolonial, tribal/lineage-based society.[23] I believe at least some aspects of women's subordination stem from precolonial times. Analyses that posit a precolonial sexual equality are at best romantic and at worst help to subordinate women under the rubric of "custom and tradition."

Both the Shona and Ndebele peoples were patrilineal, patrilocal, polygynous, and strongly male-dominated. Both societies conformed broadly to what has been termed a "lineage" mode of production[24] in which elders were dominant and able to control the labor of women and of junior men to an extent. Among the Shona (throughout the rest of the chapter only Shona peoples will be discussed unless otherwise stated, as they were the subjects of study) women were not men's social equals, but they could gain status through bearing children (especially sons), agricultural labor, and (as with men) with age.[25] Women also possessed rights, which included having a socially-defined minimum amount of land on which to grow women's crops (such as groundnuts), protection by a husband's family in case of maltreatment, and to having children and a satisfactory sexual relationship. Women's rights of redress were particularly protected through social expectations. Because landholdings were held communally (i.e., by the headman) and because men relied upon their fathers and elders to provide cattle for bridewealth (*lobola*) which enabled them to marry, men could not afford to flout the opinion of elders and the community.[26]

Consequently, women were not totally subordinated. During the colonial period, however, the position of both Shona and Ndebele women deteriorated. Under colonial law, women were deemed legal minors,[27] unable to enter into contracts (including marriage) or to represent themselves in court without permission of, and representation by, a male guardian. Shona women often lost customary rights of various sorts, including their rights to land for women's crops. With the increased importance of remittances from migrant labor and of money from cash-cropping (where this was possible), younger men began to gain independence from lineage elders; for the first time, they were able to obtain cattle and other goods for their own *lobola* payments. This situation also meant that appeals to the husbands' family by the wife often had little effect, since the family's influence over him had diminished. Reportedly, arbitrary behavior on the part of men increased,[28] as did the incidence of divorce without just cause.[29]

This situation was and is rendered even more complex by the system of marriage law enacted in Rhodesia, under which Africans could (and can) marry either under customary or civil law. The most important difference is that Christian or civil marriage must be technically monogamous. However, some men manage to combine both systems; it is common for a man married in a Christian marriage to take a second wife under customary law, even though this is bigamous and an offense.[30] Many women today realistically fear arbitrary divorce or expulsion. The lessening of community influence and rising incidence of divorce leave many women without effective means of control over their husbands' actions. They often dare not go against the husbands' wishes for fear of divorce and destitution, and they are afraid to leave violent marriages for fear of losing their children (divorcées are only granted custody of children in unusual circumstances[31]). Widowhood is also feared, since widows are often left destitute even after years of stable marriage; estates are in many cases appropriated by the husband's lineage relatives.[32] It must be emphasized that such insecurity besets nearly all married black women in Zimbabwe, irrespective of class.[33] The only women partially protected against economic insecurity are those few with sufficient independent incomes or their own capital.

CONTRADICTIONS OF POSTINDEPENDENCE POLICIES

While some policies, such as those concerning marriage law or fertility, are specifically oriented to women, other policies, such as those regarding employment, education, or agriculture, may operate as if gender-neutral, their gendered content unmentioned. This section uses examples of both policy types to illustrate the state's contradictory policies regarding women.

Contradictions can be seen in various spheres, some of which have already been mentioned concerning ideology. In the organizational sphere, the Ministry for Community Development and Women's Affairs, for instance, was created after independence to take cognizance of women's problems, but it has remained weak and underfunded, concentrating on income-generating projects for women (usually handicraft).[34]

In many ways, government welfare reforms have benefited women. Programs for national nutrition, explanation of birth control, and village health workers[35] have improved the health of many women and children, despite decreases in funding due to intervention by the IMF (International

Monetary Fund). Free or low-cost primary education has benefited girls as well as boys. Recent legal changes may begin to have important repercussions.

Three major pieces of legislation concerning women have been enacted recently, or soon will be, two of which are straightforwardly beneficial to women; the third is more ambivalent. The December 1985 Matrimonial Causes Act changes the grounds for divorce from desertion, adultery, cruelty, and insanity to either irretrievable breakdown or illness, thus making civil marriages dissoluble on no-fault grounds. This clause does not apply to customary marriages; a second clause stipulating that upon divorce assets should be divided between spouses, applies to all marriages. In addition, custody should now theoretically be awarded to the spouse best suited to care for children of the marriage.[36]

The Succession Bill is now being enacted. Its intent is to give widows the rights to guardianship of their children and to inherit husbands' estates in intestacy, thereby helping to protect them against destitution.[37]

The Legal Age of Majority Act (LAMA) took effect in December 1982. Its main aim was to grant all Zimbabweans, male and female, the right to vote at age eighteen. As a result, women entered into full contractual capacity at the age of eighteen and shed their "minority" status. However, these consequences were never spelled out explicitly, and it was soon established that provisions of the LAMA contradicted sections of the African Marriages Act that requires the consent of a male guardian for a black woman's marriage.[38] A woman still cannot marry of her own volition.

However, some see the LAMA as having revolutionary implications.[39] That this sentiment has some basis was borne out by a Supreme Court decision in 1984 (*Katekwe* vs. *Muchabaiwa*), in which it was ruled that a father could not claim damages for seduction of his daughter, since a twenty-year-old woman was a legal major. The ambiguities of the LAMA have not yet been clarified, and debate about its provisions continues. Given these ambiguities and the extreme emotions it has aroused, LAMA is a prime example of the state's contradictory policy toward women. It is one that particularly embodies conflicts between reformist and traditionalist viewpoints.

With these three pieces of legislation, Zimbabwe can be said to have the most progressive record in the region concerning women's legal entitlement. Here Marxist and Western ideological strands have converged and agree that women should be formally free adult individuals. However, the actual effects of the law upon women, especially rural women, is another matter.[40] Women often know little about the law, and the effort and material resources involved in bringing matters to a Primary Court are too great. Additionally, local courts rarely make judgments in women's favor.[41]

The negative aspects of the contradictions regarding woman-oriented policies are twofold, the first being employment policy toward women or, rather, lack thereof. Postindependence figures for private-sector employment of women are not available. In 1980, however, 16 percent of semiskilled and skilled employees in Professional and Technical categories were African women; 8 percent of Professional, skilled and semiskilled workers were female, including European women.[42] J. Kazembe notes that in 1982, the number of black and white female employees in the public sector had risen to over 44 percent,[43] but most of that figure was accounted for by employment of women in the Ministries of Health, Community Development and Women's Affairs, and Education. This rise is explained by some postindependence openings for black women, both in usual female areas of employment (nursing) and in white-collar, or petty bourgeois/ semiproletarianized, office work formerly reserved for white women. With this important exception, employment prospects for women seem relatively static.

A second negative feature of state policy toward women is evidenced in the "clean-up" campaign that took place between October and November 1983; it was directed against women labeled as urban prostitutes. During this campaign, thousands of urban women were arrested and held at police stations, some released upon production of a marriage certificate. Others, however, were sent to a resettlement camp in the hot and humid Zambezi valley. Although some women were arrested while walking alone or at night, others were on their way home from work, were accompanied by male partners, and/or had babies on their backs. The Ministry of Community Development and Women's Affairs was informed only after the arrests had occurred, and it protested against the arrests but was unable to affect decisions made at the cabinet level.

In attempting to contextualize the "clean-up" campaign, two factors should be considered. One is that such campaigns directed against women are not unique for Zimbabwe; they were enforced throughout colonial Africa, most recently by the governments of Kenya, Tanzania, and Mozambique.[44] The second factor is that the clean-ups took place at the same time that roundups were made of male and female squatters and others designated as vagrants or beggars; they were sent to the same camp as the women. The clean-up sweep of "prostitutes" was clearly linked with other types of urban influx control[45] but was directed against women as a gender group in a way that roundups of squatters were not.[46]

Although women of all classes and races were arrested, the campaign was particularly directed against younger, better-off-than-average women who appeared to be beyond "traditional" patriarchal controls; that is, against women for whom some employment opportunities have opened up recently. In general, the campaigns against the women, squatters, and "vagrants" can be seen as attempts on the part of the governing stratum to show strength and power; this was especially necessary given the gap between the government's rhetoric and ability to improve such issues as unemployment.

At the same time, moves against urban women gained popular support from several quarters. Many rural women blamed urban females (rather than their own husbands) for taking male earnings, and consequently supported the campaign. Some men, already worried by the LAMA, saw the potential inclusion of women in the "new middle classes" or urban petty bourgeois waged sector as threats to their own social and employment position. Others were perhaps reassured by the activities of a government that presented itself as strong and in favor of "purity." These campaigns reflected the weakness and instability felt by the ruling group, and hence its tendency to stigmatize marginal, weak social sectors.

WOMEN AND LAND RESETTLEMENT

I now turn to the resettlement case study in order to discuss how a specific, ostensibly gender-neutral state policy has affected women. The resettlement (or land redistribution) program has been one of the most significant state-directed reforms mentioned above. This is especially so given the importance of the demands of rural producers in the war of liberation[47] and given the program's importance as a sign that the state is attempting to meet the demands of one of its main constituencies. The resettlement program entails redistribution of land formerly owned exclusively by white large-scale capitalist farmers; today some five hundred such farms are owned by black commercial farmers.[48] The primary official aims of resettlement are to redistribute land to the poorest rural cultivators, be they landless laborers or smallholding peasants or migrant workers; to encourage productive activity; and to establish different forms of individual and collective production.[49] There are several models of resettlement, of which the two most important[50] are:

Model A: in which 12 A./5 ha. plots with variable grazing rights are distributed to individual families or, more specifically, to individual household heads;

Model B: or production cooperatives in which land is communally held. Individuals, not families, hold membership rights in Model B cooperatives.

This study is based on research conducted in 1984 in Mashonaland Central, Mashonaland East, and Manicaland provinces, all in northeastern Zimbabwe on Model A and B schemes. These were relatively fertile and nondrought-stricken areas in a year of drought. Most settlers studied were Shona speaking; the areas studied were also ones of widespread ZANU support. The project was undertaken independently while the author was a research associate of the Ministry of Community Development and Women's Affairs. Research methods, carried out both on Model A and Model B schemes, included observation, 325 individual interviews, and twenty-five group meetings.

Although the resettlement program has not kept pace with official targets[51] and only begins to fulfill the great need for land in the communal areas (see below), the program is still one of the largest of its kind in Africa.[52] By late 1985, nearly 38,000 families had been resettled, approximately 35,000 of which were Model A schemes, approximately 2,500 on Model B schemes, and a small number of other types.[53]

Model A smallholdings have been given more priority than Model B co-ops in spite of statements regarding the need for socialism in agriculture for various reasons, including international pressures and conflicts within Ministries.[54] It is also true that individual family farming is far more popular than formally organized cooperatives, which are often distrusted. But the weight (and financing) given to Model A settlement indicates that a "petty capitalist road" in agricultural reform is being pursued.[55]

This statement raises the question of the class nature of the models. By class nature we are referring to the groups the reforms are intended to benefit. If they are indeed benefited, how will their class (and social) positions be altered? How do the different models tie in with different strategies of transition? Such a discussion is made more problematic by the fact that Marxists, agrarian socialists, and others have never agreed on the ideal socialist agrarian program or transition.[56] Production cooperatives are not necessarily "socialist" units, since they must function in a capitalist system as collectively organized profit-making entities. It is not clear whether production cooperatives in Zimbabwe are intended to remain as such or should be amalgamated into larger units in view of a transition toward large-scale, collective agriculture. Presently, however, these cooperatives have a degree of socialist, collective content in their production systems as well as in their intent.

Model A farming is individualized in its structure and aims to encourage petty capitalist production and establish a black "yeomanry." In granting heads of households twelve acres, the intent is presumably that households/males should at least be able to attain the positions of self-sufficient "middle" peasants (petty-commodity producers) or even to become more well-to-do (or small capitalist farmers). This is to be accomplished without the aid of remittances upon which so many southern African households depend[57] since a secondary official aim of Model A farming is to end the migrant labor system within resettlements and to establish a permanently settled peasantry.

This chapter investigates the impact of this reformist state measure for the women included in the resettlement program. If the intended class result of the Model A program is to encourage a "middle" or "wealthier" peasantry, how does the Model B program differ? Does the nature of either program have specific effects upon women?

One aspect of the above queries can be answered straightforwardly in regard to both programs. The Model A resettlement program, in assigning land to household heads, excludes married women. It thus continues the tradition, discussed above, of exclusion of females. The land distributed to settlers is not owned by them as such, but is held on a series of permits that are potentially retractable by government; the head of the household holds these permits. In Zimbabwe, unless a woman is unmarried, widowed, or divorced or unless very unusual circumstances exist, the head of household is always considered to be the husband. Widows or divorcées with children are eligible to apply, and some are resettled, but their numbers are small. If one intent of Model A resettlement is to allow certain groups to become or remain middle or "wealthy" peasants, then women are excluded from entry into these strata of the peasantry because they do not hold permits; they remain dependents of men. Such exclusion is, of course, not specific to Zimbabwe.[58]

In case of divorce, a married female settler loses any right to stay on the Model A scheme. Resettled women are as subject as other women to divorce or expulsion, so all of the issues discussed above concerning women's legal and customary status remain paramount (as they do for most Zimbabwean women). This means that gender issues structure men's and women's class positions differently. In particular, the class positions women assume alongside of or (perhaps more accurately) in subordination to men may be temporary because they may lose their positions as wives. They are determined not only by capitalist market forces and production processes, but also by their individual relationships with men.

In Model B cooperatives, however, women are included as formally equal participants. Membership in state production cooperatives is on an individual basis regardless of marital status. Accordingly, a divorced woman does not lose her right to remain on a cooperative.

Later on, I will analyze the main contradictions for women involved in individual family and cooperative resettlement. Initially, the matter can be posed as simple opposition: Although married women have been excluded from Model A resettlement in the sense that they cannot hold land, they express, for the most part, great "happiness" with resettlement. Although women have been formally included in Model B resettlement, many expressed dissatisfaction with the schemes.

These general sentiments were indicative less of how different types of resettlement affected the respondents as women than of how women perceived resettlement to affect their socioeconomic and class positions as well as those of their husbands. Nearly all Model A settlers are better off than they were before they had their twelve-acres plots, whereas many Zimbabwean cooperatives are suffering from underfunding and financial hardship. Model B settlers often complain of their impoverishment.[59] So, the most immediate feelings women expressed about resettlement directly reflected their standards of living.

Nevertheless, the two models do affect women's gender positions. The following two sections treat the more specific features of Model A and B schemes that affect women as a gender group.

WOMEN AND MODEL A:
INDIVIDUAL FAMILY RESETTLEMENT

The most significant negative effect of Model A resettlement, women's exclusion, has already been discussed. This is a direct effect of state policy, but it also operates at the level of common sense expectations. Ministry officials[60] have not stipulated that heads of households are to be male. It is simply that the social expectation is that men are heads of household. Accordingly, most women do not feel that they can apply for resettlement. In my sample, 88 percent of the married women asked, felt that they could not apply for resettlement and only one woman did apply on her household's behalf.

Class relations[61] are developing between resettled households, although such relationships are still fairly rudimentary and do affect women. Resettlement has not, however, created rural differentiation; it already exists in the communal areas despite their name. The National Household Capability Survey 1983/4 showed that about 50 percent of CA land is controlled by about 20 percent of the households, and almost 6 percent of all households are landless.[62] Even before resettlement, men and families in this sample held differing amounts of property. In this sample, 68 percent of which was from the CAs, nearly one quarter of the people—a high percentage—were formerly landless and 31 percent held under two acres of land. However, 6 percent of the settlers had larger holdings of twelve acres or more. Just under one-third of the settlers held either no cattle or else had over five head. In Mashonaland East Province, over half of the farmers had no cattle, and about one-quarter held between one to five head.[63] Thirty percent of the settlers did not own a plough, whereas 6 percent owned two or three (some of these also owned other agricultural equipment). These assets may either be hired out to or rented from neighbors so that nearly 7 percent of the settlers hired out equipment, whereas one-third had to rent equipment from other settlers.

These differences in what is sometimes called "agricultural capability" among groups of settlers may reflect the differing and somewhat contradictory aims of government in resettlement. So while the landless are being resettled, the above figures indicate that other groups who are better off than average CA farmers are resettled as well.

Another indication of differentiation is that landholdings are not equal within the settlements, even though all households are allocated twelve acres to cultivate. Resettlement land is being rented out, usually by settlers who lack labor, draught animals, or equipment with which to cultivate, to those who are able to do so. About 5 percent of the settlers admitted to holdings of between fourteen and thirty-seven acres.[64] The extent of class differentiation mentioned here should not be exaggerated—the difference between effective holdings of six and thirty-seven acres is not huge—but neither should the resettlement areas be seen as egalitarian communities.

Wives will assume somewhat different class positions within resettlement villages, according to the extent of their husband's resources. However, what is likely to be equally important for the socioeconomic positions of women and their husbands is the extent to which men are willing to redistribute resources within the household. This may depend in turn upon the extent to which wives can influence husbands; in any case, fierce gender struggles may take place over this issue.[65]

In an attempt to measure women's power within the household, I constructed a scale comprised of scores relating to such items as polygyny, decisionmaking, sexual division of labor, and attitudes concerning wife beating. "Middle"[66] peasant women in the sample gained the lowest "power" scores. "Middle" peasant men are most likely to rely on wifely labor to accumulate capital, and are unlikely to have the resources to hire many laborers or to mechanize.

Additionally, "middle" peasant men had high rates of polygyny (43 percent). The sample as a whole had fairly high polygyny rates of 27 percent for men, although poorer men had the lowest rates. There are no official national or regional figures for rates of polygyny in Zimbabwe, but Weinrich found a 10 percent rate for rural Shona people in general.[67] Although about a quarter of the sample consisted of people of the Vaspostori (Apostolic) faith, which encourages polygyny, the phenomenon was spread among most religious groups.

No generalizations can be made about other resettlement areas, of course, but this study suggests that some men may hope to pursue polygyny, as a strategy for accumulating capital through accumulation of wives. In her study of an African Purchase Area (now known as Small Scale Commercial Farming Areas) in southern Zimbabwe, Weinrich found that up to 47 percent of the households were polygynous;[68] in another APA study, A. Cheater found lower polygyny rates of approximately 20 percent.[69] In a subsequent study, Cheater found that the more educated and "modern" APA entrepreneurs were less likely to be polygynists[70]; however, in my sample, education had little effect upon the extent of polygyny.[71] It is assumed that the effects upon women of high polygyny rates will be negative, since in the studies cited small capitalist farmers who were polygynists treated wives (especially younger ones) virtually as laborers. Polygyny is certainly unpopular among most women.[72]

Although class differentiation is an indirect consequence of state policy encouraging petty-capitalist agriculture, this particular effect of resettlement has nothing to do with government policy. Indeed, among state officials, a Westernized nuclear family model is probably more dominant than a lineage-based one; it is rather a consequence of the choices of individual men.[73]

I now turn to aspects of Model A resettlement which I adjudge to be beneficial to the welfare of women settlers and which they also perceive so. There are three such aspects.

First, there has been a marked shift in the sexual division of labor within resettlements, with men performing far more farm work, especially ploughing, than is common in Communal Areas.[74] For instance, no one reported that women ploughed by themselves; this would have been common in CAs. Nearly 70 percent of the married women said they and their husbands ploughed together, and 17 percent said that men ploughed alone. Concerning weeding, work more commonly assigned to women, about 85 percent of the women said they weeded together with the men. Men also perform domestic duties more commonly, sometimes fetching water and occasionally even cooking or tending children, although these chores are very strictly defined as female tasks. For instance, 10 percent of the women said their spouses helped to fetch water. In general, the amount of work that resettled men do in the farm and in the household appears to have increased.

More settlers now live in nuclear families than in the past. There is no comprehensive data on family types in Zimbabwe; and certainly in some areas and situations, many people do not live in patrilineal extended families, although this remains a norm in rural households. However, when asked whether they preferred to live alone (i.e., in monogamous or polygynous nuclear families) or in extended families, 63 percent of the settlers vociferously supported the nuclear family. This preference was expressed by both males and females. The most common reason given for the preference—by 43 percent—was that "misunderstandings occur" in extended families so that "we will come to hate one another." Strong words indeed in a society in which social propriety is of great importance. The predominance of the nuclear family over a patrilineal extended family is analyzed as beneficial because it weakens the power of the husband's relatives and places more emphasis on the couple as a unit. Although the change could mean that a wife is more at the mercy of an unreasonable spouse, having little recourse to other relatives, it also means that the husband is far more dependent upon his wife or wives.[75]

Third, women in general say that marital relations have improved with resettlement. Flagrant abuse of wives—persistent wife beating, husbands' spending large amounts of money on women outside the household, male drunkenness—have all been reduced in the Resettlement Areas studied. Thirty percent of the women said that their husbands regarded them more highly in resettlement than before: only one woman said that her husband regarded her less highly. Resettled women often perceive themselves as having increased influence within the household and over their husbands.

These positive changes in men's behavior and in women's position are mainly due to two factors. Most important is the power that the resettlement officer has within settlements. Resettlement Areas are, for the time being,[76] each administered by a resettlement officer, a state-appointed official who is invested with very wide-ranging powers. These powers include some judicial powers, as well as the right to remove lazy or offending settlers. Some of the above-mentioned improvements in male behavior can be traced directly to the presence of the resettlement officer. For instance, men generally drink less partly because beer halls are now further away (transport in Resettlement Areas is very poor) but, more importantly, because they know they must be "on good behavior" and hard at work in the fields. The power of resettlement officers may have replaced some of the social controls previously exerted by lineage elders and the community in general. The simple and direct social control that resettlement officers can exert is based on power and authority emanating directly from the state; this was seen by settlers as legitimate authority.

The second factor underlying these shifts in behavior concerns changes in ideology. A strong ethos of "getting ahead" influences both men and women in Model A resettlements. This ethos is certainly encouraged by resettlement officers, as well as by the structure of the Model A program. However, in the schemes I studied, there existed little need for encouragement since the ethic was also indigenous. One corollary of this is an emphasis upon directing energies and resources into individual households. Another is an emphasis upon the individual family unit itself, related, obviously, to the fact that people more commonly live in nucleated families. Because of this emphasis and because wives now work more closely with their husbands, wives report that they have more ability to influence the men's decisions over crops, money, schooling, and so on. The focus upon the individual family has various causes. As indicated above, people often choose to live in this sort of family, both for their own individual reasons and possibly because of the influence of Westernized family ideology. In addition, in granting land to households, albeit to the household head, state policy has implicitly defined the individual household as a significant unit.

The combination of their households' increased access to land and various gender-specific factors operates to improve conditions for many married women in Model A resettlements. The contradiction, however, is that their lack of entitlement in the Model A schemes remains so that they therefore continue to lack any concrete hold over the disposition of resources. Because of the general insecurities which beset women in Zimbabwe, the positions in resettlement they assume by virtue of their husbands' class may be only temporary. It appears to be a strong possibility, given the prevalence of polygyny, that a sector of men will use this lack of female autonomy in order to exploit the labor of multiple wives.

WOMEN AND MODEL B:
COOPERATIVE RESETTLEMENT

Resettlement on Model B cooperatives has proven to be as contradictory for women as that on Model A schemes, despite their inclusion in membership of the schemes. The reasons for these contradictions have been different from those cited above, but they also reflect a combination of state policies and individual male strategies. The negative and the positive features of cooperatives are discussed below.

Three types of negative feature are examined: however, of these only one is gender-specific. The first such aspect broadly concerns the poverty of which many Model B settlers complain. Typically, Model B settlers had far more impoverished origins than did typical Model A settlers; inasmuch as cooperatives involve partial pooling of resources, few resources may exist. A far larger proportion of settlers were ex-commercial farm laborers, and a disproportionate minority were of foreign origin (either refugees from Mozambique or ex-migrant laborers). Another minority consisted of ex-squatters. The best-endowed Model B settlers, in material terms, tended to be ex-guerrillas or soldiers who had received demobilization payments shortly after independence and used these monies to settle. In official views, cooperatives tend to be seen as appropriate for the single and the poor.[77] Implicitly, this may mean that they are seen as less appropriate for those who are better off and may be used as one solution to rural poverty.

Although not all cooperatives are yet making full use of their land[78] and problems with lack of planning and management skills exist,[79] by far the most important reason for any relative or absolute poverty has been the lack of government funding. Many Model B co-ops either do not receive their expected establishment grants, or may do so only after long delays. In early 1985, the planning agency, Derude, estimated that a new cooperative needed at least Z$109,554 for a tractor, oxen, and implements and for basic building. Of the fifty-one Model B settlements at the time, however, only fifteen received any grant, and fourteen of these received less than Z$20,000.[80] When co-ops are better funded, as were two of the six studied here, it is partially due to aid from the outside (i.e., foreign) voluntary agencies. Adequate funding is so important that it tends to dominate all other issues; it is, of course, a direct result of government policy and reflects the general devaluation of and lack of attention given to cooperatives. The main reasons for this have been pressure from outside funding bodies such as the World Bank and struggles within the government,[81] so that an individual petty capitalist "road" in agrarian reform has been favored. However, official attitudes toward production cooperatives have changed over the past year, and future Zimbabwean cooperatives may receive increased support.

A second negative aspect of cooperative concerns democracy—that is, the perceived or real lack thereof in some. Two quite different phenomena are relevant here. One is a fear of state controls and state appropriation, found commonly within peasant groupings in Zimbabwe[82] and many other settings. Most Zimbabwean peasants want to hold an individual family farm,[83] and this colors many people's attitudes toward cooperatives. Interestingly, in Zimbabwe, this distrust of formal cooperation coexists with approval of informal cooperation of working together which, reportedly, was practiced both in precolonial and colonial times.

Another aspect of the problem of democracy appeared to have more direct foundation. Of the six cooperatives studied, four were each dominated by one extended family.[84] Domination occurred because of the family's numerical predominance—sometimes in conjunction with its founding of the organization; because of its control of the co-op Committee; or because of both factors. Such domination gave certain families more access to resources, better housing, certain types of work, and/or to powerful organizational positions within the cooperatives. This system of informal family domination also constitutes an important form of stratification within cooperatives. Analytically, it could be said to combine a patriarchal/pseudolineage form of control with a more modern collectivist form. But however the phenomenon is analyzed, it does not partake of egalitarian principles of organization.

Two points should be made concerning the above discussion. The first concerns the state's role in such matters. The fear of state intervention appears to emanate more from fears already held than to the co-operator's direct experiences.[85] In this author's direct experience, regional officials seemed concerned to promote democratic practices within co-ops. Notably, the interventions witnessed were in fact to halt abuses arising from what I term family domination. Second, neither of these aspects has specific gender content. Females were somewhat more distrustful of cooperation than were males, but many people on both Model A and B schemes favored individual family farming. On family dominated cooperatives, women who were members of the appropriate families benefited, although they were rarely in controlling positions.

One aspect of the negative features of cooperatives is negative specifically for women. On most cooperatives studied, men appropriated the use of advanced technology such as tractors and harvesters. It has been noted in other settings[86] that where any relatively advanced technology is available, men tend to dominate its use, and tractors and combine harvesters are available on some larger co-ops. Men tend to justify this situation by thinking they have greater skills. Women are commonly found in servicing and processing roles (e.g., weeding and husking coffee beans); they complain of the roles they have been assigned and that men refuse to teach them how to operate advanced machinery.[87] If anything, then, the sexual division of labor may be on the increase in cooperatives, although this has nothing to do with the organization of cooperatives per se or with the state's role. Rather, it can be seen as an informal, collective male strategy of control.

These problems, while difficult, can all be rectified or at least tackled. Cooperatives deserve particular attention because they offer some potential for improving women's status. It is not being argued that, aside from the factor of technology mentioned, cooperatives are diminishing women's position, simply that neither are they greatly improving it.

This is unfortunate, since several aspects intrinsic to the structure of state-production co-ops in Zimbabwe should improve women's status. One, mentioned above, is that membership in cooperatives is on an individual basis, so that stability of membership is afforded despite the insecurity of marriage. Another is that women members, like men, have their work points calculated on an individual basis and therefore receive individual yearly incomes, based on the cooperative's profits. A third is that the cooperative's Committee—its executive and administrative body—has the power to intervene in many spheres of life. All co-op members can vote for the Committee, and many cooperatives have a majority of female members. And a fourth, nonstructural but still significant factor, is that cooperatives have what amounts to an official ideology of egalitarianism.

However, none of these potentially beneficial factors operate as strongly as they might. With regard to income, for instance: a women's income earned on the cooperative is—perhaps because of egalitarian ideology—usually seen as legitimately hers; however, as elsewhere, husbands often appropriate this income in the name of customary law. Concerning co-op committees: those I studied reportedly at times intervened in marital relationships. However such action must have been exceptional, as in general women did not feel empowered on the Committee and said that male Committee members ignored their needs. Explanations which they gave for this powerlessness centered around their lack of education, feelings of not being articulate, and the fact that men would not listen to them in any case!

State policies could encompass the employment of cooperatives as a means to alter women's social position. This would, however, necessitate specific attention to women's needs and, probably, specific programs. Given the class and gender orientation of state policies discussed above, however, such programs are only likely to be placed on the agenda through gender struggles.

CONCLUSION

Women's most immediate responses to resettlement in Model A and Model B schemes had less to do with gender concerns than with how resettlement had affected their general socioeconomic situations and those of their households. For most women, however, and certainly for rural women in Zimbabwe, economic needs are structured by gender.

This becomes evident in discussing the main concerns women expressed in group meetings[88] which were not to do with resettlement per se but instead were related to their situations as women. They were concerned about the provision of safe birth control methods which would not be visible to men;[89] the right to refuse sex, and the need for independent sources of cash. The common theme of these demands is women's wish for a measure of personal autonomy and independence. This wish operates both in the connected spheres of sexuality and economics.

Although many aspects of state policy toward women have been contradictory, there has been less conflict with women's wish for personal autonomy. While current legislation does seek to ameliorate the most detrimental aspects of women's situation, the policy has been to continue seeing women as dependents of men. Women's needs have either been neglected or indirectly excluded in many spheres of state policy, including the resettlement program. These stances also relate to the class orientation of the state. In Model B schemes, this aspect emerges in the lack of funding and educational and organizational attention given to co-ops, and in the preference exhibited for individual family farming. In such a situation, where financial constraints become paramount, gender concerns are inevitably given a low priority. In policies regarding Model A schemes, women have been marginalized.

To an extent, women have also been treated as class competitors, as in the clean-up campaign. One—although not the only—tendency of state policy appears to downplay, or even to react against, processes that threaten to enable some women to become equal participants in the class system. The fact that such a threat is not at present a reality and could in any case only apply to a few women, does not lessen its perceived importance. This stance relates to the ruling stratum's own ambiguous position and to the pulls of differing ideologies to which it is subject with regard to gender issues. As racial divisions come to be overshadowed by those of class among Africans in independent Zimbabwe, questions may arise as to what "place" women have in such a system. The usual answer given in class societies is that women are differentiated by class while remaining structurally subordinate to men: in a socialist scenario, the answer might differ.

NOTES

Thanks to Peter Phillips for his helpful comments, particularly on the section concerning the state, and to Graham Trickey and Alan Sillitoe. Any misinterpretations, omissions, or errors, however, are entirely my own.

1. Mouzelis, *Modern Greece: Facets of Underdevelopment.*
2. Folbre, "Patriarchal Social Formations in Zimbabwe."
3. Pankhurst and Jacobs, "Land Tenure, Gender Relations and Agricultural Production: The Case of Zimbabwe's Peasantry."
4. Johnson, *The Middle Classes in Dependent Countries*, 176.
5. Stoneman, *Zimbabwe's Inheritance*, 114–123; Clarke, *Foreign*

Companies and International Investment in Zimbabwe; Astrow, *Zimbabwe: The Revolution that Lost Its Way*, 166.

6. Freund, *The Making of Contemporary Africa*, 239. With the possible exception of South Africa in recent years.

7. Astrow.

8. Definitions of the terms petty bourgeois, and middle class have, of course, excited much debate within sociological and Marxist writings. See, for instance, Giddens, *The Class Structure of the Advanced Societies*; Poulantzas, *Classes in Contemporary Capitalism*; Abercrombie and Urry, *Capital, Labour and the Middle Classes*; Wright, *Class, Crisis and the State* and *Classes*.

Here the Zimbabwean governing class is termed petty bourgeois in the sense that it comprises part of the "new" petty bourgeoisie/middle class, which encompasses, among other sectors, managers, technocrats, and bureaucratic officials. Like the "old" petty bourgeoisie, which engaged in petty commodity production, the "new" groupings are placed between capital and labor, and are in what E.O. Wright terms "ambiguous" class positions. As a result, their class consciousness and class action are often ambiguous as well. Wright, *Class, Crisis* and *Classes*.

Some scholars have reached other conclusions. Ibo Mandaza identifies the governing class and trainee professionals in Zimbabwe as petty bourgeois. Some are even "emergent bourgeoisie." *Zimbabwe: The Political Economy of Transition*, 49. Gibbon and Neocosmos have a more static conception, arguing that "by petty bourgeoisie is meant . . . a group of persons corresponding to or associated with economic, ideological or political practices of a certain kind." "Some Problems in the Political Economy of African Socialism," 190. To some extent, Mandaza, Gibbon, and Neocosmos use petty bourgeois as a pejorative label.

9. Moore, "What was Left of Liberation in Zimbabwe?" 48–49.

10. Weiner, "Land and Agricultural Productivity"; P. Phillips, personal correspondence, November 2, 1987.

11. Gibbon and Neocosmos, 157.

12. Roberts, "Feminism in Africa, Feminism and Africa," 183; Jacobs and Howard, "Women in Zimbabwe," 29–30.

13. The Zimbabwean petty bourgeoisie does, of course, contain women, and in increasing numbers. Historically, however, their numbers have been small, and this has been a very male class.

14. See Arrighi, "Labor Supplies in Historical Perspective" and "The Political Economy of Rhodesia"; Bush and Cliffe, "Labor Migration and Agrarian Strategy"; Duggan, "The Native Land Husbandry Act"; Palmer, *:Land and Racial Domination in Rhodesia*; Palmer and Parsons, *The Roots of Rural Poverty*; Phiminster, "Peasant Production and Underdevelopment"; Weinrich, *African Farmers in Rhodesia*.

15. Encouraged by sectors of capital that wished to see a stabilized peasantry and working class, the Native Land Husbandry Act was passed by the Todd government in the 1950s. It attempted to establish a settled peasantry in the TTLs (reserves) and a settled black proletariat in the towns. Blacks and whites both resisted the Act for different reasons, and attempts to enforce it were abandoned.

16. Moyo, "The Land Question," 187.

17. Folbre, "Zimbabwe and the Lineage of Patriarchal Capitalism," 23.

18. First, *Studies in Black and Gold*; Bush and Cliffe. First and Bush and Cliffe use this term to describe the situation of southern African agriculturalists/wage laborers. They use the term "farmer-housewives" to describe the situation of women.

19. van Onselen, *Chibaro*, 182.

20. Weinrich, *Women and Racial Discrimination in Rhodesia*, 35.

21. Clarke, *Agricultural and Plantation Workers in Rhodesia*, 28.

22. Mubi et al., "Women in Agricultural Projects"; Muchena, *The Situation of Women*; Pankhurst, "Women's Control over Resources," in Pankhurst and Jacobs.

23. The debate has both academic and political resonance because African socialist and nationalist ideology often make reference to "African custom and tradition," in which the role of women has central importance. One consequence is that Western feminism is sometimes portrayed as a corrupting influence of cultural imperialism. As with most "traditions," what actually occurred in the past is often less important than a "tradition's" use in the present. See, for instance, Hobsbawm and Ranger, *The Invention of Tradition*.

24. Terray's *Marxism and "Primitive" Societies* and Kahn's "Marxist Anthropology and Segmentary Societies" use this term. Folbre's use of the term "patriarchal mode of production" bears some similarity to this usage with perhaps greater emphasis upon transhistorical patriarchal power. I prefer the term "lineage mode of production" when referring to segmentary societies.

25. See Holleman, *Shona Customary Law*; Bourdillon, *The Shona*; Weinrich, *Women* and *African Marriage in Zimbabwe*.

26. Chigwedere, *Lobola*, 36.

27. Some argue that neither men nor women in precolonial times could be seen as legal adults since no younger people operated autonomously and all were under the tutelage of elders. Cf. R. Milroy, *The Herald*, October 31, 1982, February 27, 1983.

28. Pankhurst, "Wives and Husbands."

29. In Shona customary law, just causes for a man to divorce his wife included failure to keep house or to cook properly; failure to feed the family; repeated adultery; infertility; witchcraft; insubordination, including public disagreement with the husband, or rudeness to the man's relatives; and refusal of sexual relations with the husband. See Holleman; Bourdillon; and May, *Zimbabwean Women in Customary and Colonial Law*.

30. May, 80–81; Weinrich, *African Marriage*, 47.

31. Mpofu, "Some Observable Sources of Women's Subordination in Zimbabwe," 30.

32. Mpofu, 35; Folter and Deck, "A Study of Bereavement among Women."

33. Under current interpretation of customary law by some courts and many husbands, a woman's income, even if from wages, is usually considered the husband's within marriage, and "her" property may revert to his relatives upon divorce or widowhood. Customarily, a woman's *mavoko* or "hands" property, was her own. However, income now earned by other than purely

traditional means (beer brewing, herbalism, or midwifery) is considered to belong to the husband or his relatives. Kazembe, "The Woman Question," 380–82.

34. Jacobs and Howard; Seidman, "Women in Zimbabwe."

35. Davies and Sanders, "Stabilisation Policies and the Effects on Child Health in Zimbabwe."

36. ZANU, *Zimbabwe News,* "Comrade E. Zvobgo Explains New Divorce Law," 8–9 (1986).

37. *Ibid.*

38. Mpofu, 10.

39. Kazembe, 390.

40. *Ibid.*, 395.

41. May, 90; Pankhurst, "Wives and Husbands," 48.

42. GOZ, Ministry of Manpower, Planning and Development (1983). *National Manpower Survey, Vols. I–III.* Harare, Zimbabwe, 198.

43. Kazembe, 397–98.

44. See Bujra, "Postscript: Prostitution, Class and the State"; Roberts, "The State and the Regulation of Marriage"; Shaidi, "Tanzania"; Official, Mozambique Information Committee, London (1984).

45. Gaidzanwa and Women's Action Group, "Operation Clean Up," 225.

46. Jacobs and Howard.

47. Ranger, *Peasant Consciousness and Guerrilla War in Zimbabwe.*

48. Moyo, 188.

49. GOZ, 1981. *Growth with Equity.* Salisbury, paragraphs 22 to 24.

50. Six models of resettlement exist, including Model A and Model B. The others are:

- *Accelerated Resettlement* (in both Models A and B) is an attempt to respond to urgent needs for land, especially by rural squatters. Farmers are given land, but no infrastructure is provided in the short term.
- *Model C* consists of individual family holdings attached to a core estate, run either cooperatively by the farmers themselves or as a state farm. At present, three such schemes exist.
- *Model D* incorporates nearby ranches as extended grazing areas for Communal Areas farmers in arid regions IV and V (i.e., mainly in the west and south). Some have been planned for Matebeleland.
- *Model F* refers to the 1982 incorporation of new criteria for some settlement so that experienced and usually fairly well-off Master Farmers (i.e., farmers who have obtained official certificates) could be resettled in addition to the most needy.

51. In 1982, th Transitional National Development Plan revised the target for resettlement from about 35,000 households to 162,000. GOZ. 1982. *Transitional National Development Plan, Vol. I.* Salisbury; Cliffe, "Prospects for Agricultural Transformation in Zimbabwe," 13.

52. Kinsey, "Forever Gained: Resettlement and Land Policy," 13.

53. Hanlon, "Producer Cooperatives," 8.

54. *Ibid.*

55. Moyo, 187.

56. Much of the discussion among Marxist and "revisionist" writers has

concerned the relative viability of large- and small-scale farming rather than collectivization of agriculture per se. Kautsky argued that small- and medium-scale farms were more efficient than large-scale ones, as does Bidelux more recently in *Communism and Development*. In the 1920s, Bukharin and Preobrazhenskii of the USSR debated the question of collectivization, although neither envisaged Stalinist forced collectivization. See Lewin, *Russian Peasants and Soviet Power*; Cliffe, "The Collectivisation of Agriculture"; Hussain and Tribe, *Marxism and the Agrarian Question*.

57. Bush and Cliffe; Leys, 263; Harris and Weiner, "Wage Labor," 42; Pankhurst, "Women's Control," 16–19.

58. C.D. Deere, for instance, has remarked upon similar effects of the Peruvian and Chilean land reforms during the 1960s and early seventies. Deere, "Rural Women and Agrarian Reform."

59. However, such complaints should not necessarily be taken to mean that respondents' standards of living were absolutely lowered through resettlement.

60. For instance, an official in the Ministry of Lands, Resettlement and Rural Development (as it was then named) held that anyone could apply for resettlement without prejudice and that heads of households could be taken to be either men or women. Personal interview, May 1984.

61. The phenomenon referred to here does not concern differences of class but, rather, differences of a lesser nature (i.e., differentiation of *strata* among agrarian, petty bourgeois smallholders).

62. Davies and Sanders, 11.

63. Central Statistical Office. 1983–1984. *Report on a Demographic Socio-Economic Survey of the Communal Areas of Moshonaland East Province*. Harare, Zimbabwe, 12.

64. This figure almost certainly underestimates the numbers of settler households having access to more than their twelve-acre allotments, since settlers are aware that they are meant to cultivate the full twelve acres but no more.

65. Pankhurst and Jacobs.

66. Settlers in the survey were ranked as "poor," "middle," or "wealthier" peasants according to scores on questions concerning the ability to plough self-sufficiently (i.e., ownership of a plough and two or more cattle), land ownership, and hiring or performance of wage labor. Most people in the "middle" category were self-sufficient in these respects, although many settlers hired one or two laborers in order to help with clearing land, building huts, and fieldwork.

67. Weinrich, *African Marriage in Zimbabwe*, 142.

68. Weinrich, *African Farmers in Rhodesia*, 162.

69. Cheater, *Idioms of Accumulation*, xiv.

70. *Ibid.*

71. No men with secondary education were polygamists. However, there were only five such men, and three were Roman Catholics, whose rate of polygyny was 10 percent (of eleven men). Approximately 40 percent of men with grade 6 or 7 education were polygamists.

72. In a 1984 survey of widowhood and bereavement, Drs. Folter and

Deck found that only two groups of women approved of polygyny: older Tonga women and a group of younger, poor Shona women who felt their status would be enhanced as a result of marrying an older man of higher status. See Weinrich, *African Marriage*, 145.

73. Although such individual choices have their group aspect—viz the socially sanctioned choices of Apostolic men not to drink or marry several wives.

74. The research of Henny Henson (Institute of Political Studies, University of Copenhagen) in Mufurudzi Resettlement Area in 1983–1984 also supports these findings.

75. This effect is more likely to occur in monogamous households.

76. It is planned that the Resettlement Areas will eventually come under the jurisdiction of the neighboring local administration, but this has not yet been implemented.

77. Mupawose and Chengu, "The Determination of Land Policy in Zimbabwe."

78. Using data from the Ministry of Lands, Resettlement and Rural Development, Weiner estimates that between 1982 and 1983, twelve Mashonaland and cooperatives cropped only 3.9 percent of the allocated land. However, this low percentage also occurred, to a lesser extent, on Model A schemes in the better farmland (agroecological Region II): only 9 to 12 percent of the land was used due to the large amounts used for grazing.

79. Mumbengegwi, "Some Aspects of Zimbabwe's Post-Independence Producer Cooperatives"; Hanlon.

80. Hanlon, 10.

81. *Ibid.*

82. Cheater, "Rural Development Policy in Zimbabwe."

83. Bratton, "Draft Power, Draft Exchange and Farmer Organisations."

84. Of the remaining two cooperatives, one was new and composed mainly of elderly ex-commercial farm workers with few resources.

85. Few people on Model B co-ops, in any case, have extensive experience with cooperation.

86. Food and Agriculture Organization, "World Conference on Agrarian Reform and Rural Development," cited in Issacman and Stephen, 81.

87. With such tasks as weeding, sowing, and fetching water for agricultural, rather than household use, both men and women participated.

88. These meetings were held under the auspices of the Women's Clubs. Women's Clubs were first founded in the colonial era to teach African women Western-style homemaking skills. This remains one of the main functions of the Women's Clubs, though they also initiate such income-generating projects as gardening, sewing, and baking. Although linked loosely to the Ministry of Community Development and Womens Affairs, these clubs are also grassroots organizations and, to an extent, provide a forum in which women can discuss matters without men present.

89. Many men oppose the use of contraceptives without the husband's permission.

CHAPTER 10

Gender Perspectives on African States

NAOMI CHAZAN

The study of African politics has focused increasingly on the shifting characteristics of the state and on the dynamics of state-society relations on the continent. This research emphasis reflects not only the pervasive quality of state organs in twentieth-century Africa and the growing awareness of the importance of states in molding the lives and choices of their citizens, but also an enhanced sensitivity to social interaction and its impact on economic and political trends.[1] The relationship between gender and these state-related processes has, however, largely been ignored.

This book represents the first systematic effort to introduce gender into the analysis of the state in Africa. The contributions cover a broad array of topics, regions, and time periods, varying widely in mode of analysis and theoretical perspectives. Each chapter, nevertheless, addresses aspects of the connection between women and the state, supplying new insights into the main features of African states and the nature of state-society relations.

What images of women and the state in Africa emerge from these studies? In what ways does the incorporation of gender affect the understanding of links between states and social groups in different parts of the continent? Is the analysis of African states altered as a result? What are the implications of these studies for further research and conceptual clarification? This conclusion attempts to draw together some of the key findings presented in this volume, analyze commonalities and differences in approach and interpretation, and suggest several directions for future research.

Attention to the gender dimensions of politics highlights the integral relationship between the condition and prospects of women and their specific socioeconomic and political circumstances. The position of women in Africa is shaped, and at times severely circumscribed, by formal structures, officeholders, and interests. At the same time, however, women do construct their own life histories within this network of constraints, and their activities subsequently affect both the capacities of states and their coherence. By compelling the expansion of the boundaries of political analysis, the study of female experience sheds light on heretofore obscure aspects of the African political landscape and suggests alternative avenues for research and theoretical reflection.

WOMEN AND THE STATE IN AFRICA:
PROCESSES AND POLICIES

The female experience in African politics during the past century is portrayed in these pages as one of exclusion, inequality, neglect, and subsequent female consolidation and reaction. Women have neither played a significant part in the creation of the modern state system on the continent, nor have they been able to establish regular channels of access to decisionmakers. State policies toward women have, as a result, exhibited varying degrees of discrimination and coercion. While there is substantial agreement among the authors concerning the depressed status of African women and their ability to survive and even thrive in unofficial niches, the depictions of this condition vary widely, as do the reasons offered for their appearance and the significance attributed to these trends.

Women and the Origins of the Modern African State

Although African societies have a vibrant indigenous state tradition, the boundaries and institutional foundations of the contemporary state system are closely associated with the colonial intrusion into the continent.[2] The essays in this book stress several dimensions of colonial state construction inimical to women.

In the first instance, the establishment of colonial administrations, discussed by Jane Parpart and Kathleen Staudt, was tied to capitalist penetration and accompanying processes of class formation. The expansion of merchant capital worked against women, rendering them, according to most contributors herein, outside the mainstream of major economic developments during the early part of the century. More significantly, as Robert Fatton, Jr., underlines, the elaboration of state structures has been part of the process of entrenchment of a monopolistic ruling class. "In Africa, the construction of ruling class hegemony has the effect of conflating male power with class closure."[3] The forces that brought about the institutionalization of a new set of formal agencies in the public arena were marked by their male complexion.

In the second place, the close correlation between gender exclusivity and proximity to public goods was perpetuated through the continuous employment of social-control techniques that inevitably involved the imposition of limitations on female physical and social mobility. Margot Lovett shows how the centrality of women for the reproduction of labor and maintenance of the economic bases of traditional society worked to curtail the migration of women in East, Central, and southern Africa. The position of male elders was reinforced through the codification of customary marriage laws. Lovett's findings are corroborated by Karen Hansen for Zambia and by Marjorie Mbilinyi for Tanzania, who also highlight other ways in which various forms of public power were transferred into the private sphere.

New methods of accumulation added a third element to the gender divisions attendant upon the formation of the colonial state. In the rural areas, state intervention into land tenure and usage systems, according to Lovett and others, left women attached to the land but more deprived of control over its resources. Urbanization, moreover, adversely affected women's economic position. Mbilinyi, relying heavily on original archival research, shows convincingly how women were marginalized in the new towns and how this peripheralization was sanctioned through the careful construction of cultural codes that buttressed male dominance. In all the essays, the inability of women to accumulate resources (and hence, again in Lovett's terms, the formalization of the separation between production and reproduction) is viewed as one of the major by-products of colonial state bureaucracies.

In a fourth sense, too, the peculiar features of externally imposed state structures, and especially the partial nature of state hegemony, influenced the capacity of women to act in the colonial environment. Perhaps the most significant contribution of these essays to the growing literature on the roots of contemporary African states lies in their insistence on the boundaries of the reach of the state apparatus. Hansen's discussion of the black market in Lusaka is notable for its stress on the limits of the state in Zambia. Fatton, too, weighs the techniques and impact of women's individual and collective challenge to state dominance. The debate over the viability and meaning of the exit option intrudes into virtually every analysis in this volume.[4] From a greater perspective, processes of state formation in modern Africa were marked not only by their coerciveness and inequality, but also by their geographic and demographic incompleteness.

The connection between the elaboration of state institutions and gender-weighted ideologies and practices is explained in these pages in a variety of ways. One approach, best exemplified by Fatton, but also adopted by Susan Jacobs and Mbilinyi, attributes state forms and ensuing gender policies to processes of class formation. Fatton argues that the state is an instrument of the dominant class and that "the existence of a ruling class requires the existence of a state whose role is to preserve and reproduce the social, political, and economic structures of the ruling class's dominance."[5] In this perspective, women are marginal to the state apparatus because they were not a prominent part of the construction of new ruling classes and their position has therefore depended heavily on their links with powerful men. Mbilinyi and Jacobs refine this avowedly Marxist mode of analysis by demonstrating how the relationship between women and class curtails female access to resources. They distinguish between petty bourgeois and other groups of women in order to highlight the differential impact of class via the state on gender relations. In these analyses, class factors limit the extent of state autonomy.

While not dismissing the significance of class and capital, a second approach, apparent in the writings of Parpart and Staudt, Lovett, and implicit in Newbury and Schoepf, stresses the gendering of these processes as a key to understanding the origins and nature of contemporary states in Africa. As Lovett puts it: "if both state and class formation are to be fully understood, they must be seen as gendered, i.e., as having differential impacts on women and men, who consequently experience them in dissimilar ways."[6] From this vantage point, the relationship between capital penetration, class differentiation, and state formation is distinctly neither unidirectional nor gender-neutral. The influence of colonial states on women, therefore, is also somewhat more nuanced than in the uniquely class-rooted approach. Ingrained in this perspective is an assumption regarding the relative autonomy of the state.

Most of the chapters is this collection fall into the materialist category of political analysis in all its diversity. Nevertheless, glimpses of other conceptual approaches are also evident. Some of the contributors do not explicitly address the issue of state formation (Nina Mba and Monica Munachonga, for example). In their essays they accept the state as given and do not delve into its roots, thereby implying that the contemporary state is an outgrowth of historical processes, particularly of the colonial experience. In this third view that state is perceived as an arena for socioeconomic and political activity, perhaps even as a manager, but not necessarily as an independent purveyor of its own interests.

Hansen offers a fourth approach to the origins of twentieth-century states in Africa. She suggests that states on the continent cannot be grasped in monolithic terms, thus implying that their derivation cannot be attributed to any one discrete set of factors. By intimating the existence of a variety of state entities, she raises important questions about their strength, potential influence on social relations, and centrality as primary agents in the lives of their inhabitants. "The state is comprised of administrative, legal, and coercive apparatuses and their changing and complex relationships. Their effects on distinct social segments are highly variable in historical terms and likely differ from one country to the next. In their turn, a society's segments relate to the state's structures in diverse and changing ways."[7] The author's appeal for historical and contextual specificity yields a more interactive and less exclusive image of the concept of the state.

The chapters in this book offer a wide variety of reasons for the entrenchment of the colonial state and its ramifications for the condition of women. They differ in their conceptual and theoretical underpinnings, geographic frame of reference (West African examples are not treated in sufficient depth), and, inevitably, in the significance they attribute to class, capital, and institutions in the process of state formation. These discrepancies are reflective of basic differences of opinion on two fundamental issues. First, there is no consensus on the extent of continuity between precolonial and colonial patterns of state construction. Second, there are latent, albeit clear-cut, disagreements about the relationship between the state in general and male domination. Some authors tend to see the state inherently as a bastion of male supremacy, whereas others are more flexible, suggesting that female opportunities and constraints vary within different state contexts. These debates have important repercussions for an understanding of both state origins and state-gender relationships.

The correlation between state formation and gender inequality discussed in these pages opens up a host of questions requiring further examination. What is the connection between military superiority and state formation? How do women enter into this process? What role do technology and control of knowledge play in the origins of the state? Do symbolic and ideological world views buttress the linkage between the emergence of states and the institutionalization of patriarchal structures, as Mbilinyi posits? Indeed, can the place of women in concrete instances of state formation be specified with greater care?[8]

Into what institutions were women incorporated, and why? Where were they notably absent? How have these trends affected the particular features of individual states? Have they also had an impact on their dynamics? What happened to the position and status of women not only during the transition from the precolonial to the colonial periods, but also after decolonization? What, in fact, are the gender components of the dynamics of state transformation in recent African history? How have these gender considerations affected the variety of states that have developed on the continent? In what ways, and why?

These and other queries, of an empirical as well as an analytical and theoretical nature, are generated by the debates contained within this volume. A subtle and nuanced view of the interaction between state consolidation and gender relations must await the answers they, along with additional case studies, will furnish.

Women's Access to State Structures

The creation of new arenas of decisionmaking inevitably raises two interrelated considerations for students of women and politics: the gender composition of these bodies and the degree of women's access to central institutions. Almost all the chapters in this collection depict a picture (familiar to students of women and politics in other parts of the globe) of inadequate female representation, sporadic participation, and blocked channels of access to leadership circles.

The first facet of women's status in the public sphere relates to the extent of female involvement in policy positions. During the colonial period, women were emphatically not a part of officialdom. This situation has endured, with few exceptions, since independence. Munachonga describes the poor political representation of women in Zambia in some detail. She indicates that while Zambian women are represented at all levels of the party system, their numbers are too low compared with those of their male counterparts to help integrate women into development.[9] The Zambian case is indicative of a strategy of female incorporation and subsequent segregation. Although women have been drawn into the political system, they have been organized in separate institutions heavily reliant on official handouts and are thereby prevented from exerting pressure in accordance with their numbers.

The Nigerian case, as discussed by Nina Mba, highlights a strategy of exclusion rather than of unequal incorporation. Until recently, Mba asserts, military rulers (much like colonial administrators) pursued a policy of purposeful female neglect. The totally male composition of army-led public bodies left women effectively outside formal power constellations.

The second facet of women's representation in politics relates to access to decisionmakers. Once again, consistently, women appear to have precious few avenues of approach to leadership at the national level. Mbilinyi demonstrates how high female party membership in Tanzania was not easily translated after independence into political influence. Mba and Munachonga highlight the low levels of female participation in central government and imply that similar patterns exist at the local level as well. Less explicitly, but nevertheless forcefully, Newbury and Schoepf's discussion of economic adjustment programs in Zaire and Jacobs' analysis of land-resettlement schemes in Zimbabwe underline the virtual absence of female influence on policy considerations.

These findings are hardly surprising: In most African states, the capacity of individuals and groups to affect policy is severely circumscribed. Elections do not take place in many countries; where they do, they are not always a good indicator of public preferences.[10] Nevertheless, less visible channels of political participation have developed, mostly of a patron-client sort. These relationships have provided an important means for citizen-ruler communication and an effective, albeit indirect, method for obtaining necessary goods and services.[11] They have also furnished linkage structures between various segments of the population and central government. None of the contributions in this book refer to the connection between women and clientage systems. Perhaps the most telling commentary on female access to state power is their virtual exclusion from these linkage networks.

The treatment of women's organizations in the chapters of this book, a third facet of the issue of female involvement in political life, reinforces the dominant image of marginalization. Only Parpart and Staudt, Munachonga, and Mba go into any detail in regard to the activities of major women's organizations. Their analyses indicate that while the specific associations they studied—the National Council of Women's Societies in Nigeria, the

Women's Brigade in Zambia—were periodically consulted by politicians, they developed a dependency on the formal apparatus that limited their utility as funnels for women's demands. Even though these studies point to a proliferation of women's groups and greater sensitivity to their demands, the fragility of large umbrella groups seems to have prompted the creation of radical organizations (such as WIN in Nigeria) with a more focused political agenda.

Indeed, most of the contributions to this book discuss female organizations not as an appendage to the state system but as vehicles for grassroots action and periodic protest. Women's groups are depicted as generally small, loosely structured, and geographically contained entities whose members come together to pursue clearly defined economic interests. The activities of women beer brewers in East and Central Africa, as described by Mbilinyi and Lovett, are two vivid cases in point. Unlike much of the literature on women's associations, these chapters stress the detachment of these female groupings from the power apparatus, while simultaneously underlining their connection to the market.[12]

The placement of women's collective action by the authors of this volume at the frontiers of formal political arrangements raises the possibility that, conceptually, women occupy the interstices of political power in many African states.[13] By filling in political spaces, they may constitute an important bridge between official institutions and informal political and economic activities. They might also, as Karen Hansen tentatively proposes, serve as preliminary indications of more deep-seated processes of political transformation.

The near-absence of women from state institutions in contemporary Africa sheds additional light on the prevalence of gender inequality while, at the same time, accentuating the ongoing importance of women's endeavors to understand political processes on the continent. Several reasons for the paucity of women in public life are offered in these pages. One set of explanations, formulated most explicitly by Mba, attributes the lack of female visibility in formal politics to the personal predispositions of rulers. Drawing on the Nigerian case, she argues that military men are particularly disinclined to incorporate women into leadership positions. Deviations from this pattern (which dates back to the colonial period) are an outcome of the preferences of particular individuals. A second approach is suggested by Munachonga, who claims that poor access to education and low female participation in wage employment have hampered women's political participation. Culturally rooted attitudes to the gender division of labor, coupled with male domination of the bureaucracy, have perpetuated inequalities which can, in her opinion, be overcome only through long-term changes in value systems. "It is argued here that [an] increase in levels of formal education is likely to promote not only some degree of awareness among women about their national role, but also confidence in women to compete and work with their male counterparts at various levels of [the] state and party structures."[14]

Both approaches to the analysis of women's political status rely heavily on the connection between regime characteristics and women's access to officeholders and the resources they control. It is interesting to note that the two chapters focusing most directly on women in the political arena are those least concerned with questions of state formation and transformation. Most of the other contributors do not deal overtly with matters of female participation in official politics because they presume that the nature of modern African states precludes substantial female involvement. From this perspective, the nature of the state, and not the specificity of regimes, underpins poor participation rates and illuminates the preference of many women for nonformal political activity.

Issues of differential gender access to decisionmakers cannot be, however, neatly dissociated from either state or regime. The composition of policy circles, although in all probability in itself an outcome of unequal access to resources, has a crucial bearing on the disposition of goods and services and hence on women's behavior and potential influence. With very few exceptions, the study of women and politics in Africa has avoided a direct confrontation with some core political questions.[15]

Very little is known about gender and citizenship in Africa. The connection between legitimacy and female political support is poorly understood, as are the links between ideology and policy in different countries (a subject referred to, but not pursued by Jacobs). More to the point, the gender dimensions of various regimes have yet to be explored in any systematic way. The rules of the political game in party mobilizing systems differ substantially from those of personal or populist regimes.[16] The position of women—or for that matter, of other social groups as well—is at least partially determined by the institutional arrangements peculiar to specific governments and regimes. The structure of women's association with the state may diverge accordingly. Without a more careful investigation of the distribution of power in African countries and of how specific groups of women are tied to both formal and informal political processes, discussions of female access to the state will continue to concentrate almost exclusively on the quantity of women in public office rather than on the substance of their involvement in political affairs.

Women and the Disposition of State Resources

The focus of many studies of women and the state, the present book included, has been less on the relationship between women and the aggregation of institutions in the public arena than on the impact of the state and its policies on women. This concern reflects a growing awareness of the state's pivotal role in the extraction and distribution of resources and its centrality in structuring social relations.

The studies in this collection stress, in some detail, various aspects of the neglect of women's interests in policy considerations and allocations. They assess the implications of ignoring women not only for the condition of women but also for their societies as a whole. The thrust of their argument is that as long as women are excluded from state benefits, African states themselves are bound to be frail and inefficient.

The first element of these analyses centers perforce on the contents of state policies. Almost all the chapters point to the utilization of the state apparatus for regulatory purposes in a manner discriminatory to women's needs and interests. Legislation regarding access to land (treated in great detail by Lovett and Fatton for the colonial period and by Jacobs for the period since independence) has imposed a variety of constraints on women. In recent years, attempts to regulate trading activities and petty manufacturing, as described especially by Hansen and Newbury and Schoepf, have placed additional barriers in the way of women's economic advancement.

Women have also suffered from neglect in distributional policies: they are generally not targeted for crucial training and educational schemes, nor is their work, in rural as well as urban areas, usually deemed worthy of formal inputs. The lack of concern for women has extended to the structural adjustment programs of the mid-1980s, that have been accompanied by the enactment of a series of measures that militate against the eradication of gender-based divisions of labor. Even extractive steps have not adequately taken into account the possible contributions women can make to increasing state revenues.

The second component of these analyses deals with the effects of these official steps on gender relations. Without exception, all the chapters in this book claim that the combination of neglect and discrimination has further hindered women's economic prospects. "The state captured men far earlier than women, but in exchange, men acquired resources and used ascendance in state institutions to consolidate control over women."[17] In the rural areas, not only do women perform different tasks than men, but more perniciously, as Newbury and Schoepf document, there is a growing differentiation between women's and men's crops. In the urban areas, trading, marketing, and wage employment are gendered. The concentration of women in certain occupations and the undervaluation of these activities has institutionalized problematic patterns of work and social exchange that are hardly conducive to development efforts.

Although there is little disagreement in these pages regarding the adverse impact of state policies on females, views on the extent of this influence—a third factor—vary. Fatton, Lovett, and Mbilinyi suggest that state actions have had an extensive influence on the shaping of women's lives. Munachonga and Jacobs are more reserved in their assessment of the effects of these measures, while Hansen and Newbury and Schoepf admit to their negative repercussions but query the degree of the actual penetration.

These differences of opinion are largely a result of divergent approaches to a fourth aspect of policy analysis, female responses to policy initiatives. It is generally conceded that the extraction of women's work from mainstream economic planning has engendered a variety of activities in the informal economic sector, or in what Mbilinyi so aptly calls "off-the-books" activities. The heavy involvement of women in petty trading, marketing, beer brewing, food cropping, and prostitution is indicative of the prevalence of these endeavors (Newbury and Schoepf actually view the informal sector in feminine terms).

Some of the contributors to this work, however, view black-market activities as an extension of the formal arena and male subjugation. As Fatton puts it: "The *magendo* persists because it serves the material and political purposes of the ruling class."[18] This evaluation is challenged by Hansen, who sees the second economy as an unintended by-product of government action. "While the state's intrusiveness in the economy, including small-scale marketing and trade, in theory forecloses some opportunities, it indirectly opens up a range of others. Conflicts between the state's apparatuses, in this case the administrative and the coercive ones . . . provide a loophole of economic opportunity."[19] Mbilinyi, too, attributes the rise of the parallel economy to capital's response to economic crisis, but highlights the relative autonomy of off-the-books activities.[20] Newbury and Schoepf take one additional step when they suggest that "off-the-books activities indicate efforts by women to direct their labor into channels where they can have some control over what is produced."[21] Parpart and Staudt, in contrast to the other authors, hint at the fact that these activities might be a sign of disengagement from the state.

What unites these discussions is the consensus that the informal economy serves as an expression of women's responses to formal policies and as an arena for launching challenges to state hegemony. The informal organization of women, albeit not always successful, "represent[s] a form of survival strategy that relies on solidarity from below and reflects the vitality of popular perceptions of exploitation."[22] Implicit in these studies, therefore, is the assertion that women indirectly affect the quantity and disbursement of state resources even though they do not, in most instances, enjoy their fruits.

The experience of African women exemplifies some of the (perhaps unintended) negative structural and human consequences of many recent policy initiatives. The considerable evidence mustered in these chapters leaves little room for doubt regarding either the subordinate condition of women or the role of policy measures in the perpetuation of this situation. Interpretations of the causes and implications of these findings do, however, differ substantially. Some authors insist that male domination, via the state, lies at the root of the problem, whereas others continue to stress the significance of the dynamic interaction between men, women, resources, values, the market, and the state.

These quite distinct approaches derive from the use of different research perspectives. Some studies are cast deliberately in macro terms. They view state structures and allied policies from above, employing the state itself as the unit of analysis and women as the object of state actions. Fatton and, to a lesser degree, Jacobs, Munachonga, and Mba proceed on this assumption. From this vantage point, African states do tend to appear central and their policies antithetical to women's interests. In contrast, other chapters rely heavily on micro techniques, detailing various aspects of women's lives and assessing the impact of macro economic and political processes on their strategies and activities (notably Hansen, Mbilinyi, and Newbury and Schoepf; perhaps also Lovett). In these studies, women serve as the springboard for investigation and analysis; formal institutions are introduced where they impinge on women's choices. From this research perspective, female agency is central. While states are important, their policies are attenuated by the actions and anticipated responses of women themselves. In these chapters, variations in policies toward different groups of women are highlighted and "the success of state policies, provoked as they so often were by women's resistance and sometimes organized struggle, was never a foregone conclusion."[23]

A second reason for the divergence of opinion concerning the sources of inequitable policies stems from different motives imputed to the state. Those who attribute female neglect to male control of the state view states as monolithic entities with conspiratorial intentions. The discriminatory practices of state managers are merely a concrete indication of these propensities. Those who submit that policies have a differential impact not only in gender terms but also on specific groups of women tend to disaggregate the state apparatus and to refine their analysis of the female population in order to account for specific patterns of social interaction (Hansen's analysis of the connection between the life cycle and women's activities is fascinating in this context.) States are perceived less in anthropomorphic and organic terms than in institutional and processual ones.

The alternative explanations of the nature and impact of political action for gender relations reveal some limitations of existing paradigms. Uniquely materialist or statist modes of analyses do not adequately take into account issues of mobilization and agency, nor do they provide sufficiently honed tools for the exploration of the diversity and complexity of gender politics. Many of the contributors to this volume, while themselves products of critical approaches to the study of African politics, are uneasy with the analytical constraints imposed by some of these conceptual frameworks. In this respect, too, concentrating on the relationship between women and the state may provide fresh insights into the study of politics on the continent.

This volume offers a rich yield of detailed studies on the impact of official policies on women and their responses to these actions. Their tantalizing results magnify the need for additional case studies and for the expansion of the geographic scope of such research.[24] They also accentuate the urgency of more systematic comparative analyses of the significance of specific state policies for women's lives. Following on Newbury and Schoepf, what changes have structural adjustment programs had on rural and urban women in other parts of the continent? Do privatization schemes further marginalize women? In what ways, and why? Can similar studies be conducted for the spheres of education and health? What will the outcomes of such research tell us about spatial and generational differences among women as well as those relating to class? How do specific groups of women respond to these measures, and why? The answers to these, and similar, questions may permit a much more comprehensive view of how women's actions actually affect policy, the as-yet poorly studied side of the relationship between the disposition of state resources and gender relations. In the same vein, further research may foster alternative approaches to development planning and more specific policy options.

Above all, however, much work has still to be done in tying the more heavily studied policy aspects of gender politics in Africa to their less-examined historical and institutional dimensions. As Parpart and Staudt state so pointedly, "It would be a mistake to overdetermine the state's relationship to women."[25] The gender outcomes of state actions will carry greater meaning if they are more integrally linked to an understanding of power structures and political processes.

WOMEN AND THE STATE IN AFRICA: INTERACTIONS AND IMPLICATIONS

A wealth of information on women and the state in Africa and a genuine intellectual curiosity punctuate these pages. The gender perspective on recent African political history supplies new possibilities for grasping some of the complexities of African states and state-society relations, offering a host of new directions for research and reflection.

The careful examination of the interaction between women and the state in Africa is symptomatic of some general patterns of state-society relations. The image of the relationship between women and state institutions revealed in these studies is one of confrontation. States and social groups are portrayed in adversarial terms. Society is engaged in a continuous effort to avoid domination by ever-expanding state bodies.[26] In this vision, few channels of linkage between formal institutions and informal networks mediate societal exposure to state impulses. Women demonstrate, perhaps more starkly than many other social groups, the broad strokes of sociopolitical conflict in contemporary Africa: formal versus informal, official versus off-the-books, manipulation versus agitation, repression versus avoidance, hegemony versus escape. The investigation of gender politics thus confirms the distinction between the official and the popular in the contemporary African experience.[27]

The innovative value of the essays in this collection lies, however, in the fact that, unlike most other studies of state-society interactions, they proceed to chart some of the processes through which previously invisible behavior has developed and is structured. Precisely because the features of the African scene are so vividly accentuated through the female lens, the historical examination of the ways in the which these forms of confrontation came into being is especially instructive. And, indeed, with a specificity absent in other perspectives, several distinct patterns of state-society relations emerge from these studies.

The first pattern, clearest in the colonial context, is one of center domination and coercion. Here, as Lovett and Fatton detail, the state is pitted against women. The official apparatus is particularly repressive, seeking to extract goods and services while denying women—and by extension perhaps other groups—control over independent resources. A second, but opposite, pattern, hinted at continuously (most notably by Parpart and Staudt) but significantly never actually corroborated, is one of social disengagement from the state. In this scheme, women, possibly the most powerless element of the populace, not only remain "uncaptured" but, through a variety of activities, consciously dissociate themselves from contact with formal institutions. In between these two extremes, several dynamic patterns of social-political interchange, reflective of various combinations of autonomy and reciprocity, have emerged. A third pattern, examined by Newbury and Schoepf, is one of individual domination.[28] In these cases, and Zaire is a good example, a particular regime has devised a multiplicity of methods to repress women. Their response has been to establish a variety of coping mechanisms without necessarily increasing their influence on overall political processes. A fourth pattern is one of unequal vertical exchange (exemplified in Mba's work on Nigeria). Here official policies have created an incontrovertible dependence of women on the state. The exit option is precluded, and autonomous female activity, where it exists, draws on the subtle manipulation of formal resources. Tanzania and Zimbabwe provide a fifth, somewhat different, pattern. In these two countries, a greater measure of structured, albeit still unequal, interaction is evident. Women have developed their own modes of popular discourse which are not easily penetrated by official organs. At the same time, however, their activities and responses have helped to shape government policies. State-society relations in this form are infrequent and intermittent.

A final pattern, most intriguingly crafted by Hansen, suggests that "The Zambian state's economic intervention in marketing the trade has left loopholes for women's black marketing because the changeable set of state apparatuses constructed to administer and coerce it are ineffectively and ambiguously applied." She goes on to "advocate an approach that accounts for the interactive roles of state policy and local cultural practices."[29] In this pattern, specific groups of women fill in the spaces not occupied by state institutions. Relations are hence less overtly conflictual, and more interactive kinds of dynamics are set in motion.

The gender outlook probes a variety of empirical possibilities for the structuring of state-society relations. Since many aspects of women's experiences are so clearly outside the purview of the official, the in-depth analysis of female behavior allows for a refinement of the understanding of the informal political world not easily attainable from other perspectives. Significantly, specific activities, particularly in the parallel market, are injected with new meaning when examined within the framework of different patterns of sociopolitical interaction. The variable interpretations of agency, and not only its importance, are magnified. The message conveyed by these essays is that the study of the female view of politics compels close attention to diversity, to the tracing of varieties of societal activities and, on this basis, to the more careful amplification of the many facets of state-society relationships.

The stress on the variety that emerges in historically specific situations has important implications for understanding the nature of states in present-day Africa. The contributors to this volume commenced their studies with quite different definitions of the state in mind. Some adopted, at the outset, a class-based conceptualization. Thus, Fatton asserts categorically that "in Africa, class power is state power, the two are fused and inseparable."[30] Jacobs joins him in seeing the state as the institutional expression of class relations, as does Mbilinyi. Other authors ventured forth with a more organizational notion of the state. Mba and Munachonga, together with Newbury and Schoepf and to a lesser extent Lovett, defined the state, perhaps less explicitly, largely in terms of the aggregate of institutions in the public domain. Parpart and Staudt, as well as Hansen, chose to view the state both in class and institutional terms.

In the course of the separate analyses, the role of the state was explicated. Most of the chapters took pains to show how the state shapes beliefs, lives, and social relations. Although some essays stress the dominance of the state and others its limitations, all the contributions gradually came to recognize the interactive, as opposed to the purely organic, qualities inherent in the contemporary African state. In Hansen's words, her analysis "seeks to qualify the idea of state intrusiveness, casting doubt on the extent to which the state may be said to determine action."[31]

A process of reconceptualization of the state has taken place during the writing of each of the chapters. If at the beginning of many of the chapters the state was viewed in unidimensional terms, by their conclusion state agencies were viewed in more disaggregated terms and the inclusivity of these structures was qualified. Substantively, policies that appeared clear-cut were gradually depicted as frequently contradictory and their consequences more disparate than originally conceived. The relations that developed between men and women, between females and the state, were perceived as the source of various types of social interactions and state forms. In brief, many of these studies raised the distinct possibility that states and state action were as much the outgrowth of women's actions as the molders of female behavior.

This book reaffirms that some recent studies have suggested: that the nature of the state in Africa is not uniform and that social and economic processes are consequently far from inexorable.[32] The relationship between states, regimes, power constellations, and political action varies, and so do gender and other forms of social interaction. The identification of different kinds of states and of the complex processes by which they came about can go a long way toward clarifying allied citizenship characteristics and consequent societal dynamics. The subtleties of the female experience underline the complexities of African states and draw attention to a wide range of issues yet to be explored.

The chapters in this book constitute a preliminary set of offerings on gender politics in Africa. By demonstrating how female activities can furnish new insights into the political process, *Women and the State in Africa* generates more questions than these essays can conceivably answer. A more detailed research agenda emerges form this undertaking. On the empirical level, less is known than is obscure about the attitudes, beliefs, and activities of women in the political realm. Women's patterns of mobilization, organization, and coalition-building need to be studied in many more areas of the continent. The supply side of women's politics has yet to be addressed over time, and its relationship to the construction of state structures explicated. Despite the increased yield of recent years, the factual vacuum on these topics is still enormous.

On the conceptual level, the feminine perspective points to intriguing directions for retheorizing the parameters of the political. In political terms, the female condition frequently lies beyond the domain of conventional political studies. By stressing the extent to which the official and the previously invisible are intertwined, these analyses press for a redefinition of political boundaries. They also suggest that political channels are deeper than they appear on the surface, that patterns of mobilization should be reviewed to account for structures of inequality, and that the gendering of social relations has important ramifications for grasping patterns of political articulation and the dynamics of political change. The insertion of new information thus leads to a rearrangement of the African political science agenda.

On the practical plane, too, more careful work needs to be done regarding the interconnection between the neglect of women's needs and the failure of many development schemes. The authors of this and other works on African women have repeatedly stressed the centrality of women to economic progress. These essays suggest that female coping mechanisms may contain both structural and practical guidelines for future policies. If women do indeed make a difference, then it is imperative to map out the intricacies of their potential contributions and the ways in which they can be advanced. The experience of African women presents a challenge both for analysis and praxis.

The inclusion of women augments the texture and reorders many of the priorities observable in the African political world. As additional information is gathered and analyzed, and as conceptual and theoretical models are readjusted accordingly, new options come to the fore and alternative possibilities arise. The gender perspective on African politics expands the range of political choice. Here lies the intellectual excitement generated by these initial explorations; here, too, stands a vital challenge both for policy-makers and researchers in the years ahead.

NOTES

1. For some of the latest literature on the state in Africa see Rothchild and Chazan, eds., *The Precarious Balance*; Chabal, ed., *Political Domination in Africa*; and Ergas, ed., *The African State in Transition*. For a broader comparative perspective see Evans, Rueschmeyher and Skocpol, eds., *Bringing the State Back In*.

2. On the precolonial state, see Alpers, "State, Merchant Capital and Gender Relations in Southern Mozambique." On the colonial origins of the state see Young, "Africa's Colonial Legacy," 25–51. Also see Sklar, "The Colonial Imprint on African Political Thought," 1–30.

3. Fatton, "Gender, Class and State in Africa," in this volume.

4. This argument was originally raised for Africa by Hyden, *Beyond Ujamaa in Tanzania*. Much of the discussion that has ensued goes back to Hirschman, *Exit, Voice and Loyalty*. For a recent major critique see Kasfir, "Are African Peasants Self-Sufficient?" 335–357 and for another exposition of this thesis, Azarya and Chazan, "Disengagement from the State in Africa," 106–131.

5. Fatton, in this volume.

6. Lovett, "Gender Relations, Class Formation and the Colonial State in Africa," in this volume.

7. Hansen, "The Black Market and Women Traders in Lusaka, Zambia," in this volume.

8. On some elements of the origins of the state in Africa see Eisenstadt, Abitbol and Chazan, eds., *The Early State in African Perspectives*.

9. Monica Munachonga, "Women and the State: Zambia's Development Policies and their Impact on Women," in this volume.

10. For an overview of elections in Africa, see Hayward, ed., *Elections in Independent Africa*.

11. For fuller discussions of patronage in Africa, see Kasfir, *State Class in Africa*, and Callaghy, *The State-Society Struggle*.

12. For a comprehensive, but early, discussion of urban women's

organizations, see Little, *African Women in Towns*.

13. This terminology is taken from Hirschmann, "Women and Politics in Commonwealth Africa."

14. Munachonga, in this volume.

15. For some early examples, see Filomena C. Steady, The Structure and Function of Women's Voluntary Association in an African City: A Study of the Associative Press among Women in Freetown (D. Phil. Dissertation, Oxford University, 1973). Also see her "Protestant Women's Associations in Freetown, Sierra Leone," 183–212.

16. These terms are borrowed from Chazan, Mortimer, Ravenhill and Rothchild, *Politics and Society in Contemporary Africa*.

17. Parpart and Staudt, "Introduction: Women and the State in Africa," in this volume.

18. Fatton, in this volume.

19. Hansen, in this volume.

20. Mbilinyi, "'This is an Unforgettable Business': Colonial State Intervention in Urban Tanzania," in this volume.

21. Newbury and Schoepf, "State, Peasantry and Agrarian Crisis in Zaire: Does Gender Make a Difference?" in this volume.

22. *Ibid.*

23. Mbilinyi, in this volume.

24. For an in-depth study from West Africa, see Guyer, *Family and Farm in Southern Cameroon*.

25. Parpart and Staudt, in this volume.

26. Bayart, "Civil Society in Africa," 109–125, presents this image with particular skill.

27. See Cooper in "Who is the Populist?" 99–104. Also see Barber's seminal analysis, "Popular Arts in Africa," 1–78.

28. Again, the terms used here are drawn from Chazan *et al.*, *Politics and Society in Contemporary Africa*, 212–213.

29. Hansen, in this volume.

30. Fatton, in this volume.

31. Hansen, in this volume.

32. See Chazan, "State and Society in Africa: Images and Challenges," 325–341.

Bibliography ⎯⎯⎯⎯⎯⎯⎯⎯⎯⎯

Aaby, Peter. 1977. "Engels and Women." *Critique of Anthropology* 3, 9–10:25–53.

Abercrombie, Nicholas, and John Urry. 1983. *Capital, Labour and the Middle Classes*. London: Allen and Unwin.

Abernathy, D. B. 1985. "Reflections on a Continent in Crisis." In Gerald J. Bender et al., eds., *African Crisis Areas and U.S. Foreign Policy*. Berkeley: University of California Press.

Achola, P. P. W. 1983. "Where Have the Women Gone? Education, Gender and Inequality in Zambia." Paper presented at a Seminar on the Role of Women in Development, Ridgeway Campus, University of Zambia. November 21–25.

Acker, Joan. 1988. "Class, Gender, and the Relations of Distribution." *SIGNS* 13, 3: 473–497.

Adams, Lois. 1980. "Women in Zaire: Disparate Status and Roles." In Beverly Lindsay, ed., *Comparative Perspectives on Third World Women*. New York: Praeger.

Afigbo, A. E. 1980. "Nigerian politics in the 1980s: Political horoscope for the Second Republic." Lecture, the Institute of Management and Technology, Enugu, Nigeria, February 12.

Afshar, Haleh, ed. 1987. *Women, State and Ideology*. London: Macmillan.

Ajayi, S. F. A., and B. Ikara. 1985. *Evolution of Political Culture in Nigeria*. Ibadan: Ibadan University Press.

Ake, Claude. 1981. *A Political Economy of Africa*. New York: Longman.

Akerele, O. 1979. *Women Workers in Ghana, Kenya and Zambia*. Addis Ababa: UNECA/ATRCW.

Alavi, Hamza. 1972. "The State in Post-Colonial Societies: Pakistan and Bangladesh." *New Left Review* 74: 59–81.

Alpers, Ned. 1975. *Ivory and Slaves in East Central Africa*. Berkeley and Los Angeles: University of California Press.

———. 1985. "State, Merchant Capital and Gender Relations in Southern Mozambique." *AEH* 13:23–55.

Amin, Samir. 1974. *Accumulation on a World Scale: A Critique of the Theory of Underdevelopment*. New York: Monthly Review Press.

———. 1978. *Imperialism and Unequal Development*. Sussex: Harvester.

Anderson, David, and David Throup. 1985. "Africans and Agricultural Production in Colonial Kenya: The Myth of the War as a Watershed." *JAH* 26,4: 327–346.

Arrighi, Giovanni. 1973. "Labor Supplies in Historical Perspective" and "The Political Economy of Rhodesia." In G. Arrighi and J. Saul, *Essays on the Political Economy of Africa*. New York: Monthly Review.

Astrow, Andre. 1983. *Zimbabwe: The Revolution that Lost Its Way*. London: Zed Press.

Ault, James. 1983. "Making 'Modern' Marriage 'Traditional'": State Power and the Regulation of Marriage in Colonial Zambia." *Theory and Society* 12: 181–210.

Awe, Bolanle. *Iyalode Efunsetan Aniwura*. Forthcoming.

Azarya, Victor, and Naomi Chazan. 1987. "Disengagement from the State in Africa: Reflections on the Experience of Ghana and Guinea." *Comparative Studies in Society and History* 29, 1: 106–131.

Baldwin, Richard E. 1969. *Economic Development and Export Growth: A Study of Northern Rhodesia 1920–1960*. Berkeley: University of California Press.

Barber, Karen. 1987. "Popular Arts in Africa." *ASR* 30, 3: 1–78.

Bardouille, Raj. 1981. "University of Zambia Students' Career Expectations." *Manpower Research Report*, No. 9. Lusaka: Institute for African Studies, University of Zambia.

Barker, Jonathan, ed. 1984. *The Politics of Agriculture in Tropical Africa*. Beverly Hills: Sage Publications.

Barrett, Michele. 1980. *Women's Oppression Today: Problems in Marxist Feminist Analysis*. London: Verso Publications.

Bates, Robert. 1981. *Markets and States in Tropical Africa: The Political Basis of Agricultural Policies*. Berkeley and Los Angeles: University of California Press.

Bay, Edna, ed. 1982. *Women and Work in Africa*. Boulder: Westview.

Bayart, Jean-Francois. 1986. "Civil Society in Africa." In Chabal.

Beeckmans, R. 1983. "Afrique-Actualites: Decembre 1982." *Zaire-Afrique*, 172.

Beinart, William. 1979. "Joyini Inkomo: Cattle Advances and the Origins of Migrancy from Pondoland." *JSAS* 5, 2: 199–219.

Beneria, Lourdes. 1979. "Reproduction, Production and the Sexual Division of Labour." *Cambridge Journal of Economics* 3, 3: 203–225.

———, ed. 1981. *Women and Development: The Sexual Division of Labor in Rural Societies*. New York: Praeger.

Beneria, Lourdes, and Gita Sen. 1981. "Accumulation, Reproduction, and Women's Role in Economic Development." *SIGNS*. 7, 2: 279–298.

Berg, Robert, and Jennifer Whitaker, eds. 1986. *Strategies for African Development*. Berkeley: University of California Press.

Berman, Bruce. 1984. "Structure and Process in the Bureaucratic States of Colonial Africa." *Development and Change* 15: 161–202.

Bernstein, Harry. 1979. "African Peasantries: A Theoretical Framework." *JPS* 6, 4: 421–443.

Berry, Sara. 1984. "The Food Crisis and Agrarian Change in Africa: Review Essay." *ASR* 27, 2: 59–112.

Bettison, David. 1960. "The Poverty Datum Line in Central Africa." *The*

Rhodes-Livingstone Journal, 27.

Bettison, David, and P. J. Rigby. 1961. *Patterns of Income and Expenditure, Blantyre-Limbe, Nyasaland*. Lusaka: The Rhodes-Livingstone Institute, Rhodes-Livingstone Communication No. 20.

Beveridge, Andrew A., and Anthony Oberschall. 1979. *African Businessmen and Development in Zambia*. Princeton: Princeton University Press.

Bhagavan, M. R. 1978. *Zambia: Impact of Industrial Strategy on Regional Imbalance and Social Inequality*. Uppsala, Sweden: Scandinavian Institute of African Studies.

Bideleux, Robert. 1985. *Communism and Development*. New York: Methuen.

Biersteker, Thomas. 1986. "Self-Reliance in Theory and Practice in Tanzanian Trade Relations." In Ravenhill.

Block, Fred. 1977. "The Ruling Class Does Not Rule: Notes on the Marxist Theory of the State." *Socialist Register* 7, 3: 6–28.

Bonani, B. n.d.. "Une première approche des structures d'intégration de la femme du milieu rural de l'aire du Projet Nord-Shaba au processus du développement," Kongolo, Zaire: PNS, Document de Base No. 8.

Boserup, Ester. 1970. *Woman's Role in Economic Development*. New York: St. Martin's Press.

Bottomore, T. B., L. Harris, V. G. Kiemen, and R. Miliband, eds. 1983. *A Dictionary of Marxist Thought*. Oxford: Basil Blackwell.

Bourdillon, M. 1982. *The Shona Peoples*. Gweru, Zimbabwe: Mambo Press.

Bratton, Michael. 1984. "Draft Power, Draft Exchange and Farmer Organisations." Dept. of Land Management, University of Zimbabwe, Working Paper 9/84.

Bryceson, Deborah, and M. Mbilinyi. 1980. "The Changing Role of Tanzanian Women in Production." *Jipemoyo* 2: 85–116. Uppsala, Sweden: Scandinavian Institute of African Studies.

Bujra, Janet. 1975. "Women 'Entrepreneurs' of Early Nairobi." *CJAS* 9, 2: 213–235.

———. 1982. "Women 'Entrepreneurs' of Early Nairobi" and "Postscript: Prostitution, Class and the State." In Colin Sumner, ed., *Crime, Justice and Underdevelopment*. London: Heinemann.

———. 1983. "Class, Gender and Capitalist Penetration in Africa." *Africa Development* 8, 3: 17–42.

———. 1986. "Urging Women to Redouble Their Efforts: Class, Gender and Capitalist Transformation in Africa." In Robertson and Berger.

Bush, R., and L. Cliffe. 1982. "Labour Migration and Agrarian Strategy in the Transformation to Socialism in Southern Africa: Zimbabwe as a Case." *ROAPE* Conference, Leeds.

———. 1984. "Land Reform or Transformation in Zimbabwe?" *ROAPE* 29, July: 77–94.

Bush, R., L. Cliffe, and V. Jansen. 1986. "The Crisis in the Reproduction of Migrant Labour in Southern Africa." In Lawrence.

Callaghy, Thomas. 1984. *The State-Society Struggle: Zaire in Comparative Perspective*. New York: Columbia University.

———. 1986. "The International Community and Zaire's Debt Crisis." In Nzongola-Ntalaja.

———. 1987. "The State as Lame Leviathan: The Patrimonial Administrative State in Africa." In Ergas.

Carnoy, Martin. 1984. *The State and Political Theory*. Princeton: Princeton University Press.

Carter, Gwendolyn, and Patrick O'Meara, eds. 1985. *African Independence: The First Twenty-Five Years*. Bloomington: Indiana University.

Chabal, Patrick, ed. 1986. *Political Domination in Africa: Reflections on the Limits of Power*. London: Cambridge University.

Chanock, Martin. 1977. "Agricultural Change and Continuity in Malawi." In Palmer and Parsons.

———. 1982. "Making Customary Law: Men, Women, and Courts in Colonial Northern Rhodesia." In Hay and Wright.

———. 1985. *Law, Custom and Social Order: The Colonial Experience in Malawi and Zambia*. Cambridge: Cambridge University Press.

Chazan, Naomi. 1988. "State and Society in Africa: Images and Challenges." In Rothchild and Chazan.

Chazan, Naomi, R. Mortimer, J. Ravenhill, and D. Rothchild. 1988. *Politics and Society in Contemporary Africa*. Boulder, Colorado: Lynne Rienner.

Chauncey, George, Jr. 1981. "The Locus of Reproduction: Women's Labour in the Zambian Copperbelt, 1927–1953," *JSAS* 7, 2: 135–164.

Cheater, A. 1981. "Rural Development Policy in Zimbabwe: Past and Future." Harare, Zimbabwe: unpublished.

———. 1985. *Idioms of Accumulation*. Gweru, Zimbabwe: Mambo Press.

Chigwedere, A. 1982. *Lobola*. Harare, Zimbabwe: Books for Africa.

Chilivumbo, A., and J. Kanyangwa. 1985. "Women's Participation in Rural Development Programmes: The Case of SIDA Lima Programme," Occasional Papers, No. 22. Lusaka: Rural Development Studies Bureau, University of Zambia.

Clark, Alice. 1919. *Working Life of Women in the Seventeenth Century*. London: Dutton.

Clarke, D. G. 1977. *Agricultural and Plantation Workers in Rhodesia*. Gweru, Zimbabwe: Mambo Press.

———. 1980. *Foreign Companies and International Investment in Zimbabwe*, Catholic Institute for International Relations. Gweru, Zimbabwe: Mambo Press.

Cliff, T. 1972. "The Collectivisation of Agriculture." *International Socialist Journal* 19.

Cliffe, Lionel. 1978. "Labour Migration and Peasant Differentiation: Zambian Experiences." *JPS* 5, 3: 326–346.

———. 1986. "Prospects for Agricultural Transformation in Zimbabwe." Paper submitted to Government of Zimbabwe, unpublished.

Cohen, Abner. 1969. *Custom and Politics in Urban Africa*. Berkeley: University of California.

Colson, Elizabeth. 1980. "The Resilience of Matriliny: Gwembe and Plateau Tonga Adaptations." In Linda A. Cordell and Stephen J. Beckerman, eds., *The Versatility of Kinship*. New York: Academic Press.

Commins, Stephen K., et al., eds. 1980. *Africa's Agrarian Crisis: The Roots of Famine*. Boulder, Colorado: Lynne Rienner.

Cooper, Fred. 1981. "Africa and the World Economy." *ASR* 24, 2/3: 1–86.
———. 1987. "Who is the Populist?" *ASR* 30, 3: 99–104.
Coulson, Andrew. 1977. "Agricultural Policies in Mainland Tanzania." *ROAPE* 10: 74–101.
Cox, Terry S. 1976. *Civil-Military Relations in Sierra Leone.* Cambridge: Harvard University Press.
———. 1986. *Peasants, Class and Capitalism.* Oxford: Oxford University Press.
Davies, R., and D. Saunders. 1987. "Stabilisation Policies and the Effects on Child Health in Zimbabwe." *ROAPE* 38, April: 3–23.
de Beauvoir, S. 1974. *The Second Sex.* New York: Vintage Books.
Deere, Carmen D. 1976. "Rural Women's Subsistence Production in the Capitalist Periphery." *RRPE* 8, 1: 9–17.
———. 1986. "Rural Women and Agrarian Reform in Peru, Chile and Cuba." In J. Nash and H. Safa, *Women and Change in Latin America.* New York: Bergin and Garvey.
Depelchin, Jacques. 1983. The 'Beggar Problem' in Dar es Salaam in the 1930s. University of Dar es Salaam (UDSM), history seminar paper.
Depelchin, J., and S. J. LeMelle. 1979. Some Aspects of Capital Accumulation in Tanganyika 1920–1940. UDSM, history seminar paper.
Dewar, D., and V. Watson. 1982. "Urbanization, Unemployment and Petty Commodity Production and Trading: Comparative Cases in Cape Town." In David Smith.
Dinham, B., and C. Hines, eds. 1984. *Agribusiness in Africa.* Trenton, N.J.: Africa World Press.
Dixon-Fyle, Mac. 1977. "Agricultural Improvement and Political Protest on the Tonga Plateau, Northern Rhodesia." *JAH* 18, 4: 579–596.
———. 1983. "Reflections on Economic and Social Change Among the Plateau Tonga of Northern Rhodesia, c. 1980–1935." *IJAHS* 16, 3: 423–441.
Dudley, B. J. 1982. *Introduction to Nigerian Government and Politics.* London: Macmillan.
Duggan, W. R. 1980. "The Native Land Husbandry Act and the African Middle Classes of S. Rhodesia." *African Affairs* 79: 227–241.
Eisenstadt, S. N., Michael Abitbol, and Naomi Chazan, eds. 1988. *The Early State in African Perspective: Culture, Power and Division of Labour.* Leiden: E.J. Brill.
Eisenstein, Zillah. 1981. *The Radical Future of Liberal Feminism.* London: Longman.
———. 1984. *Feminism and Sexual Equality: Crisis in Liberal America.* New York: Monthly Review.
Elwert, G. 1984. "Conflicts Inside and Outside the Household: A West African Case Study." In Smith et al.
Epstein, A. L. 1981. *Urbanization and Kinship. The Domestic Domain on the Copperbelt of Zambia 1950–56.* New York: Academic Press.
Ergas, Zaki, ed. 1987. *The African State in Transition.* London: Macmillan.
Evans, Peter. 1979. *Dependent Development.* Princeton: Princeton University.
Evans, Peter, R. Rueschemeyer, and Theda Skocpol, eds. 1985. *Bringing the*

State Back In. Cambridge: Cambridge University Press.

Fagen, Richard, C. D. Deere, and J. L. Coraggio, eds. *Transition and Development: Problems of Third World Socialism.* New York: Monthly Review.

Fatton, Robert, Jr. 1987. *The Making of a Liberal Democracy: Senegal's Passive Revolution, 1975–1985.* Boulder: Lynne Rienner.

Fauré, W. A., and J. F. Medard, eds. 1982. *État et bourgeoisie en Côte d'Ivoire.* Paris: Editions Karthala.

Fearn, H. 1961. *An African Economy: A Study of the Economic Development of the Nyanza Province of Kenya, 1903–1953.* London: Oxford University.

Fee, Terry. 1976. "Domestic Labour: An Analysis of Housework and its Relation to the Production Process." *RRPE* 8, 1: 1–8.

First, Ruth. 1982. *Studies in Black and Gold: The Mozambiquan Miner from Peasant to Proletarian.* Sussex: Harvester.

Folbre, Nancy. 1983. "Zimbabwe and the Lineage of Patriarchal Capitalism," unpublished.

————. 1988. "Patriarchal Social Formations in Zimbabwe." In Stichter and Parpart.

Folter, and Deck. 1984. A Study of Bereavement Among Women. Paper, Department of Sociology, University of Zimbabwe, April.

Foster-Carter, Aidan. 1978. "The Modes of Production Controversy." *New Left Review* 107 (Jan.–Feb.): 47–78.

Freund, B. 1984. *The Making of Contemporary Africa.* London: Macmillan.

Fundanga, Caleb M. 1981. "Shortages of Essential Commodities and the Urban Poor in Lusaka." In International Labour Office, ed., *Zambia. Basic Needs in an Economy Under Pressure.* Addis Ababa: Jobs and Skills Programme for Africa. Technical Paper, 11.

Gaidzanwa, R., and Women's Action Group. 1987. "Operation Clean Up." In M. Davies, ed., *Third World, Second Sex.* London: Zed Press.

Galli, R. E. 1987. "The Food Crisis and the Socialist State in Lusophone Africa." *ASR* 30, 1, March: 19–44.

Geiger, Susan. 1987. "Women in Nationalist Struggle: TANU Activists in Dar es Salaam." *IJAHS* 20, 1: 1–26.

Geisler, Gisela. 1987. "Sisters under the Skin: Women and the Women's League in Zambia." *JMAS* 25, 1: 43–66.

Gertzel, Cherry, Carolyn Baylies, Morris Szeftel, eds. 1984. *The Dynamics of the One-Party State in Zambia.* Manchester: Manchester University.

Geshiere, P. 1984. "La paysannerie africaine—est-elle captivé?" *Politique Africaine* 14: 13–33.

Gibbon, P., and M. Neocosmos. 1985. "Some Problems in the Political Economy of African Socialism." In Henry Bernstein and Bonnie Campbell, eds., *Contradictions of Accumulation in Africa.* Beverly Hills: Sage.

Giddens, Anthony. 1981. *The Class Structure of the Advanced Societies.* London: Hutchinson.

————. 1985. *The Nation-State and Violence.* Berkeley: University of California.

Gould, David. 1980. *Bureaucratic Corruption and Underdevelopment in the Third World: The Case of Zaire.* New York: Pergamon Press.

Gramsci, Antonio. 1971. *Selections from the Prison Notebook*. London: Lawrence and Wishart.

Gran, Guy, ed. 1979. *Zaire: The Political Economy of Underdevelopment*. New York: Praeger.

―――. 1979. "An Introduction to Zaire's Permanent Development Crisis." In Gran.

―――. 1983. *Development by People*. New York: Praeger.

Gray, R. F., and P. H. Gulliver, eds. 1964. *The Family Estate in Africa*. London: Routledge and Kegan Paul.

Green, Reginald. 1984. "Consolidation and Accelerated Development of African Agriculture: What Agendas for Action?" *ASR* 27, 4: 17–34.

Green, Reginald, and C. Allison. 1986. "The World Bank's Agenda for Accelerated Development: Dialectics, Doubts and Dialogues." In Ravenhill.

Green, Reginald, and X. Kadhani. 1986. "Zimbabwe: Transition to Economic Crises: 1981–83: Retrospect and Prospect." *World Development* 14, 8.

Guha, Ranajit. 1983. "The Prose of Counter-Insurgency." In Ranajit Guha, ed., *Subaltern Studies II*. Delhi: Oxford University.

Gulliver, Phillip H. 1955. *Labour Migration is a Rural Economy*. Kampala: East African Institute of Social Research.

―――. 1964. "The Arusha Family." In Gray and Gulliver.

Guyer, Jane. 1984a. *Family and Farm in Southern Cameroon*. Boston: Boston University.

―――. 1984b. "Women in the Rural Economy: Contemporary Variations." In Hay and Stichter.

Hafkin, Nancy, and Edna Bay. 1976. *Women in Africa: Studies in Social and Economical Change*. Stanford: Stanford University.

Hamilton, Roberta. 1978. *The Liberation of Women*. London: George Allen & Unwin.

Hanlon, J. 1986. "Producer Cooperatives and the Government in Zimbabwe," unpublished.

Hansen, Art, and Della E. McMillan, eds. 1986. *Food in Sub-Saharan Africa*. Boulder, Colo.: Lynne Rienner.

Hansen, Karen Tranberg. 1975. "Married Women and Work: Explorations from an Urban Case Study." *African Social Research* 20: 777–799.

―――. 1980a. "When Sex Becomes a Critical Variable: Married Women and Extra-Domestic Work in Lusaka, Zambia." *African Social Research* 30: 831–849.

―――. 1980b. "The Urban Informal Sector as a Development Issue: Poor Women and Work in Lusaka, Zambia," *Urban Anthropology* 9, 2: 199–225.

―――. 1982. "Lusaka's Squatters" Past and Present." *African Studies Review* 25, 2/3: 117–136.

―――. 1984. "Negotiating Sex and Gender in Urban Zambia." *JSAS* 10, 2: 219–238.

―――. 1986. "Household Work as a Man's Job," *Anthropology Today* 2, 3: 18–23.

Hardt, T. L. 1981. "Decision Making Roles in the Rural Household and the Adoption and Diffusion of an Improved Maize Variety in Northern Shaba Region, Zaire." Ph.D. diss., Iowa State University.

Harries-Jones, Peter. 1975. *Freedom and Labour. Mobilisation and Political Control on the Zambian Copperbelt.* Oxford: Basil Blackwell.

Harris, Alfred, and Grace Harris. 1964. "Property and the Cycle of Domestic Groups in Taita." In Gray and Gulliver.

Harris, T., and D. Weiner. 1986. "Wage Labor, Environment and Peasant Agriculture in the Labor Reserves of Zimbabwe," unpublished.

Hay, Margaret Jean. 1976. "Luo Women and Economic Change During the Colonial Period." In Hafkin and Bay.

————. 1982. "Women as Owners, Occupants, and Managers of Property in Colonial Western Kenya." In Hay and Wright.

Hay, Margaret Jean, and Marcia Wright, eds. 1982. *African Women and the Law: Historical Perspectives.* Boston: Boston University Papers on Africa, no. VII.

Hay, Margaret Jean, and S. Stichter, eds. 1984. *African Women South of the Sahara.* London: Longman.

Hayward, Fred, ed. 1986. *Elections in Independent Africa.* Boulder, Colo.: Westview Press.

Heisler, Helmuth. 1974. *Urbanisation and the Government of Migration: The Inter-Relation of Urban and Rural Life in Zambia.* New York: St. Martin's Press.

Henn, Jean. 1984. "Women in the Rural Economy: Past, Present and Future." In Hay and Stichter.

Hermitte, E. 1974. "An Economic History of Barotseland, 1800–1940." Ph.D. diss., Northwestern University.

Hirschmann, Albert. 1970. *Exit, Voice and Loyalty: Responses to Decline in Firms, Organizations and States.* Cambridge: Harvard University Press.

————. 1981. *Essays in Trespassing: Economics to Politics and Beyond.* Cambridge: Cambridge University.

Hirschmann, David. 1986. "Women and Politics in Commonwealth Africa: Operating at the Interstices of Power." Paper presented at African Studies Association, Madison, Wisconsin.

Hobsbawm, Eric, and Terence O. Ranger. 1983. *The Invention of Tradition.* Cambridge: Cambridge University.

Holleman, J. F. 1952. *Shona Customary Law.* Cape Town: Oxford University.

Hurlich, Susan. 1986. *Women in Zambia.* Consultancy report prepared for the Canadian International Development Agency (April).

Hussain, A., and K. Tribe. 1983. *Marxism and the Agrarian Question.* London: Macmillan.

Huybrechts, A. 1985. "Zaire: Economy." *Africa South of the Sahara 1986.* London: Europa Publications.

Hyden, Goran. 1980. *Beyond Ujamaa: Underdevelopment and an Uncaptured Peasantry.* Los Angeles: University of California Press.

————. 1983. *No Shortcuts to Progress: African Development Management in Perspective.* Los Angeles: University of California Press.

IBRD/The World Bank. 1981. *Accelerated Development in Sub-Saharan Africa: An Agenda for Action.* Washington, D.C.: The World Bank.

Iliffe, John. 1979. *A Modern History of Tanganyika.* Cambridge: Cambridge University.

INSTRAW. *National Machineries for the Advancement of Women: Selected Case Studies.* New York: UN.

Isaacman, Barbara, and June Stephen. 1980. *Mozambique: Women, the Law and Agrarian Reform.* Addis Ababa: UN/ECA.

Jackson, Lynette. 1987. "Uncontrollable Women in a Colonial African Town: Bulawayo Location, 1893–1958." M.A. thesis, Columbia University.

Jacobs, Susan. 1984. "Women and Land Resettlement in Zimbabwe." *ROAPE*, 27/8, March: 33–42.

Jacobs, S., and T. Howard. 1987. "Women in Zimbabwe: Stated Policy and State Action." In Afshar.

Jacquet, I. 1987. "Viens, je t'emmène de l'autre coté des nuages . . . Aspects de la vie quotidienne au Zaire." *Politique Africaine* 27 (Sept.–Oct.): 101–106.

Johnson, D. 1985. *The Middle Classes in Dependent Countries.* Beverly Hills: Sage.

Jules-Rosette, Bennetta. 1981. *Symbols of Change: Urban Transition in a Zambian Community.* Norwood, N.J.: Ablex Publishing Corporation.

Kabongo, I. 1984. "Déroutante Afrique ou la syncope d'un discours." *CJAS* 18, 1: 13–22.

Kabwit, G. C. 1979. "Zaire: The Roots of the Continuing Crisis." *JMAS* 17, 3: 381–407.

———. n.d. "The Potential for Grassroots Development in Zaire: A Blueprint for Self-Help in Africa," unpublished.

Kahn, J. 1981. "Marxist Anthropology and Segmentary Societies: A Review of the Literature." In J. Kahn and J. Llobera, eds., *The Anthropology of Pre-Capitalist Societies.* London: Macmillan.

Kalenda, N. M. 1985. "La femme zairoise et les droits de l'homme." *Zaire-Afrique* 196: 363–371.

Kasfir, Nelson. 1984. "State, Magendo and Class Formation in Uganda" and "Relating Class to State in Africa," in his *State and Class in Africa.* London: Frank Cass.

———. 1986. "Are African Peasants Self-Sufficient?" *Development and Change* 17, 2: 335–357.

Kazembe, J. 1984. "The Woman Question." In Mandaza.

Keller, Bonnie B. 1978. "Marriage and Medicine: Women's Search for Love and Luck." *African Social Research* 26: 489–505.

———. 1979. "Marriage by Elopement." *African Social Research* 27: 565–585.

———. 1984a. *The Integration of Zambian Women in Development.* Lusaka: Norad.

———. 1984b. "Development for Rural Zambian Women." Paper prepared for FAO, Human Resources, Institutions and Agrarian Reform Division, Rome.

Kerner, Donna. 1986. "'Hard Work' and Informal Sector Trade in Tanzania." Paper presented to American Anthropological Association, Philadelphia.

King, Kenneth. 1977. *The African Artisan. Education and the Informal Sector in Kenya.* London: Heinemann.

Kinsey, B. 1982. "Forever Gained: Resettlement and Land Policy in the Context of National Development in Zimbabwe." *Africa* 32, 3.

———. 1983. "Emerging Policy Issues in Zimbabwe's Land Resettlement

Programme." *Development Policy Review* 1, 2, November.

Kirk-Greene, Anthony, and Douglas Rimmer. 1981. *Nigeria since Nineteen Seventy: A Political and Economic Outline.* New York: Holmes and Meier.

Krasner, Stephen. 1978. *Defending the National Interest: Raw Materials Investments and U.S. Foreign Policy.* Princeton: Princeton University.

Kruks, S., and B. Wisner. 1984. "The State, the Party and the Female Peasantry in Mozambique." *JSAS* 11, 1: 106–128.

Kuhn, Annette, and Annmarie Wolpe, eds. 1978. *Feminism and Materialism: Women and Modes of Production.* London: Routledge and Kegan Paul.

Laitin, David. 1986. *Hegemony and Culture: Politics and Religious Change Among the Yoruba.* Chicago: University of Chicago.

Lambrechts, A., and G. Bernier. 1961. *Enquête alimenatire et agricole dans les populations rurales du Haut-Katanga.* Lubumbashi, Zaire: Centre d'Etude des Problems Sociaux Indigènes, Mémoires II.

Lancaster, Chet. 1976. "Women, Horticulture and Society in Subsaharan Africa." *American Anthropologist* 78, 3: 539–564.

————. 1979. "Battle of the Sexes in Zambias: A Reply to Karla Poewe." *American Anthropologist* 81, 1: 117–119.

Langdon, S. 1977. "The State and Capitalism in Kenya." *ROAPE* 8, (January/April): 90–97.

Lawrence, Peter, ed. 1986. *The World Recession and the Food Crisis in Africa.* London: James Currey.

Lemarchand, Rene. 1979. "The Politics of Penury in Rural Zaire: The View from Bandundu." In Gran.

Lerner, G. 1986. *The Creation of Patriarchy.* New York: Cambridge University.

Leslie, J. A. K. 1983. *A Survey of Dar es Salaam.* London: Oxford University.

Leslie, Winsome. 1986. "The World Bank and Zaire." In Nzongola-Ntalaja.

————. 1987. *The World Bank and Structural Transformation in Developing Countries: The Case of Zaire.* Boulder, Colo.: Lynne Rienner.

LeVine, Robert A. 1964. "The Gusii Family." In Gray and Gulliver.

Lewin, Moshe. 1968. *Russian Peasants and Soviet Power.* London: Allen and Unwin.

Lewis, Jane. 1985. "The Debate on Sex and Class." *New Left Review* 149 (January/February): 108–120.

Leys, Colin. 1975. *Underdevelopment in Kenya: The Political Economy of Neo-Colonialism.* London: Heinemann.

Leys, R. 1986. "Drought and Drought Relief in Southern Zimbabwe." In Lawrence.

Little, Kenneth. 1973. *African Women in Towns.* Cambridge: Cambridge University Press.

Lofchie, Michael. 1985. "Africa's Agrarian Malaise." In Carter and O'Meara.

Lonsdale, John. 1981. "States and Social Processes in Africa: A Historiographical Survey." *ASR* 24, 2–3: 139–225.

Lonsdale, John, and Bruce Berman. 1979. "Coping with the Contradictions: The Development of the Colonial State in Kenya, 1895–1914." *JAH* 20: 487–505.

————. 1980. "Crises of Accumulation, Coercion and the Colonial State: The Development of the Labour Control System in Kenya, 1919–1929." *CJAS*

14, 1: 55–81.

Lovett, Margot. 1986. "From Wives to Slaves: Twentieth-Century Male Labour Migration from Nyasaland, 1903–1953." Paper presented to African Studies Association, Madison, Wisconsin.

Loxley, John. 1984. "The World Bank and the Model of Accumulation." In Barker.

Lubeck, Paul, ed., 1987. *The African Bourgeoisie: Capitalist Development in Nigeria, Kenya, and the Ivory Coast.* Boulder: Lynne Rienner.

Lumpungu, K. 1977. "Land Tenure Systems and the Agricultural Crisis in Zaire." *African Environment* 2, 4 and 3, 1: 57–71.

Maasdorp, Gavin. 1982. "Informal Housing and Informal Employment: Case Studies in the Durban Metropolitan Region." In D. M. Smith.

MacGaffey, Janet. 1983. "How to Survive and Become Rich Amidst Devastation: The Second Economy in Zaire." *African Affairs* 82, 328: 351–366.

———. 1986a. "Fending-for-Yourself: The Organization of the Second Economy in Zaire." In Nzongola-Ntalaja.

———. 1986b. "Women and Class Formation in a Dependent Economy: Kisangani Entrepreneurs." In Robertson and Berger.

———. 1988. "Economic Disengagement and Class Formation in Zaire." In Rothchild and Chazan.

MacKinnon, Catherine. 1982. "Feminism, Marxism, Method, and the State: An Agenda for Theory." *SIGNS* 7, 3: 515–544.

———. 1983. "Feminism, Marxism, Method and the State: Towards Feminist Jurisprudence." *SIGNS* 8, 4: 635–658.

Maka, M. K. 1985. "Des paysans an marche: Changements dans quelques villages d'Idiofa." *Zaire-Afrique* 199: 521–532.

Mamdani, M. 1985. "Disaster Prevention: Defining the Problem." *ROAPE* 33: 92–96.

Mandala, Elias. 1982. "Peasant Cotton Agriculture, Gender and Intergenerational Relationships: The Lower Tchiri (Shire) Valley of Malawi, 1906–1940." *ASR* 25, 2–3: 27–44.

———. 1984. "Capitalism, Kinship and Gender in the Lower Tchiri (Shire) Valley of Malawi, 1860–1960: An Alternative Theoretical Framework." *AEH* 13: 137–170.

Mandaza, Ibo., ed. 1986. *Zimbabwe: The Political Economy of Transition.* Dakar, Senegal: Codeseria.

Markovitz, Irving L. 1987. "The Consolidation of Power: Women's Role in Political and Economic Transformations." In Irving L. Markovitz, ed., *Studies in Power and Class in Africa.* New York: Oxford University.

Martin, Richard J. 1974. "Housing in Lusaka." In Nigel Hawkesworth, ed., *Local Government in Lusaka.* Lusaka: City Council.

Marx, Karl. 1973. *The Grundrisse.* Harmondsworth, England: Penguin.

Mascarenhas, Ophelia, and M. Mbilinyi. 1983. *Women in Tanzania* Uppsala: Sweden: Scandinavian Institute of African Studies.

Maxon, Robert M. 1980. *John Ainsworth and the Making of Kenya.* Lanham, MD: University Press of America.

May, Joan. 1983. *Zimbabwean Women in Customary and Colonial Law.*

Gweru, Zimbabwe: Mambo Press.

Mba, Nina. 1982. *Nigerian Women Mobilized: Women's Political Activity in Southern Nigeria, 1900–1965*. Berkeley: University of California Institute of International Studies, Research Series #48.

Mbilinyi, Marjorie. 1985. "'City' and 'Countryside' in Colonial Tanganyika." *Economic and Political Weekly* 20, 43: WS-88–96.

———. 1986. "Agribusiness and Casual Labour in Tanzania." *African Economic History* 16: 107–142.

———. 1988. "Runaway Wives in Colonial Tanganyika: Forced Labour and Forced Marriage in Rungwe District: c. 1919–1961." *International Journal of the Sociology of Law* 16, 1.

———. In press. *This is the Big Slavery: Agribusiness and Women Peasants and Workers in Tanzania*. Dar es Salaam: University Press.

McDonough, R., and R. Harrison. 1978. "Patriarchy and Relations of Production." In Kuhn and Wolpe.

McIntosh, M. 1978. "The State and the Oppression of Women." In Kuhn and Wolpe.

McNeil, Leslie. 1978. "Women of Mali: A Study in Sexual Stratification." B.A. Thesis, Harvard University, 1979.

Meillassoux, Claude. 1964. *Anthropologie economique des Gouro de Côte d'Ivoire*. Paris: Mouton.

Milliband, Ralph. 1977. *Marxism and Politics*. New York: Oxford University.

———. 1983. *Class Power and State Power*. London: Verso.

Miracle, Marvin. 1962. "Apparent Changes in the Structure of African Commerce, Lusaka 1954–59." *Northern Rhodesia Journal* 5, 2: 170–175.

Mitchell, J. Clyde. 1956. *The Kalela Dance*. Manchester, England: Manchester University. The Rhodes-Livingstone Papers, 27.

Molohan, M. J. B. 1957. *Detribalisation*. Dar es Salaam, Tanganyika.

Molyneux, M. 1977. "Androcentrism in Marxist Anthropology." *Critique of Anthropology* 3, 9–10: 55–81.

Moore, D. 1988. "What was Left of Liberation in Zimbabwe? Struggles for Socialism and Democracy within the Struggle for Independence." Paper presented to the Department of Politics, Liverpool, March.

Morgan, Robin, ed. 1984. *Sisterhood is Global*. Garden City, New York: Anchor Press.

Mouzelis, Nicos. 1978. *Modern Greece: Facts of Underdevelopment*. London: Macmillan.

Moyo, Sam. 1986. "The Land Question." In Mandaza.

Mpofu, J. 1983. "Some Observable Sources of Women's Subordination in Zimbabwe." Centre for Applied Social Studies, University of Zimbabwe, April.

Mubi, M., et al. 1983. "Women in Agricultural Projects in Zimbabwe: Final Report." Harare, Zimbabwe: Agritex, August.

Muchena, Olivia. 1982. *Report on the Situation of Women in Zimbabwe*. Harare, Zimbabwe: unpublished. Ministry of Community Development and Women's Affairs.

Mukohya, V. 1982. "African Traders in Butembo, Eastern Zaire 1960–1980." Ph.D. diss., University of Wisconsin-Madison.

Mumbengegwi, C. 1984. "Some Aspects of Zimbabwe's Post-Independence Producer Cooperatives: A Profile and Preliminary Assessment." Harare, Zimbabwe: unpublished.

Munachonga, M. L. 1986. "Conjugal Relations in Urban Zambia: Aspects of Marriage Under the Marriage Ordinance." M.Phil. thesis, University of Sussex, England.

———. 1988. "The Place of Women in National Development: The Role of the University of Zambia." *Zambia Educational Review* 7, 1–2: 69–80. School of Education, University of Zambia.

Muntemba, M. Shimwayi. 1982. "Women and Agricultural Change in the Railway Region of Zambia: Dispossession and Counterstrategies, 1930–1970." In Bay.

Mupawose, R., and E. Chengu. 1982. "The Determination of Land Policy in Zimbabwe." Paper, Workshop on Agricultural Production, Gaberone, Botswana, unpublished.

Mvuga, Mphanza P. 1978. "A Call for Reform in the Law of Succession in Zambia." *Zango: Zambian Journal of Contemporary Issues* 4/5: 18–23.

Nelson, Nici. 1978/79. "Female Centered Families: Changing Patterns of Marriage and Family Among Buzaa Brewers of Mathare Valley." *African Urban Studies* 3: 85–103.

Newbury, Catharine. 1984a. "*Ebutumwa Bw'Emiogo*: The Tyranny of Cassava. A Women's Tax Revolt in Eastern Zaire." *CJAS* 18, 1:35–54.

———. 1984b. "Dead and Buried or Just Underground? The Privatization of the State in Zaire." *CJAS* 18, 1: 112–115.

———. 1985. "From Bananas to Cassava: Women and Changing Food Production among the Tembo of Eastern Zaire." Paper at ASA, New Orleans, November.

———. 1986. "Survival Strategies in Rural Zaire: Realities of Coping with Crisis." In Nzongola-Ntalaja.

Newbury, David. 1986. "From 'Frontier to Boundary': Some Historical Roots of Peasant Strategies of Survival in Zaire." In Nzongola-Ntalaja.

Nordlinger, Eric. A. 1981. *On the Autonomy of the Democratic State.* Cambridge: Harvard University.

Norwood, H. C. 1975. "Informal Industry in Developing Countries." *Town Planning Review* 46, 1: 83–94.

Nwabueze, B. O. 1982. *The Presidential Constitution of Nigeria.* London: C. Hurst and Enugu Nwamife Publishers.

———. 1985. *Nigeria's Presidential Constitution.* London: Longman.

Nyirenda, A. A. 1957. "African Market Vendors in Lusaka with a Note on the Recent Boycott." *Rhodes-Livingstone Journal* 22: 31–63.

Nzongola-Ntalaja. 1979. "The Continuing Struggle for National Liberation in Zaire." *JMAS* 17, 4: 595–614.

———. 1982. *Class Struggles and National Liberation in Africa.* Roxbury, Mass.: Omenana.

———. 1984. "Bureaucracy, Elite, New Class: Who Serves Whom and Why in Mobutu's Zaire?" *CJAS* 18, 1: 99–102.

———, ed. 1986. *The Crisis in Zaire: Myths and Realities.* Trenton, N.J.: Africa World Press.

O'Barr, Jean. 1984. "African Women in Politics." In Hay and Stichter.

Obbo, Christine, 1980. *African Women: Their Struggle for Economic Independence.* London: Zed Press.

Oberschall, Anthony. 1972. "Lusaka Market Vendors: Then and Now." *Urban Anthropology* 1, 1: 107–123.

Oboler, Regina. 1985. *Women, Power, and Economic Change: The Nandi of Kenya.* Stanford, Calif.: Stanford University.

Odetola, T. O. 1978. *Military Politics in Nigeria: Economic Development and Political Stability.* New Brunswick: Transaction Books.

———. 1982. *Military Regimes and Development.* London: George Allen and Unwin.

Okeyo, Achola Pala. 1980. "Daughters of the Lakes and Rivers: Colonization and the Land Rights of Luo Women." In M. Etienne and E. Leacock, eds., *Women and Colonization: Anthropological Perspectives.* New York: Praeger.

Okonjo, Kamene. 1976. "The Dual Sex Political System in Operation: Igbo Women and Community Politics in Midwestern Nigeria." In Hafkin and Bay.

O'Laughlin, B. 1975. "Marxist Approaches in Anthropology." *Annual Review of Anthropology.*

Ollawa, Patrick. 1979. *Participatory Democracy in Zambia: The Political Economy of National Development.* Elms Court: Arthur H. Stockwell Ltd.

Ong, B. N. 1984. "Women and the Transition to Socialism in Saharan Africa," unpublished.

Oooko-Ombaka, O. 1980. "An Assessment of National Machinery for Women." *Assignment Children* 49/50.

Oppong, Christine. 1980. "From Love to Institution: Indicators of Change in Akan Marriage." *Journal of Family History* 5, 2: 197–209.

Orde Browne, G. [1933] 1967. *The African Labourer.* London: Frank Cass.

Organization of Angolan Women (OMA). 1984. *Angolan Women Building the Future.* Translated by Marga Holness. London: Zed Press.

Oyediran, O., ed., 1979. *Nigerian Government and Politics under Military Rule.* London: Macmillan.

Palmer, Ingrid. 1981. "Seasonal Dimensions of Women's Roles." In R. Chambers et al., eds. *Seasonal Dimensions of Rural Poverty.* London: Frances Pinter.

Palmer, Robin. 1977a. "The Agricultural History of Rhodesia." In Palmer and Parsons.

———. 1977b. *Land and Racial Domination in Rhodesia.* London: Heinemann.

Palmer, Robin, and N. Parsons, eds. 1977. *The Roots of Rural Poverty in Central and Southern Africa.* London: Heinemann.

Pankhurst, D. 1986a. "Women's Control over Resources: Implications for Development in Zimbabwe's Communal Lands." Paper, ROAPE Conference, Liverpool, England, September.

———. 1986b. "Wives and Husbands: Rules and Practice." Unpublished.

Pankhurst, D., and S,. Jacobs. 1988. "Land Tenure, Gender Relations and Agricultural Production: The Case of Zimbabwe's Peasantry." In Jean Davison, ed., *Women and Land Tenure in Africa.* Boulder: Westview.

Parpart, Jane, and Timothy M. Shaw. 1983. "Contradiction and Coalition: Class Fractions in Zambia, 1964–1984." *Africa Today* 30, 3: 23–50.

———. 1985. *Working Class Wives and Collective Labor Action on the Northern Rhodesian Copperbelt, 1926–1964.* Boston: Boston University African Studies Center Working Paper No. 98.

———. 1986. "Class and Gender on the Copperbelt: Women in Northern Rhodesian Copper Mining Communities." In Robertson and Berger.

———. 1988a. "Women and the State." In Rothchild and Chazan.

———. 1988b. "Sexuality and Power on the Zambian Copperbelt, 1926–1964." In Stichter and Parpart.

Paul, J. C. N. 1984. "The World Bank's Agenda for the Crises in Agriculture and Rural Development in Africa: An Introduction to Debate." *African Studies Review* 27, 4: 1–8.

Peemans, J. P. 1975. "The Social and Economic Development of Zaire since Independence: An Historical Outline." *African Affairs* 74, 295: 148–179.

———. 1986. "Accumulation and Underdevelopment in Zaire: General Aspects in Relation to the Evolution of the Agrarian Crisis." In Nzongola-Ntalaja.

Peil, Margaret. 1976. *Nigerian Politics: The People's View.* London: Cassell.

Perlman, M. L. 1966. "The Changing Status and Role of Women in Toro (Western Uganda)". *Cahiers d'Études Africaines* 6, 4: 564–591.

Peters, David. 1960. *Land Usage in Barotseland.* Lusaka: The Rhodes-Livingstone Institute, Rhodes-Livingstone Communication No. 19.

Pettman, J. 1974. *Zambia: Security and Conflict.* Blandford Heights, Dorset, England: Davidson Publishing.

Phillips, A. 1987. *Divided Loyalties: Dilemma of Sex and Class.* London: Virago.

Phimister, Ian. 1975. "Peasant Production and Underdevelopment in Rhodesia, 1898–1914." *African Affairs* 73, 291: 217–228.

———. 1978. "African Labour Conditions and Health in the Southern Rhodesian Mining Industry, 1898–1953.:" In I. R. Phimister and C. van Onselen, eds., *Studies in the History of African Mine Labour in Colonial Zimbabwe.* Gweru, Zimbabwe: Mambo Press.

Poewe, Karla. 1978. "Matriliny in the Throes of Change: Kinship, Descent and Marriage in Luapula, Zambia." *Africa* 48, 3 & 4: 205–219; 335–365.

———. 1980. "Matrilineal Ideology: The Economic Activities of Women in Luapula Zambia." In L. S. Cordell and S. J. Beckerman, eds., *The Versatility of Kinship.* New York: Academic Press.

Pottier, Johan. 1983. "Defunct Labour Reserve?: Mambwe Villages in the Post-Migratory Economy." *Africa* 53, 2: 1–22.

Poulantzas, Nicos. 1973. *Political Power and Social Classes.* London: New Left Review.

———. 1975. *Classes in Contemporary Capitalism.* London: New Left Books.

———. 1978. *State, Power, and Socialism.* London: New Left Books.

Raikes, P. 1978. "Rural Differentiation and Class Formation in Tanzania." *JPS* 5, 3: 285–325.

Ranger, Terence. 1983. "The Invention of Tradition in Colonial Africa." In E. Hobsbawm and T. Ranger, eds., *The Invention of Tradition.* Cambridge: Cambridge University.

————. 1985. *Peasant Consciousness and Guerrilla War in Zimbabwe*. London: Currey.

Rapp, Rayna. 1977. "Gender and Class: An Archeology of Knowledge Concerning the Origin of the State." *Dialectical Anthropology* 2: 309–316.

Ravenhill, John. 1986. "Africa's Continuing Crises: The Elusiveness of Development" and "Collective Self-Reliance or Collective Self-Delusion." In his *Africa in Economic Crisis*. New York: Columbia University.

Riddell, R. C. 1978. *CIIR: From Rhodesia to Zimbabwe, No. 2: The Land Question*. London: CIIR.

Roberts, Andrew. 1976. *A History of Zambia*. New York: Africana.

Roberts, Penelope. 1984. "Feminism in Africa: Feminism and Africa." *ROAPE* 27/8: 175–184.

————. 1987. "The State and the Regulation of Marriage: Sefwi Wiawso (Ghana), 1900–1940." In Afshar.

Robertson, Claire. 1983. "The Death of Makola and Other Tragedies, Male Strategies Against a Female-Dominated System." *CJAS* 17, 3: 674–695.

————. 1984. *Sharing the Same Bowl: A Socioeconomic History of Women and Class in Accra, Ghana*. Bloomington: Indiana University.

————. 1986. "Women's Education and Class Formation in Africa, 1950–1980." In Robertson and Berger.

Robertson, Claire, and J. Berger. 1986. "Introduction." In their *Women and Class in Africa*. New York: Africana.

Rodney, Walter. 1972. *How Europe Underdeveloped Africa*. Washington: Howard University.

Rosenberg, E. M. 1980. "Demographic Effects of Sex Differential Nutrition." In N. W. Jerome et al., eds., *Nutritional Anthropology: Contemporary Approaches to Diet and Culture*. Pleasantville, N.Y.: Redgrave.

Rothchild, Donald, and Naomi Chazan, eds. 1988. *The Precarious Balance: State and Society in Africa*. Boulder: Westview.

Rothman, Norman C. 1978. "The Liquor Authority and Welfare Administration in Lusaka." *African Urban Studies*, 1.

Sacks, Karen. 1979. *Sisters and Wives: The Past and Future of Sexual Equality*. Urbana: Illinois University.

Safilios-Rothschild, C. 1985. "Policy Implications on the Roles of Women in Agriculture in Zambia." *Planning Division Special Studies*, No. 20 (November). National Commission for Development Planning.

Sandbrook, Richard. 1985. *The Politics of Africa's Economic Stagnation*. Cambridge: Cambridge University Press.

Sanyal, B. C., J. Case, P. Dow, and M. E. Jackman. 1976. *Higher Education and the Labour Market in Zambia: Expectations and Performance*. Lusaka: The UNESCO Press, University of Zambia.

Sato, M. 1986. "The Cooperative Movement and Peasant Struggles in Southern Africa." Paper, ROAPE Conference, Liverpool, September.

Saul, John. 1986. "The Role of Ideology in Transition to Socialism." In R. Fagen, C. D. Deere, and J. L. Coraggio, eds., *Transition and Development: Problems of Third World Socialism*. New York: Monthly Review.

Schatz, Sayre. 1984. "Pirate Capitalism and the Inert Economy of Nigeria." *JMAS* 22, 1: 45–57.

Schatzberg, Michael. 1980. *Politics and Class in Zaire: Bureaucracy, Business and Beer in Lisala.* New York: Africana.

Schoepf, Brooke. 1975. "Zaire's Rural Development: History, Problems and Prospects; Continuity and Discontinuity in Perspective." Paper presented at the Societies for Applied Anthropology, Amsterdam.

———. 1983. "Unintended Consequences and Structural Predictability: Man and Biosphere in the Lufira Valley." *Human Organization* 42, 4 (Winter): 361–367.

———. 1984. "The Political Economy of Agrarian Research in Zaire: Man and Biosphere in the Lufira Valley." In Jonathan Barker.

———. 1985a. "Food Crisis and Class Formation: An Example from Shaba." *ROAPE* 23: 33–43.

———. 1985b. "The 'Wild,' the 'Lazy' and the 'Matriarchal'": Nutrition and Cultural Survival in the Zairian Copperbelt." Michigan State University, Women in International Development *Working Papers*, No. 96.

———. 1986. "Food Crisis and Class Formation in Zaire: Political Ecology in Shaba." In Lawrence.

———. 1987. "Social Structure, Women's Status and Sex Differential Nutrition in the Zairian Copperbelt." *Urban Anthropology* 16, 1: 73–102.

———. In press. "Women, Health and Economic Crisis in Central Africa." *CJAS.*

Schoepf, Brooke, and Claude Schoepf. 1981. "Zaire's Rural Development in Perspective." In B. G. Schoepf, ed., *The Role of U.S. Universities in International Rural and Agricultural Development.* Tuskegee Institute: Center for Rural Development.

———. 1984. "Peasants, Capitalists and the State in the Lufira Valley." *CJAS* 18, 1: 89–93.

———. 1987a. "Food Crisis and Agrarian Change in the Eastern Highlands of Zaire." *Urban Anthropology* 16, 1: 5–37.

———. 1987b. "Gender, Land and Hunger in Eastern Kivu, Zaire." *Urban Anthropology.*

———. In press. "Gender, Land and Hunger in Eastern Kivu, Zaire." In R. Huss-Ashmore and S. Katz, eds., *African Famine and Food Supply.* New York and London: Gordon and Breach.

Schoepf, B. G., Rukarangura-wa-Nkera et al. 1988. "AIDS and Society in Central Africa: A View from Zaire." In N. Miller and R. Rockwell, eds., *AIDS in Africa: Social and Policy Impact.* Lewiston, N.Y.: Edwin Mellen.

Schuster, Ilsa. 1979. *New Women of Lusaka.* Palo Alto, Calif.: Mayfield Publishing Company.

Schwarz, A. 1972. "Illusion d'une émancipation at aliénation réelle de l'ouvrière zairoise.: *CJAS* 6, 2: 183–212.

Scott, Joan. 1986a. "Gender: A Useful Category of Historical Analysis." *American Historical Review* 91, 5: 1053–1075.

———. 1986b. "Women in *The Making of the English Working Class*," unpublished paper.

Seccombe, Walter. 1974. "The Housewife and her Labour under Capitalism." *New Left Review* 83: 5–24.

Seddon, David, ed. 1986. *Relations of Production: Marxist Approaches to*

Economic Anthropology (1978). Translated by Helen Lackner. London: Cambridge University.

Seidman, Ann. 1974. "The Distorted Growth of Import-Substitution Industry: The Zambian Case." *JMAS* 12, 4: 601–631.

Seidman, G. W. 1984. "Women in Zimbabwe: Post-Independence Struggles." *Feminist Studies* 10 3 (Fall): 419–440.

Sen, Gita, and Caren Grown, eds. 1987. *Development, Crises and Alternative Visions: Third World Women"s Perspectives*. New York: Monthly Review Press.

Shaidi, L. P. 1984. "Tanzania: The Human Resources Deployment Act, 1983— A Desperate Measure to Contain a Desperate Situation." *ROAPE* 31 (December): 82–86.

Shaw, Timothy M. and O. Aluko, eds. 1985. *Africa Projected: From Recession to Renaissance by the Year 2000?* London: Macmillan Press.

Shifferaw, M. 1982. "Educational Policy and Practice Affecting Females in Zambian Secondary Schools." Ph.D. thesis, University of Wisconsin, Milwaukee.

Shorter, Edward. 1976. *The Making of the Modern Family*. New York: Basic Books.

Sikaneta, S. 1986. "Analysis of the Women's League of Zambia." Report for a Commonwealth-Sponsored SADCC (Southern African Development Coordination Conference) Workshop on Policy Development, presented in Harare, Zimbabwe.

Sivard, Ruth. 1985. *Women . . . A World Survey*. Washington, D.C.: World Priorities.

Sklar, Richard. 1979. "The Nature of Class Domination in Africa." *JMAS* 17: 351–353.

———. 1985. "The Colonial Imprint on African Political Thought." In Carter and O'Meara.

Skocpol, Theda. 1979. *States and Social Revolutions*. Cambridge: Cambridge University Press.

———. 1981. "Political Responses to Capitalist Crisis: Neo-Marxist Theories of the State and the Case of the New Deal." *Politics and Society* 10, 2: 155–201.

———. 1985. "Bringing the State Back In: Strategies of Analysis in Current Research." In Evans, Rueschemeyer, and Skocpol.

Smith, David, ed. 1982. *Living under Apartheid: Aspects of Urbanization and Social Change in South Africa*. London: George Allen and Unwin.

Smith, J., I. Wallerstein, and H. Evers, eds. 1984. *Households and the World-Economy*. Beverly Hills, CA: Sage Publications.

Smith, Tony. 1979. "The Underdevelopment of Development Literature: The Case of Dependency Theory." *World Politics* 31, 2 (January).

Sosne, Elinor. 1986. "Colonial Peasantization and Contemporary Underdevelopment: A View from a Kivu Village." In Gran.

Southall, Aidan. W., and Peter C. W. Gutkind. 1957. *Townsmen in the Making: Kampala and Its Suburbs*. Kampala, Uganda: East African Institute of Social Research.

Southall, Tony. 1980. "Zambia: Class Formation and Government Policy in the 1970s." *JSAS* 7, 1: 91–108.

Stamp, Patricia. 1976. "Perceptions of Change and Economic Strategy Among Kikuyu Women of Mitero, Kenya." *Rural Africana* 29.

Staudt, Kathleen. 1978. "Administrative Resources, Political Patrons, and Redressing Sex Inequalities: The Case from Western Kenya." *The Journal of Developing Areas* 12, 4: 399–414.

———. 1982. "Sex, Ethnic and Class Consciousness in Western Kenya." *Comparative Politics* 14, 2: 149–167.

———. 1984. Review of Hyden, *No Shortcuts to Progress.* In *Journal of Developing Areas* 18, 4: 530–532.

———. 1986a. "Stratification: Implications for Women's Politics." In Robertson and Berger.

———. 1986b. "Women, Development and the State: On the Theoretical Impasse." *Development and Change* 17, 2.

———. 1987a. "Uncaptured or Unmotivated?" *Rural Sociology* 52, 1: 37–55.

———. 1987b. "Women's Politics, the State, and Capitalist Transformation in Africa." In Markovitz.

———. "The State and Gender in Colonial Africa: Anthropological Perspectives." In S. E. Charlton, J. Everett, and K. Staudt, eds., *Women, the State and Development.* Albany: SUNY Albany. Forthcoming.

Steady, Filomina. 1975. *Female Power in African Politics: The National Congress of Sierra Leone Women.* Pasadena: Munger Africana Library, California Institute of Technology.

———. 1976. "Protestant Women's Association in Freetown, Sierra Leone." In Hafkin and Bay.

Stichter, Sharon. 1975–75. "Women and the Labor Force in Kenya, 1985–1964." *Rural Africana* 29 (Winter).

———. 1985. *Migrant Laborers.* New York: Cambridge University.

Stichter, Sharon, and Jane Parpart, eds. 1988. *Patriarchy and Class: African Women in the Home and the Workforce.* Boulder: Westview.

Stoneman, C., ed. 1981. *Zimbabwe's Inheritance.* London: Macmillan.

Strobel, Margaret, 1984. "Women in Religion and in Secular Ideology." In Hay and Stichter.

Sutton, J. E. G. 1970. "Dar es Salaam: A Sketch of A Hundred Years." *Tanzania Notes and Records* 71: 1–19.

Swantz, Marja L. 1985. *Women in Development: A Creative Role Denied?* London: C. Hurst.

Tadesse, Z. 1979. "The Impact of Land Reform on Women: The Case of Ethiopia." *Women, Land and Food Production, ISIS Bulletin* No. 11: 18–21.

Tambila, K. 1983. "A Plantation Labour Magnet: The Tanga Case." In W. Rodney, K. Tambila, and L. Sago, eds., *Migrant Labour in Tanzania During the Colonial Period.* Hamburg: Institut fur Afrika-Kunde.

Tembo, L. P. 1984. *A National Survey on Sex Biases in Zambian Textbooks in Primary and Junior Secondary Schools and Their Implications for Education in Zambia.* Paris: UNESCO; and Lusaka: Zambia National Commission for UNESCO.

Terray, E. 1972. *Marxism and 'Primitive' Societies.* New York: Monthly Review.

Thornton, Stephen. 1977–78. "The Struggle for Profit and Participation by an Emerging African Petty-Bourgeoisie in Bulawayo, 1893–1933." In *The Societies of Southern Africa in the 19th and 20th Centuries*, vol. 9. University of London: Institute of Commonwealth Studies, collected Seminar Papers No. 24.

Todd, David M., and C. Shaw. 1980. "The Informal Sector and Zambia's Employment Crisis." *JMAS* 18, 3: 411–425.

Tosh, John. 1978. "Lango Agriculture During the Early Colonial Period: Land and Labour in a Cash-Crop Economy." *JAH* 19, 3: 415–440.

UN. 1985. *Report of the World Conference to Review and Appraise the Achievements of the United Nations Decade for Women: Equality, Development and Peace*. Nairobi: United Nations.

Urdang, Stephanie. 1979. *Fighting Two Colonialisms: Women in Guinea-Bissau*. New York: Monthly Review.

———. 1984. "The Last Transition? Women and Development in Mozambique." *ROAPE* 27/28: 8–32.

Vail, Leroy. 1983. "The Political Economy of East-Central Africa." In D. Birmingham and P. Martin, eds., *History of Central Africa*, vol. 2. New York: Longman.

Van Allen, Judith. 1972. "Sitting on a Man: Colonialism and the Lost Political Institutions of Igbo Women." *CJAS* 6, 2: 165–182.

van Onselen, C. 1980. *Chibaro: Mine Labour in S. Rhodesia: 1900–1933*. Johannesburg: Pluto.

van Zwanenberg, R. 1972. "History and Theory of Urban Poverty in Nairobi: The Problem of Slum Development." *Journal of East African Research and Development* 2, 2.

———. 1975. *Colonial Capitalism and Labour in Kenya, 1919–1939*. Nairobi: East African Literature Bureau.

Vincent, Joan. 1970. "The Dar es Salaam Townsman . . ." *Tanzania Notes and Records* 71: 149–156.

Vogel, Lise. 1983. *Marxism and the Oppression of Women*. New Brunswick, N.J.: Rutgers University.

von Freyhold, M. 1977. "The Post-Colonial State and its Tanzanian Version." *ROAPE* 8 (January–April): 75–89.

Wallerstein, I. 1974. *The Modern World System*. New York: Academic Press.

Warren, Bill. 1980. *Imperialism: Pioneer of Capitalism*. London: New Left Books.

Waruzi, B., 1982. "Peasant, State, and Rural Development in Post-Independent Zaire: A Case Study of 'Reforme Rurale' and Its Implications." Ph.D. diss., University of Wisconsin-Madison.

Weiner, D., S. Moyo, B. Munslow, and P. O'Keefe. 1985. "Land Use and Agricultural Productivity in Zimbabwe." *JMAS* 23, 2: 251–286.

Weinrich, A. K. H. 1975. *African Farmers in Rhodesia*. Oxford: Oxford University.

———. 1979. *Women and Racial Discrimination in Rhodesia*. Paris: UNESCO.

———. 1982. *African Marriage in Zimbabwe*. Gweru, Zimbabwe: Mambo Press.

White, Luise. 1980. "Women's Domestic Labor in Colonial Kenya:

Prostitution in Nairobi, 1909–1950." Boston: Boston University African Studies Center Working Paper No. 30. Revised version in Stichter and Parpart.

———. 1983. "A Colonial State and an African Petty Bourgeoisie: Prostitution, Property, and Class Struggle in Nairobi, 1936–1940." In F. Cooper, ed., *Struggle for the City: Migrant Labor, Capital, and the State in Urban Africa*. Beverly Hills: Sage Publications.

Willame, J. C. 1984. "Zaire: Système de survie et fiction d'Etat." *CJAS* 18, 1: 83–88.

Williams, Raymond. 1973. *The Country and the City*. Oxford: Oxford University Press.

Wilson, Godfrey. 1941–42. *An Essay on the Economics of Detribalization in Northern Rhodesia* Part I and II. Manchester: Manchester University Press. The Rhodes-Livingstone Papers, 5 and 6.

Winans, E. V. 1964. "The Shambala Family." In Gray and Gulliver.

Wipper, Audrey. 1972. "African Women, Fashion, and Scapegoating." *CJAS* 6, 2: 329–350.

Wolpe, Harold. 1974. "Capitalism and Cheap Labour-Power in South Africa: From Segregation to Apartheid." *Economy and Society* 3: 425–456.

Women in Nigeria Editorial Committee. 1985. *Women in Nigeria Today*. London: Zed Books.

Wright, Erik O. 1978. *Class, Crisis and the State*. New York: New Left Books.

———. 1985. *Classes*. London: Verso.

Wright, Marcia. 1982. "Justice, Women and the Social Order in Abercorn, Northeastern Rhodesia, 1897–1903." In Hay and Wright.

———. 1983. "Technology, Marriage and Women's Work in the History of Maize-Growers in Mazabuka, Zambia: A Reconnaissance." *JSAS*, 10, 1: 71–85.

Wrigley, C. C. 1959. *Crops and Wealth in Uganda*. Kampala, Uganda: East African Institute of Social Research.

Yahaya, A. D. 1979. "The Struggle for Power in Nigeria 1966–1979." In Oyediran.

Young, Alistair. 1973. *Industrial Diversification in Zambia*. New York: Praeger.

Young, Crawford. 1978. "Zaire: The Unending Crisis." *Foreign Affairs* 57, 1: 169–185.

———. 1982. "Patterns of Social Conflict: State,. Class and Ethnicity." *DAEDALUS*, 2.

———. 1984. "Zaire: Is There a State?" *CJAS* 18, 1: 80–82.

———. 1988. "The African Colonial State and Its Political Legacy." In Rothchild and Chazan.

Young, Crawford, and T. Turner. 1985. *The Rise and Decline of the Zairian State*. Madison: University of Wisconsin.

Young, K., C. Wolkowitz, and R. McCullagh, eds. 1981. *Of Marriage and the Market: Women's Subordination in International Perspective*. London: Routledge & Kegan Paul

Zambia Association for Research and Development. 1985. *Women's Rights in Zambia*. Proceedings of the Second National Women's Rights Conference held at Mindolo Ecumenical Foundation, Kitwe, Zambia, 22–24 March.

Zaretsky, E. 1976. *Capitalism, the Family and Personal Life*. London: Pluto.

Index

Accumulation, 6, 8, 11, 32, 33; capital, 2, 11, 13, 26, 97–98, 104; polygyny as capital accumulation strategy, 173, 175; state in capitalist accumulation, 43(n54), 59, 111; women accumulators, 6, 103, 111, 113, 116–122, 173. *See also* Beer brewing; Traders

Afigbo, A. E., 70

Agriculture, 2, 12, 91–105, 164, 170, 182(n56); bias against peasants, 13, 100–104; cash crops, 23, 37–39, 101, 112, 127, 165; male preference in subsidy, 12, 25, 37–38, 98–104, 130, 177; women in, 25, 27, 36, 37, 57–58, 61, 92, 98–104, 130, 164–165. *See also* International development agencies; Public policies

AIDS, 105

Akrinrinade, Chief, 77, 78, 82

Angola, 10

Association of African Women for Research and Development, 15

Awe, Bolanle, 88–89(n11)

Azarya, Victor, 157

Babangida, Maj. Gen., 84

Barrett, Michele, 49

Beer-brewing, 5, 10, 12, 14, 24, 31, 34, 35, 101, 111, 113, 115–122, 132, 145–147, 150, 191. *See also* Traders; Economy, "second"

Benin, 10

Berger, Iris, 4

Berman, Bruce, 16(n14), 25, 26

Berry, Sara, 97

Biafra, 72

Birth control, 166, 179

Botswana, 152

Buhari, Maj. Gen., 83

Bujra, Janet, 51, 63

Callaghy, Thomas, 6, 9

Cameroon, 9

Capitalism, 2, 57–58, 111; capitalist ideology, 175; international, 2, 4, 7, 112, 127, 162; precapitalism, 25

Chanock, Martin, 7, 30

Chauncey, Jr., George, 31

Chazan, Naomi, 15, 157, 185–200

Cheater, Angela, 173

Clark, Alice, 58

Class, 2–6, 13, 35, 36, 170; class formation, 24–40; gendered class formation, 23–40, 163; ruling class, 13, 47–66, 97, 162–163, 186–187; women and, 4–5, 48–52, 77, 86–87, 124–125, 138, 173, 178; women's politics, 56, 77, 138

Colonialism, 7, 11; agriculture in, 98, 164; army in, 69; colonial state, 5, 13, 24–40, 164–166; family policy, 115–116; officials, 8, 11, 111–122, 165, 187; precolonial, 26, 27, 165; racism in, 14, 113, 116, 124, 126, 134, 164; similarity to military regime, 69–70, 87; women under, 130, 134, 164–165, 111–127, 190–191

Constitutional reform, 75–78, 109(n54), 137. *See also* Legal inequality

Cooper, Frederick, 57

Customary law, 7, 28, 30, 40, 85, 132, 178

deBeauvoir, Simone, 53, 176–177

Democracy, 3, 54, 192

Dependency theory, 2, 16(n10)

225

Domestic service, 146, 150, 152–154, 164
Dudley, B. J., 72

Economy, "second" (magendo), 8–9, 11–
  12, 14, 18(n14), 61, 102, 105, 111,
  116–122, 125–126, 144–154, 194,
  196; modernization of, 70
Education, 12, 131–134, 150, 167; home
  economics, 131, 133, 136, 184(n88)
Eisenstein, Zillah, 5
Electoral franchise (female suffrage), 70–
  71, 73, 76, 176
Elite women, 71, 73, 77. See alsso Class
Elwert, George, 10
Employment, 12, 61, 112–113, 131–132,
  144–145, 150; as extension of
  reproduction, 34; wage levels, 27, 124,
  126, 164–165, 167–168
Ethiopia, 13
European state formation, 7

Fatton, Robert, 3, 4, 13, 47–64, 186–187,
  193, 194, 197, 198
Feminist analysis, 5, 14; anthropology, 7;
  and class, 4; dependency, 2; political
  agenda, 53–54, 61; state, 5. See also
  Gender approach; Politics; Women's
  resistance
Feminization of poverty, 12
Folbre, Nancy, 161

Gambo, Sawaba, 76, 79
Geisler, Gisela, 10
Ghana, 60
Geiger, Susan, 124
Gender approach, 1, 16(n3), 24–40;
  conflict, 5–7, 10–11, 100–101, 173;
  critique of neutrality, 1, 11, 23, 163,
  166, 169, 188; ideology, 10, 11, 36,
  163. See also Feminist analysis;
  Ideology; State, internal contradictions
Government cabinet, 8, 9, 18(n39);
  legislatures, 8, 9, 70, 117, 134, 137;
  local government, 75–77, 86, 96, 125;
  officials (civil service), 72–74, 83, 131,
  133, 136–137, 174–175, 177; regime
  type, 9, 192. See also Politics; State
Gowon, Lt. Col., 72–74, 76
Gramsci, Antonio, 14, 52–62
Guinea-Bissau, 10
Guyer, Jane, 105

Hamilton, Roberta, 50

Hansen, Karen, 2, 6, 12, 14, 143–158,
  187, 188, 191, 193, 194, 195, 197–198
Hay, Margaret Jean, 12
Hegemony, 52–62
Hirschmann, Albert O., 103
Households: assumptions of income
  pooling, 7, 16(n10), 132; cycles, 143–
  156; husbands' control of income, 25,
  36, 37, 39, 150, 155, 173, 178; income
  for wives' autonomy, 35, 156, 178;
  interdependence, 36, 174; men's
  dependency on women, 36; nuclear or
  extended, 15, 174, 177; policy treats
  men as heads, 171–172; women heads
  of, 130, 149, 153–154
Housing, 33, 44(n69), 113, 124, 144,
  151–153
Hyden, Goran, 57, 59, 60, 100, 104

Ideology, 3, 5, 10, 13, 17(n27), 37, 163,
  167, 175, 178; colonial, 130;
  international capitalist, 162. See also
  Hegemony
Iliffe, John, 113, 123
International development agencies, 12,
  14, 92, 94, 98, 100, 104, 140. See also
  IMF; U.S. AID; World Bank
Ironsi, Maj. Gen., 71–72
Islam, 33, 70, 73–76, 82, 85, 124, 125
Ivory Coast, 10, 65(n37)

Jacobs, Susan, 2, 4, 6, 10, 11, 13, 15,
  161–179, 190, 192–193, 195, 198

Kaunda, Kenneth, 133–134, 137
Kenya, 12, 27, 29, 32, 33, 35, 38,
  65(n37), 117, 168

Lagos Plan of Action, 2, 83
Land, male control of, 12, 13, 23, 25, 28,
  37–39, 59, 61, 94, 98, 104, 108(n28),
  131, 164–165, 187, 193. See also
  Resettlement
League of Women Voters (Nigeria), 79–85,
  109(n54)
Legal inequality, 15, 26, 59, 78, 85, 102,
  131–132, 137–138, 165–166, 167, 171
Lemarchand, René, 101
Lonsdale, John, 6, 25, 26
Lovett, Margot, 4, 8, 13, 23–40, 86, 187,
  188, 191, 193, 197, 198

MacGaffey, Janet, 11, 12

MacKinnon, Catherine, 49, 50, 55
Malawi (Nyasaland), 7, 9, 24, 26, 30, 152, 153
Mali, 10
Marital exchange systems, 8, 12, 28, 29, 30, 42–43(n44), 115, 132, 165–166
Markovitz, Irving Leonard, 56
Marriage and divorce laws, 15, 26, 29, 30–59, 85, 132, 138, 166–167
Marx, Karl, 1, 58, 143
Marxists: on agriculture, 170, 182–183(n56); critique of dependency theory, 2; feminism, 4, 49, 163; productive-reproductive labor debate, 40(n3); rhetoric, 13; on the state, 3, 4, 157, 187
Matrilineality, 29, 149, 156, 157, 160(n39)
Mba, Nina, 7, 9, 10, 14, 69–88, 188, 190, 191,. 195, 197–198
Mbilinyi, Marjorie, 5–7, 11, 14, 100, 111–127, 187, 189–191, 193–194, 198
Migrant labor, 23, 24, 26–29, 33, 58, 105, 111–113, 115, 144, 145, 164, 170, 186; restrictions on female movement, 24, 28–29, 36
Military, 9, 14, 191; civil servant links, 72, 74, 83; governments, 69–88; women in, 70–72, 83, 134, 191
Mining, 24, 93, 112, 144, 146; mine marriages, 30; women in area, 31, 35, 139
Missions, Christian, 12, 37, 96, 166
Mode of production, 3, 16(n14), 27, 57, 165, 181(n24)
Mohammed, Gen. Murtala, 74
Mozambique, 10, 13, 168, 176
Munachonga, Monica, 10, 14, 130–140, 188, 190, 191, 193, 195, 198

National Council of Women's Societies (Nigeria), 71, 75, 80, 83–87
Newbury, Catharine, 2, 11, 14, 88, 91–105, 190, 193, 194, 195, 197, 198
Nigeria, 7, 9, 10, 69–90; women's war in, 69
Nwapa, Flora, 72

Obasanjo, Lt. Gen., 74, 76
Odinamado, Oyibo, 80–81
Obbo, Christine, 11, 48, 53, 61
Oooko-Ombaka, Ooki, 9

Patrilineality, 8, 12, 25, 29, 149, 160(n39), 165
Parpart, Jane, 1–15, 103, 186, 188, 190, 194, 196–198
Peasant "capture," 57–62, 100; grassroots resistance, 103–104
Politics: elites, 5, 8; female exclusion, 4, 8–11, 14, 48, 72–74, 75, 83–84, 134, 189, 190–191; institutions, 3, 134; insufficient attention to, 3, 199–200; parties, 9, 10, 14, 59, 62, 70, 72, 79–82, 133–136, 154, 190; personal politics, 1, 6–8, 36, 49, 157, 173; women legislators and officials, 71, 74, 82, 85, 134, 190; women's organizations, 7, 10, 11, 71, 79, 84, 125, 133, 138–140, 184(n88), 190–191; women's withdrawal from, 11, 48, 55, 187, 197–198. See also Government, Public policies, States; Women's bureau
Polygyny, 15, 101, 132, 138, 149, 151, 153, 173–175
Privatization, 93–105
Poulantzas, Nicos, 4, 143
Property rights, 138, 156, 160(n39), 166, 181(n33), 166–167. See also Land; Legal inequalities
Prostitution, 12, 24, 32–34, 60, 61, 105, 110(n73), 115–116, 126, 139, 145, 164, 168
Public policies: "gender-specific effects," 11–13, 130–133, 137–138, 161–180, 192–193; and agricultural development, 91–100, 172–178; implementation limited, 137; macroeconomic, 14, 91–104. See also Gender neutrality critiqued; International development agencies; Politics; Women's bureaus

Ranger, T. O., 8
Rapp, Rayna, 7
Ravenhill, John, 2
Reproduction, 2, 4, 10, 27, 32, 34, 40, 41(n3), 50, 112, 124; production and, 13, 23, 25, 39, 40, 41(n3), 58
Resettlement schemes, 13, 15, 131, 161–162, 169–177, 182(n50); class and, 170, 172–173
Revolution, 4, 10, 13, 63; revolutionary submission, 102
Roberts, Pepe, 53–54
Robertson, Claire, 4, 58, 60

Rwanda, 9

Schoepf, Brooke, 2, 11, 14, 91–105, 188, 190, 193–195, 197–198
Seko, Mobutu Sese, 102
Senegal, 9, 65(n37)
Shagari, President, 82–83
Skocpol, Theda, 4, 17(n17)
Sierre Leone, 10
Socialist economy, transition to, 3; for women, 50, 179
Southern African Development Coordination Conference, 15, 142(n29)
State, 2–13; autonomy, 4, 5, 47–48, 54, 56, 188; and class, 47–64, 97, 162, 180(n8), 188; formation, 5, 7, 8, 186–189; as gendered, 1, 5, 6, 48, 59, 143, 163–169, 185–200; internal contradictions, 6, 26, 27, 32, 43(n54), 143, 148–149, 153, 157, 161–163, 167–169, 197–198; liberal-pluralist conceptions, 3; overdeterminism, 6, 14, 15, 157, 196–199; socialist, 10, 50; Weberian conceptions, 4, 9
Staudt, Kathleen, 1–15, 55–56, 62, 102, 103, 186, 188, 190, 194, 196–198
Steady, Filomena, 10
Swaziland, 152

Tadesse, Zen, 13
Tanzania, 5, 7, 10, 13, 14, 30, 33, 111–127, 168
Traders, women, 10, 11, 14, 34, 58, 60, 61, 93, 103, 115, 132, 143–158; household demographics, 154; international, 102; police harassment, 60, 132, 148–149, 151–152, 154, 158; politics of, 72, 80, 86, 139, 143;

scapegoats, 60, 103, 105, 168; in war, 73; women producers exploited, 94, 95, 107(n18). *See also* Beer brewing; Economy, "second"

Uganda, 11
United Nations, 8, 9, 15, 126; Decade for Women, 132–133, 136, 137, 139
U.S. Agency for International Development, 100–101
Urban areas, 14, 24, 28, 30–36, 43(n54), 93, 111–127, 143–158, 187
Urdang, Stephanie, 10

Vincent, Joan, 123
Vogel, Lise, 49, 51

Weinrich, C., 164, 173
White, Louise, 33
Wife abuse, 166, 173–174
Women in Nigeria (WIN), 85, 87, 191
Women's bureaus/ministries, 9, 10, 13, 15, 78, 82, 136–137, 166, 168–169, 184(n88)
Women's resistance, 13, 15, 24–25, 29, 30, 48, 96, 101, 111, 122, 162
World Bank, 92, 127, 131, 176
Wright, Marcia, 8

Young, M. Crawford, 5

Zaire, 9, 11, 12, 14, 49, 91–105, 152–153, 197
Zambia (Northern Rhodesia), 6, 7, 10, 11, 14, 24, 26, 28, 30, 35, 44(n72), 130–140, 143–158
Zimbabwe, 6, 10, 13, 15, 32, 33, 35, 44(nn69,70), 152, 153, 161–179

About the Book

In this book, the authors assert the particularity of women's relation to the state in Africa and, accordingly, the need to study gender-state relations in order to understand both the nature of the state and women's place in it. Exploring women's degree of access to the apparatus of the state, the consequences of their underrepresentation, and the mechanisms they have evolved to cope with their slim hold on the levers of power, the book includes discussions of general theoretical debates followed by case studies from Nigeria, Zaire, Tanzania, Zambia, and Zimbabwe. An analytical conclusion places the material in a global context.